™

References for the Rest of Us!®

W9-BKB-122

Hungry Minds™

1/01

Home Networking For Dummies®

Cheat Sheet

Networking Jargon at a Glance

Tear out this handy list of frequently used networking terms and stick it to a wall, the dog, or anything else that doesn't move much. If you encounter terms that don't appear in this list (or if you're just looking for something to do until dinner's ready), turn to the glossary at the back of this book for more networking lingo.

10Base-T cable: Network cable that looks like telephone wire. Also called *twisted-pair cable*.

administrator: The person in charge of maintaining the network — probably you.

backup: A copy of the files on your computer that can be used to restore data in the event that a computer in your network meets with disaster.

bus: Frequently used to refer to a slot on the motherboard, a bus is actually the data transmission path from the card in the slot to the processor.

client: A computer that uses hardware and services on another computer (called the *server*).

client/server network: A network model in which one computer (the *server*) provides services for the other computers (the *clients*).

concentrator: The home base of a 10Base-T network to which all lengths of cable from the network computers are attached. Commonly referred to as a *hub*.

Dial-Up Networking: A feature in Windows that enables your modem to connect to the Internet through an Internet service provider.

driver: Software that enables the hardware in your computer to communicate with the operating system.

IP address: A number that identifies a computer's location on the Internet.

IRQ (Interrupt Request): A communication channel assigned to a device so that it can communicate with the PC's processor.

ISP (Internet service provider): A company that provides Internet access to individuals and businesses.

Kbps: Thousands of bits per second *(kilobits per second)*. A measurement of the speed at which data can be transmitted through a modem.

LAN (local area network): Multiple computers connected by cable.

NetBIOS (Network Basic Input/Output System): A communication system in networks that enables the various applications running on computers in the network to communicate with other computers on a network.

network: Two or more computers connected to each other with network interface cards, cable, and networking software to communicate and exchange data.

NIC (network interface card): A hardware device that enables networking by providing the features necessary for cable (or wireless) communication.

peer-to-peer network: A network model in which each computer has the same capabilities as the others, and each computer can communicate with all the other computers.

protocol: A set of rules (sometimes referred to as a *language*) that computers use to communicate with each other across networks.

RJ-45: The connector at the end of 10Base-T cable. Looks like the connector at the end of telephone cable.

server: A computer that provides services for other computers (called *workstations* or *clients*) on a network. Also called a *host*.

shared Internet connection: A system that permits all the computers on a network to be logged on to the Internet at the same time.

shared resources: Resources such as files, folders, printers, and other peripherals that are attached to one computer and configured for access by users on other network computers.

TCP/IP (Transmission Control Protocol/Internet Protocol): The basic communication language *(protocol)* of the Internet. TCP/IP also can be used as a protocol for networks.

workstation: A network computer that uses the resources of one or more servers. Also called a *client*.

Home Networking For Dummies®

Stuff I Need to Know About My Network Computers

A time may come when one of the computers on your home network goes down and you have to reconnect the network settings. Rebuilding your network settings is a lot easier if you don't have to start from scratch — you shouldn't waste time trying to find the original documentation if you don't have to. You can find the essential information you need to get in, set up the connection, and get out again by double-clicking the Network icon in the Control Panel. Then select each item and click Properties to see that item's settings. Write down the specifications and keep them in a safe place — just in case Murphy's Law comes a-calling. I set up my lists like this:

Computer 1

Computer name:

NIC brand:

NIC IRQ:

NIC I/O address:

Network components installed:

Computer 2

Computer name:

NIC brand:

NIC IRQ:

NIC I/O address:

Network components installed:

Computer 3

Computer name:

NIC brand:

NIC IRQ:

NIC I/O address:

Network components installed:

Stuff I Need to Know About My Network Printers

Every day, you have a list of important things you need to remember. (You remember that you need to fill the car up with gas, but you can't remember where you left your car keys, where you left the car, and you sure as heck don't remember why there's a list of networking terms pinned to the dog.) Simplify your life — write down the important stuff once (and only once), leave the list in a handy place (don't forget where you put it!), and go on with your life until you really need to know about toner and shared resources. My lists look like this:

Printer 1

Printer manufacturer and model:

Ink or toner cartridge part number:

Attached to Computer #:

Shared as (share name):

Printer 2

Printer manufacturer and model:

Ink or toner cartridge part number:

Attached to Computer #:

Shared as (share name):

For Dummies®: Bestselling Book Series for Beginners

Home Networking

FOR

DUMMIES®

Home Networking FOR DUMMIES®

by Kathy Ivens

Hungry Minds™

HUNGRY MINDS, INC.

New York, NY ◆ Cleveland, OH ◆ Indianapolis, IN

Home Networking For Dummies®

Published by
Hungry Minds, Inc.
909 Third Avenue
New York, NY 10022
www.hungryminds.com
www.dummies.com

Library of Congress Control Number: 2001089111

ISBN: 0-7645-0857-1

Printed in the United States of America

10 9 8 7 6 5 4

1O/SQ/QU/QR/IN

Distributed in the United States by Hungry Minds, Inc.

Distributed by CDG Books Canada Inc. for Canada; by Transworld Publishers Limited in the United Kingdom; by IDG Norge Books for Norway; by IDG Sweden Books for Sweden; by IDG Books Australia Publishing Corporation Pty. Ltd. for Australia and New Zealand; by TransQuest Publishers Pte Ltd. for Singapore, Malaysia, Thailand, Indonesia, and Hong Kong; by Gotop Information Inc. for Taiwan; by ICG Muse, Inc. for Japan; by Intersoft for South Africa; by Eyrolles for France; by International Thomson Publishing for Germany, Austria and Switzerland; by Distribuidora Cuspide for Argentina; by LR International for Brazil; by Galileo Libros for Chile; by Ediciones ZETA S.C.R. Ltda. for Peru; by WS Computer Publishing Corporation, Inc., for the Philippines; by Contemporanea de Ediciones for Venezuela; by Express Computer Distributors for the Caribbean and West Indies; by Micronesia Media Distributor, Inc. for Micronesia; by Chips Computadoras S.A. de C.V. for Mexico; by Editorial Norma de Panama S.A. for Panama; by American Bookshops for Finland.

For general information on Hungry Minds' products and services please contact our Customer Care Department within the U.S. at 800-762-2974, outside the U.S. at 317-572-3993 or fax 317-572-4002.

For sales inquiries and reseller information, including discounts, premium and bulk quantity sales, and foreign-language translations, please contact our Customer Care Department at 800-434-3422, fax 317-572-4002, or write to Hungry Minds, Inc., Attn: Customer Care Department, 10475 Crosspoint Boulevard, Indianapolis, IN 46256.

For information on licensing foreign or domestic rights, please contact our Sub-Rights Customer Care Department at 212-884-5000.

For information on using Hungry Minds' products and services in the classroom or for ordering examination copies, please contact our Educational Sales Department at 800-434-2086 or fax 317-572-4005.

Please contact our Public Relations Department at 212-884-5163 for press review copies or 212-884-5000 for author interviews and other publicity information or fax 212-884-5400.

For authorization to photocopy items for corporate, personal, or educational use, please contact Copyright Clearance Center, 222 Rosewood Drive, Danvers, MA 01923, or fax 978-750-4470.

Hungry Minds™ is a trademark of Hungry Minds, Inc.

About the Author

Kathy Ivens has written more than four-dozen books about computers and has spent lots of years installing corporate networks. She's a columnist for *Windows 2000 Magazine* and has an internationally syndicated column for home computer users. She runs multiple computer networks in her own home.

Dedication

I used to be in television, and whenever we "blew" a commercial, we had to run it again at the next available commercial opening. That second running is called a "makegood." This book is dedicated to David Rogelberg, and it's a "makegood."

Author's Acknowledgments

A lot of super-talented people at Hungry Minds, Inc. worked as hard as I did (sometimes harder) to make sure this book provided good, up-to-date information in a format that makes it easy for you to perform all the technical tasks involved in setting up a home network. Steven Hayes is a joy to work with — a thorough professional with all the right "attitudes." Nicole Haims is a terrific Project Editor who cares as much as any author does about accuracy and good writing (trust me, that's not a global norm in the publishing business). Kim Darosett and Beth Parlon toiled long and hard to cut through all the geeky language to make sure I didn't embarrass myself (and my English teachers) with language errors. Lee Musick's expertise made it possible for me to say "the stuff in here is technically correct" with confidence. I am grateful to all of them for their hard work and their outstanding abilities.

Publisher's Acknowledgments

We're proud of this book; please send us your comments through our Online Registration Form located at www.dummies.com.

Some of the people who helped bring this book to market include the following:

Acquisitions, Editorial, and Media Development

Senior Project Editor: Nicole Haims

Senior Acquisitions Editor: Steven Hayes

Senior Copy Editor: Kim Darosett

Copy Editor: Beth Parlon

Technical Editor: Lee Musick

Media Development Coordinator: Marisa Pearman

Editorial Manager: Leah Cameron

Media Development Manager: Laura Carpenter

Media Development Supervisor: Richard Graves

Editorial Assistants: Candace Nicholson, Jean Rogers

Production

Project Coordinator: Regina Snyder

Layout and Graphics: Gabrielle McCann, Shelley Norris, Kristen Pickett, Heather Pope, Jacque Schneider, Brian Torwelle, Jeremey Unger

Proofreaders: John Greenough, York Production Services, Inc.

Indexer: York Production Services, Inc.

Special Help
Becky Huehls, Rebecca Senninger

General and Administrative

Hungry Minds, Inc.: John Kilcullen, CEO; Bill Barry, President and COO; John Ball, Executive VP, Operations & Administration; John Harris, CFO

Hungry Minds Technology Publishing Group: Richard Swadley, Senior Vice President and Publisher; Mary Bednarek, Vice President and Publisher, Networking and Certification; Walter R. Bruce III, Vice President and Publisher, General User and Design Professional; Joseph Wikert, Vice President and Publisher, Programming; Mary C. Corder, Editorial Director, Branded Technology Editorial; Andy Cummings, Publishing Director, General User and Design Professional; Barry Pruett, Publishing Director, Visual

Hungry Minds Manufacturing: Ivor Parker, Vice President, Manufacturing

Hungry Minds Marketing: John Helmus, Assistant Vice President, Director of Marketing

Hungry Minds Production for Branded Press: Debbie Stailey, Production Director

Hungry Minds Sales: Roland Elgey, Senior Vice President, Sales and Marketing; Michael Violano, Vice President, International Sales and Sub Rights

◆

The publisher would like to give special thanks to Patrick J. McGovern, without whom this book would not have been possible.

◆

Contents at a Glance

Cartoons at a Glance

By Rich Tennant

"Oddly enough, it came with a PCI bus slot."

page 263

"That reminds me—I installed the NICs for our telephone line last week."

page 7

"If it works, it works. I've just never seen network cabling connected with Chinese handcuffs before."

page 209

"IT WAS CLASHING WITH THE SOUTHWESTERN MOTIF."

page 67

"I think Doreen is trying to send me a message. She set up the vacuum cleaner for sharing."

page 147

Cartoon Information:
Fax: 978-546-7747
E-Mail: richtennant@the5thwave.com
World Wide Web: www.the5thwave.com

Table of Contents

Introduction

I think that if you have more than one computer in your home, you should have a network. That belief has its roots in the fact that I'm generally lazy, and I believe everyone should do everything in the easiest possible manner.

Using multiple computers is just easier if you have a network. You don't have to remember which computer you were using when you started that letter to Uncle Harry because you can just reach across the network to finish it using any computer in the house. A home network allows you to do the work you have to do better and more efficiently.

One of the best reasons to set up a home network is that when you install it, you become the *network administrator,* the person who controls which files your spouse and children can access, as well as which printers they can use. Talk about power! And the wonderful thing about being a network administrator is that the title makes it sound like you do a lot of hard work.

About This Book

This book isn't a novel or a mystery, so you don't have to start at page one and read every chapter in order — you can't spoil the ending. This book is meant to be digested on a subject-by-subject, not a chapter-by-chapter, basis. Each chapter is self-contained, covering a specific subject.

However, because the process of creating the network requires that tasks be performed in a certain order, I recommend that you check out the chapters in either Part I or Part II before you go to any of the other chapters.

After you get up to speed on the basics, you can decide which chapters you want to look at next and figure out which network features you want to add to your home network.

Conventions Used in This Book

Keeping things consistent makes them easier to understand. In this book, those consistent elements are *conventions*. Notice how the word *conventions* is in italics? In this book, I put new terms in italics and then define them so that you know what they mean. Because I know your life wouldn't be complete without all the networking jargon you could ever want located in one place, the glossary at the back of the book has many more terms than I could work into my sentences.

Here are some other conventions I use in this book:

- ✔ When you have to type something in a text box, I put it in **bold** type so that it is easy to see.
- ✔ When I cite URLs (Web addresses) within a paragraph, they appear in monofont: `www.symantec.com`. Similarly, all text formatted as *code* (commands you have to type) also appears in monofont.

What You Don't Need to Read

I've learned that some people are really curious about why some computer functions work the way they do. Other people don't care why; they just want to find out *how* to perform those functions.

I put technical explanations that you don't need to read, but may be of interest to the little computer geek in your head, in sidebars or passages of text marked with a Technical Stuff icon. You can safely skip this information if you don't care about those details. (I'll never know.)

Foolish Assumptions

I am making several assumptions:

- ✔ You use PCs that run either Windows 95, Windows 98, Windows Me, or Windows 2000 Professional.
- ✔ You want to share computers on a network, whether they're desktop computers or laptops.
- ✔ You have more people in the household than computers, so more than one person may use any single computer.

Regarding the differences between the various versions of Windows, I discuss the operating systems separately when a difference exists in the way they work. Otherwise, I just use the term *Windows*.

How This Book Is Organized

This book is divided into six parts to make it easier to find what you need. Each part has a number of chapters (some have more than others).

Part 1: Network Basics: The Hardware

Part I helps you plan and install your home network. You have some decisions to make and some hardware to buy. You also have to play architect as you design the placement of computers around the house. This part shows you how to put it all together:

- ✔ Planning your network and buying the hardware (Chapter 1)
- ✔ Installing the networking hardware in your computers (Chapter 2)
- ✔ Cabling your house to connect the computers (Chapter 3)
- ✔ Using other connection schemes: telephone lines, wireless connections, and so on (Chapter 4)

The information you find here may seem geeky and complicated, but it really isn't as complex as it sounds. If you perform each step in the right order, building a network is no harder than assembling a complicated toy for your kids. To make things as easy as possible, I take you through each task one step at a time.

Part 11: Setting Up the Computers

After you've installed all the network hardware, you have to perform some software tasks, including the following:

- ✔ Installing the files that Windows needs for networking (Chapter 5)
- ✔ Sharing an Internet connection with everybody on the network (Chapter 6)
- ✔ Setting up each computer to share stuff — and keep other stuff private (Chapter 7)
- ✔ Setting up users and learning about logins (Chapter 8)

This part tells you how to fine-tune your network — getting the computers to talk to each other and setting up users so everyone can maintain his or her own, personalized computer-configuration options.

Part 111: Communicating Across the Network

This part introduces you to the meat of networking. Here's where you get to put all your setup work into action:

✔ Setting up network printing (Chapter 9)

✔ Moving stuff around the network, from computer to computer (Chapter 10)

✔ Using files from other computers while you're working in software (Chapter 11)

The fun of networking is actually doing stuff across the network. Time to test it all out. Sit in front of any computer on the network and get stuff from any other computer. Ahhh, the power!

Part IV: Network Security and Maintenance

If you're going to create a network, any network, whether in the office or at home, that makes you the network administrator. After all the work you do creating this network, you'll want to make sure the network is safe and happy. The chapters in Part IV cover the following:

✔ Protecting the computers against harm from viruses and Internet intruders (Chapter 12)

✔ Preparing for disaster by making sure you don't lose your data when a computer dies (Chapter 13)

✔ Keeping computers healthy with the aid of some nifty tools (Chapter 14)

Part V: The Part of Tens

In true *For Dummies* style, this book includes a Part of Tens. These chapters introduce lists of ten items about a variety of informative topics. Here you find additional resources, hints, and tips, plus other gold nuggets of knowledge. The Part of Tens is a resource you can turn to again and again.

Appendixes

The appendixes take you one step farther down the road toward geekdom. In Appendix A, I explain how to write a program that backs up the data that you and the other members of your family create. Backing up regularly is easier if you have the right tool, and this program is a tool that's so easy to use you'll never fail to back up your data. Appendix B is a glossary of terms that I use throughout the book.

Icons Used in This Book

To make your experience with this book easier, I use various icons in the margins of the book to indicate particular points of interest.

This icon points out technical stuff that computer nerds or highly curious people may find interesting. You can accomplish all the important tasks in this book without reading any of the material next to these icons.

This icon means, "Read this or suffer the consequences." You find it wherever problems may arise if you don't pay attention.

Pay attention to the text this icon flags if you want to make setting up and using your network easier (and who wouldn't want that?). Think of this cute little target as a gift from one network administrator (me) to another (you).

This icon is a friendly reminder or a marker for something that you want to make sure that you cache in your memory for later use.

Where to Go from Here

Go ahead — check out the Table of Contents to see which neat networking feature you want to install first. But I do suggest that you check out Parts I and II for some networking basics.

It's quite possible that members of your family have opinions about the order in which you should install networking features — especially the kids, who seem to be born with an advanced knowledge of computing. Have a family meeting and listen to everyone's opinions — make sure the person who has the strongest views about which features should be implemented "volunteers" to help you install and maintain your network. (In my family, when one of my children is urging the family to do something, I listen carefully and then say, "Great idea, honey, you do it, and don't forget to let us know how you're doing.")

Creating a home network is satisfying, fun, and incredibly useful. Have a good time. You're on the cutting edge of computer technology. By reading this book, you prove that you're a networking nerd — and that's a compliment.

Part I
Network Basics:
The Hardware

The 5th Wave   By Rich Tennant

"That reminds me-I installed the NICs for our telephone line last week."

In this part . . .

Part I of this book covers all the hardware components required for building a network. You can't jump into this project willy-nilly; you have to plan and design your network before you actually build it. The stuff you need to know isn't complicated, and the hardware installation is very easy — anyone can do it (even your grandparents who discovered the world of computers last week).

Lots of different types of hardware are available, so you need to decide what hardware to use in your network; Chapter 1 helps you through that process. After you make your hardware decisions, you have to install the hardware, which you find out how to do in the other chapters in this part.

You're starting a great adventure, and when you cross the finish line, you'll be a network expert. You'll even be able to throw technical jargon into your conversations, words like *NIC, Ethernet,* and *hub* (don't worry; before you finish Chapter 1, you'll know what those words mean). Then all of your non-expert friends, who have no idea how easy this stuff is, will be amazed by your geekiness.

Chapter 1

What's the Big Deal about Home Networking, Anyway?

In This Chapter

▶ Deciding to create a home network

▶ Honing in on the right operating system

▶ Understanding how networks work

▶ Figuring out what hardware you need

▶ Purchasing kits or individual components

A *network* is a system of two or more connected computers so that each computer has access to the files and peripheral equipment (such as printers or modems) on another computer. You create those connections with the following elements:

✔ Hardware in each computer that permits the computer to communicate

✔ A cable or a wireless technology that sends data between the computers (using the hardware you installed)

✔ Software (called a *driver*) that operates the hardware

Installing all this stuff may not seem like a piece of cake, but if you take it one step at a time, it's amazingly logical and simple: If you can turn on a computer and use the keyboard and mouse, you can create a network in a matter of minutes.

In this chapter, I explain some reasons for setting up a network in your home, explain your software and hardware alternatives, and tell you more about how different networks *work.* I also discuss some of the technology that's available for your network.

Why Would I Even Want a Home Network?

I think that if you have more than one computer in your home, you should definitely have a network. That belief has its roots in the fact that I'm generally lazy and miserly, and I believe everyone should do everything in the easiest and cheapest manner. Here's a list of how a home network can benefit your whole household:

- **You won't have to get out of bed if you don't want to.** Say you decide it would be cozy and comfy to use your laptop, in bed, to finish an important presentation that's due tomorrow at 8 a.m. Suddenly you realize that when you were working on the presentation *yesterday,* you were sitting at the kitchen computer, slaving away at the presentation while eating a turkey sandwich. You don't have to leave your cozy bed and stumble downstairs to find the most recently saved version of the document — just grab the file across the network.

- **Your kids won't have as much to argue about.** Sally doesn't have to stop using the computer in the den because Bobby needs to retrieve his homework assignment from it. Bobby can go to the computer in the basement and grab the file from the computer in the den across the network. And because you can set up network software that lets everyone use the Internet at the same time, those arguments about whose turn it is to surf the Net are also a thing of the past.

- **You can buy yourself a diamond ring with the money you save on peripherals.** Okay, not quite, but you will save money because you won't have to buy a printer and modem every time you buy a computer — because everyone shares those tools across the network. Even better, the sharing is simultaneous, so you can avoid "It's my turn" arguments.

- **You can become a god (or goddess).** Another benefit of setting up a home network is that when you install it, you become the *network administrator* (that's what the people who installed the network at your office are called). That makes you a computer geek. Because I think that being called a computer geek is a compliment, I offer my congratulations to you.

Supporting a Network with an Operating System (Without Surgery)

You don't have to start creating your network with computers that already contain the hardware and software required for networking because you can easily install that stuff yourself (with the help of this book). However, you must have an operating system that can participate in a network environment.

You can use the following versions of Windows for your network:

- Windows 2000
- Windows NT
- Windows Me
- Windows 98 or Windows 98 Second Edition (SE)
- Windows 95

In this book, I'm assuming that at least one computer in your home is running a later version of Windows (Windows 98, 2000, or Me). Check out the Introduction of this book for other assumptions I've so flippantly made about you, and read on to find out why these versions of Windows can optimize your home network.

Which Windows versions have Internet sharing?

One of the most compelling reasons to set up a home network is to share an Internet connection. Everybody in the household can be on the Internet at the same time (well, everyone who's in front of a computer — few households have as many computers as family members). The most recent versions of Windows (Windows 98 SE, Windows Me, and Windows 2000) include the Internet connection-sharing feature. Only one of your computers needs to be running one of these operating systems; the other computers can be running on Windows 95 or Windows 98.

You can use the functions of the Internet connection-sharing feature to perform the following tasks:

- **Set up a host computer.** The *host computer* has the modem and the version of Windows that enables you to share an Internet connection with the other computers in your network.

- **Set up all the client computers.** The *client computers* are the other computers that share the host's Internet connection. The client computers don't need to run a version of Windows that has Internet connection sharing built in because these computers get the Internet connection-sharing feature from the host computer, which running one of the Windows versions I mention earlier in this chapter. That's why you need only one computer in the house that's running Windows.

What can I do if I don't have the right version?

If you don't have one computer running a version of Windows that has Internet connection sharing built in, you can still create a shared Internet connection using software that's available from stores and on the Internet. Chapter 6 contains all the instructions for setting up Internet connection sharing, and you can find some sources for the appropriate software. On the other hand, if your computer has the right hardware and processor, you could upgrade to Windows 98SE or one of the other operating systems.

Network Types — Just Like Personality Types

You can configure networks to operate in any of several *modes,* or configuration types. Like personality types, some network configuration types are interested in controlling computer users; other network types are more relaxed about controls. You can choose a mode for your current needs, and then easily change your network to another mode if the circumstances warrant. The basic hardware and configuration stuff that goes into creating a network (and that I cover in this book) doesn't change much among the network types, so your choices mostly depend upon how you want to communicate among computers.

Client/server networks for control freaks

Networking schemes that operate in *client/server* mode are common in businesses. These schemes include a main computer (a *server*) that controls users and holds files and peripherals shared by all the other computers (*clients* or *workstations*).

One of the most important reasons to install a client/server network is user authentication. The server on a client/server network checks to see if a Suzie Q. User is who she says she is and controls whether she can join the network. If she's eligible, the server continues to control her network tasks, determining what she can do. For example, perhaps she can read files but not delete them. The good news is that if you set up the network, you can control *everything.* (Heh, heh, heh.)

All the client computers are connected in a way that gives them physical access to the server. Everyone who works at a client computer can use files and peripherals that are on his or her individual computer (the local computer) or on the server. Look at Figure 1-1 to see the communication between computers in a client/server environment.

Even though all the computers are connected to each other, each client communicates with the server. The clients aren't usually configured to talk directly to each other.

Large client/server networks (usually found in the workplace) frequently have multiple servers, and each server has a specific job. For example, one server is used for authenticating users, one for e-mail, one for the accounting software, and yet another has the word-processing software. The common network operating systems used for servers on client/server networks are Windows NT, Windows 2000, Novell NetWare, and UNIX/Linux. These kinds of networks may be a *little* more than you need — unless you're thinking of running an enormous enterprise-like business out of your home — or you have a *really* big family.

Peer-to-peer networks are more relaxed about controls

Peer-to-peer networks permit all the computers on a network to communicate with each other. In Figure 1-2, you can see a typical peer-to-peer network communication structure.

If you have computers running Windows (95/98/Me/NT/2000), you can have a peer-to-peer network because the support for this type of network is built in to the operating system.

In fact, this book is about creating a peer-to-peer network in your home, so I assume that you have one of those Windows operating systems on every PC in your house.

With a peer-to-peer network, you can impose security on some resources, such as files, but the security levels don't come close to the security of a client/server network.

However, if your peer-to-peer network is running Windows NT or Windows 2000, the security is much stronger because people have to know the right password to use the computer.

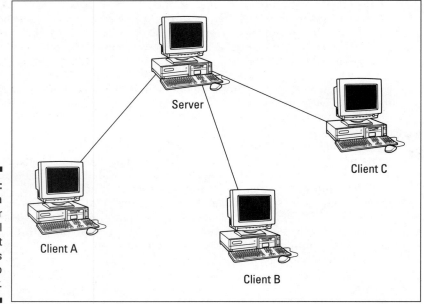

Figure 1-1:
In a client/server network, all the client computers connect to the server.

Server

Client C

Client A

Client B

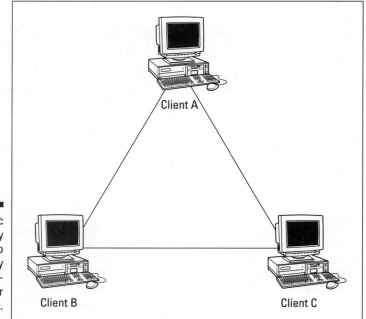

Figure 1-2:
Everybody talks to everybody in a peer-to-peer network.

Client A

Client B

Client C

Mixed networks fit all types

Just so that you don't think that the computer world is rigid, I'll point out that some networks are both client/server and peer-to-peer at the same time. Users log on to the network server and then use it to access software and store the documents that they create. Because the peer-to-peer network is built in to the operating system, users can also transfer files from other clients and access printers connected to other clients. A mixed network is the best-of-all-worlds scenario for many businesses.

The Nuts and Bolts of Hardware

The primary hardware device that you need is a network adapter, also called a *network interface card* (NIC). A NIC must be installed in each computer on the network. NICs are traditionally connected via cable. I say *traditionally* because wireless solutions are also available for small networks, and you may prefer to take that route. Also, even though the term NIC is still commonly used, not all network interface devices are cards anymore. Today, you can connect a network interface adapter device to a Universal Serial Bus (USB) or a parallel port (the printer port). However, because of the widespread use of the jargon *NIC*, I'll use that term generically.

The only rule for creating a network is that you must install a NIC in each computer. Beyond that, you have enough choices to make your head spin. I'll try to slow down the spin rate by explaining the options before I drag you into the actual installation process (which you can find in Chapter 2).

NICs come in lots of flavors, and when you buy NICs, you must match them to two important elements:

 ✔ The type of network interface device that your computer accepts

 ✔ The type of network cabling that you want to use (See the section, "Connections: Cables, wires, and thin air," in this chapter.)

Your NIC has to get on the right bus

Forget public transportation. Bus means something else in computer jargon. A *bus* is a slot on your computer's motherboard into which you insert cards. Technically, the name of the slot is *expansion slot,* and the bus is the data path along which information flows to the card. However, the common term in computerese is *bus*.

Each card (sometimes called a *controller card*) that you insert in a bus has a specific use. Your computers may have video cards, sound cards, hard drive controller cards, or other assorted cards.

Instead of using cards, some computers have one or more of these devices built right into a chip on the motherboard. These built-in devices are called *embedded cards* or *embedded controllers*.

The NIC you purchase must go in an empty bus, and you must make sure that the NIC is manufactured for the bus type that's available on your motherboard. The common bus types are

- **ISA (Industry Standard Architecture):** ISA is a standard bus that's been used for a number of years. It's a 16-bit card, which means that it sends 16 bits of data at a time between the motherboard and the card (and any device attached to the card).

- **PCI (Peripheral Component Interconnect):** The PCI bus is built for speed. Most new computers contain a PCI bus, which comes in two configurations: 32-bit and 64-bit. Its technology is far more advanced (and complicated) than the technology of the ISA bus.

You can read the documentation that comes with your computer to find out what kind of cards you must buy. However, if you have mixed bus types on the motherboard (most of today's computers contain both PCI and ISA slots), the documentation doesn't tell you which slots are already occupied. You have to open your computer to find out what type of NIC you need to buy.

Follow these safety tips when you open your computer:

- **Don't use a magnetic screwdriver.** Magnets and disk drives do not peacefully coexist — magnetic attraction can delete data.

- **Make sure that the computer is turned off and unplugged.** Either pull the plug from the wall or pull the plug from the back of the computer.

- **Discharge any static electricity in your body before you touch anything inside the computer.** Static electricity has the power to zap chips. Discharge yourself by touching something metal.

- **Remove any metal jewelry, especially rings.** Gold is a particularly efficient conductor of electricity, including static electricity.

You can tell at a glance what type of bus is available if you know what to look for.

An ISA bus is usually black, with metal pins or teeth in the center and a small crossbar about two-thirds of the way down the slot. Check out an ISA bus in Figure 1-3.

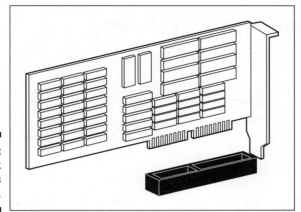

Figure 1-3:
If it's black
and long, it's
an ISA bus.

A PCI bus is usually white, and it's shorter than an ISA bus, as shown in Figure 1-4. A PCI bus has a crossbar about three-quarters of the way down its length.

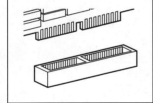

Figure 1-4:
A PCI bus.

Some NICs don't take the bus

Although motherboard NICs are the most common type of network connections, you have several other options available.

USB connectors

Most of today's computers come with a USB port (in fact, most come with two), and you can buy NICs that plug into a USB port. You don't have to worry about the bus type because all USB ports are identical. In fact, you don't even have to open your computer because USB ports are external. Look at the back of your computer to find port connectors that look like those shown in Figure 1-5.

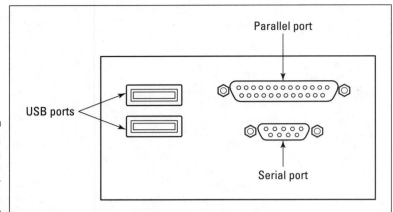

USB connectors are available for all types of network cabling and wireless connections.

Parallel port connectors

You also can skip the task of opening your computer if you decide on a networking scheme that uses parallel port connectors (usually wireless, telephone, or electric line cabling schemes). To avoid losing the use of your printer, most of these connectors include a *pass-through* device at the back of the connector into which you can attach your printer cable. The system automatically senses whether you're sending information to the printer or to the connection (or to both at once).

However, using a parallel port connector has a cost — you lose the enhanced communication powers that many printers provide (called *bidirectional communication*). If you use an enhanced printer cable, your printer can communicate better with your computer. Instead of seeing a pop-up message that the print job you just sent to the printer is encountering an error, you see specific errors, such as "printer is out of paper" or "color cartridge jammed." The pass-through connectors at the back of the parallel port network adapter connectors frequently interfere with the advanced communication between the printer and the computer. To avoid this problem, I suggest adding another parallel port to your computer, which costs about $10. Then, you have a parallel port for the printer and another for the network adapter.

Connections: Cables, wires, and thin air

You have one more decision to make before you go shopping for your hardware — you have to choose a cabling system. Your decision affects not only the type of cable you buy, but also the NIC you buy. The NIC has a device that accepts the cable connector, so the NIC must be built specifically for the cable you choose.

You have several choices for cabling your computers into a network:

- ✔ Ethernet cable
- ✔ Telephone wires already in your house
- ✔ Electrical wires already in your house
- ✔ None (wireless connections)

During the following discussions, I'm going to be mentioning the speed with which cable types transfer data among computers. Network speeds are rated in megabits per second (Mbps). A *megabit* is a million binary pulses, and the best way to put that into perspective is to think about a modem. The fastest modems transmit data at the rate of 56,000 bits per second (56 kilobits, or 56 Kbps).

Don't pooh-pooh the notion of speed; it is important. Everyone who uses computers changes his or her definition of the word *fast.* If you started using computers years ago, think about how fast the computer seemed at first, and then how impatient you became whenever you had to wait for a task to complete. Soon after you finally bought a faster computer, you got over the feeling that this was the fastest machine you'd ever seen, and impatience set in again. Waiting a long time for a file to open in a software application, or for a file to be copied from one machine to another, can drive you nuts.

Ethernet cable

Ethernet cable is the connection type of choice. It's fast, accurate, pretty much trouble-free, and simply the best. Ethernet can transfer data across the network at 100 Mbps, depending on the rated speed of the NICs and the hub. Some older NICs and hubs can send data only at 10 Mbps, but that's ten times faster than most of the other cabling technologies. Most of today's Ethernet equipment can determine the speed of individual devices on the network and automatically drop or raise the speed to match the device's capabilities.

Ethernet is the cable that you find in business networks. Today, Ethernet cable is purchased in the form of *10Base-T cable*, which is also called *twisted-pair cable* or *category 5 UTP cable*. Although Ethernet cable looks like telephone wire, it's not the same thing. Ethernet cable is designed to transmit data, rather than voice. Using 10Base-T requires the purchase of a *concentrator,* which is sometimes called a *hub.* All the network computers are connected to the concentrator, which distributes the data among the connected computers, as shown in Figure 1-6.

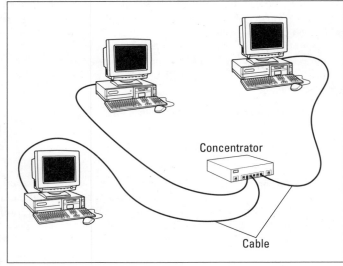

Figure 1-6:
Each
computer is
connected
to its own
port in the
concen-
trator.

Concentrator

Cable

The connector at the end of the cable looks like the connector at the end of your telephone cable, but it's actually slightly fatter. 10Base-T cable connectors are *RJ-45 connectors* — telephone connectors are *RJ-11 connectors*.

Telephone line cable

Telephone line cable is the second-best choice for wiring your home network, right behind Ethernet. It's not anywhere near as fast as the speed available with Ethernet cable, but the speed and reliability of telephone cable has improved since its introduction in the late 1990s. Most of the telephone line networking equipment that I've worked with transmits data at 1 Mbps, but newer technology is promising speeds as fast as 10 Mbps. Telephone line networking is increasing in popularity, especially because most of the computer and device manufacturers have developed and accepted standards. Having standardized technology makes it easier to buy equipment; you know it all works together. You can learn more about the technology at www.homepna.org.

To use telephone cable for home networks, you just connect a regular telephone cable between the telephone cable NIC and the telephone wall jack. Telephone cable is inexpensive and available everywhere, including your local supermarket. The networking processes use a part of your telephone line that voice communication doesn't use, so your telephone lines are still available for normal household telephone use (and for a modem).

You can use your wall jack for both a telephone and a network connection at the same time. You just have to adapt the wall jack so that it can do two things at once. Luckily, this is easy to do. You need to buy a *splitter* (the techy term is *modular duplex jack*), which is a little doo-hickey that you can purchase for a couple of bucks just about anywhere — at an office supply store, one of those super-duper big megastores, or even the supermarket. The splitter, as shown in Figure 1-7, plugs into the wall jack to give you two places to plug in phone cables instead of just one. You plug the network cable into one connector and your telephone cable into the other connector. It doesn't matter which cable goes where.

However, to avoid confusion, put some nail polish, or a little sticky star, or some other add-on near the connector on your network connection cable so you know which is which if you want to move the telephone.

For shared Internet access, only one computer needs a modem. If that computer has an external modem

1. **Plug the modem, not the telephone, into the second side of the splitter.**

2. **Plug the telephone into the appropriate connector on the modem.**

   Now you have three devices on your telephone jack: a network connection, a modem, and a telephone.

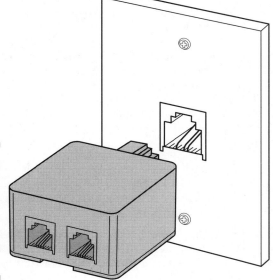

Figure 1-7: Insert a splitter to get double service from your telephone wall jack.

If the computer that's hosting the shared Internet access has an internal modem, you need a *Y-connector*, which is an adapter that looks like the capital letter Y. The bottom of the connector, where the two sides of the Y meet, plugs into the wall jack (to join the network). The two ends of the Y plug into the modem and the NIC (it doesn't matter which connector goes into which devices).

If you have multiple telephone lines in your house, all the computers on your network must be connected through the same telephone line (telephone number). Computers can't communicate across different telephone lines. (Your regular telephone service can't do this either: If someone is talking on line 1, you can't pick up a telephone connected to line 2 and eavesdrop — 'er, I mean, join the conversation.)

Here are a couple of drawbacks to using telephone wiring:

- Every computer must be near a telephone jack. Very few households have a telephone jack in every room, so this may limit your choices for computer placement.

- The maximum distance between any two computers is about 1,000 feet, but unless you live in the White House, that shouldn't be a major problem.

Electrical wires

You make electrical line connections work by plugging the manufacturer's electrical device into the power outlet on the wall. The device has an attached cable that connects to the computer, usually through the parallel port, as shown in Figure 1-8. (USB connections for electrical wires should be available at some point in the future.)

I'm not kidding when I say *wall outlet device.* Plugging it into a power strip doesn't work.

Like every networking option, using electrical wiring has its pros and cons. The only advantage of electrical line connections for a home network is that every room in the house has an electric outlet, so no matter where you place computers around the house, you can create a network. However, my advice is to install a telephone jack in a room that must have a computer; it's worth the small amount of time, money, and effort to avoid electrical wiring as a networking scheme. Here are the cons:

- **How much time do you have?** A network run on electrical wires is slow, and it's also frequently troublesome, both causing and being victimized by spasms of electrical interference. Even when no interference is present, the speed can't get much beyond 1 Mbps.

- **Um, where do you plug it in?** If your house is like most houses, only one wall outlet is near the computer, and you're already using both plugs: one for the computer and one for the monitor. Most manufacturers of electrical line networking hardware supply a special power strip into which you can plug your computer and monitor. You can plug that power strip into the plug that the network device isn't using.

- **How friendly do you want to be with your neighbor?** I could get into all the gory details about hubs and transformers and radio waves, but I'll cut to the bottom line: If your neighbor has a home network that's connected through electrical wires, then your neighbor may be able to access your network because you probably share the same transformer. That's either terribly convenient or terribly scary, depending on your relationship with your neighbor. Some manufacturers provide software to help guard your system against unauthorized users, and that software requires a separate installation and configuration process, which must be repeated whenever you add a computer to your network.

✔ **Who turned out the lights, and what happened to your novel?** Power fluctuations (a constant problem with all power companies and house-holds) can cause computers to temporarily disappear from the network. In fact, in a two-computer network, I could count on the other computer disappearing when the air conditioner compressor kicked on. On one occasion, I heard the refrigerator compressor kick on, and the file copy procedure I was performing between the computers died an ugly death. Coincidence? I think not.

✔ **Could it be any *less* user-friendly?** A limited number of vendors make electric line networking devices, and the configuration options are not as simple as those for other technologies. If you want a shared Internet connection (why wouldn't you?), you can't take advantage of the easy-to-use technology included in Windows 98SE or Windows Me. *And,* printers that are attached to computers aren't shareable; instead, you must install a network device on the printer. The printer essentially becomes another node on the network, and it looks like a computer to the network wires.

Manufacturers are just beginning to create and test standardized technolo-gies, which means that the technology should improve in the future, but not tomorrow, and probably not for a couple of years.

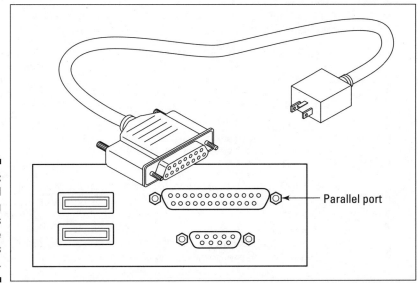

Figure 1-8:
The special plug connects to the computer's parallel port.

Parallel port

Wireless connections for the cable-phobic

Generally, people choose wireless connections because they're willing to give up speed and reliability in order to avoid dealing with any kind of cable or wire. Wireless technology also tends to be slightly more expensive than wired technology.

If you opt for wireless technology, you have two choices: radio frequency (RF) communication and infrared (IR) communication. Each has its own set of pros and cons.

Radio frequency wireless connections

RF technology isn't new; it's been around for a long time. I used it when I was a child (many eons ago) for walkie-talkie conversations with friends in the neighborhood. You probably use it today to open and close your garage door or to connect windows on upper floors to your household security system. I used to use it to unlock my car door, but I learned to hate the beeps and I set off my car alarm system so often that I had the whole system disabled. (That's my personal tale of woe, and it's also yours — even if your car doesn't beep and blink its lights at you in a parking lot as you push your little RF device to unlock it, I'm sure you're familiar with the technology.)

Here are some things to consider about RF network connections:

- They require a network adapter that's specific to RF technology, which means the adapter has to be equipped with the devices necessary to transmit and receive RF signals. Quite a few manufacturers are making RF devices, and the NICs are available for motherboards (both PCI and ISA bus types), USB ports, parallel ports, and personal computer memory card interface adapters (PCMCIA) for laptops.

- They are much slower than Ethernet connections, generally gaining a top speed of 1 Mbps. The signals can usually travel about 150 feet, moving through walls, ceilings, and floors. This distance should be sufficient for most home network schemes, but the actual distance that you can achieve may vary from manufacturer to manufacturer. If you need greater distance, you can often extend the signal by placing a special box (sometimes called a *residential gateway* or an *RF hub*) in a central location. The distance the signal travels then becomes relative to the box.

- The only things that can stop the signal dead in its tracks are metal or large bodies of water. Although you may think that only means you can't use RF technology in your castle with an iron drawbridge and moat, think again. Putting the computer (with its RF technology device attached) under a metal desk interferes with transmission. A wall that has a lot of metal plumbing pipes can also keep computers from communicating. The only problem with large bodies of water I can think of are those that crop up if you've installed a pond or swimming pool in your den, or if you're trying to communicate between two submarines or from an underwater office in a sea-world type of amusement park.

When I was testing RF technology, several manufacturers assured me that the 150-foot limit applies only indoors, assuring me that most RF devices can achieve far greater distances with no walls or floors in their way. Uh huh, thanks.

✔ You may experience interference from cell phones, pagers, home alarm systems, garage door openers, car security systems, and other wireless devices frequently found in your neighborhood. If those RF devices are properly shielded, however, you shouldn't have any problems.

✔ Technically, anyone with a computer equipped with RF technology can "join" your network without your knowledge. A neighbor or stranger could come within 150 feet of your house with a laptop, find the right frequency, and copy any files he finds. For security, some manufacturers of RF networking kits have built in a clever design feature that slows down malevolent outsiders who are trying to grab your frequency and get into your system — the frequency changes periodically. The RF signal that's sent and received across the network moves up and down within a given range (the technology is called _frequency hopping_), and this happens often enough to make it difficult to latch on to the current frequency — as soon as you get a bead on it, it moves. By the way, the idea of frequency hopping for security comes from an invention, and a patent, that is credited to a movie star named Hedy Lamarr (is anyone besides me old enough to remember her?). Read the story at `www.inventorsmuseum.com/hedylamarr.htm`.

Frequency hopping also acts as a performance enhancer. The speed is improved because you're effectively transmitting across a wider spectrum.

A downside of this choice is that most of the RF technology manufacturers provide software for setting up Internet connection sharing, instead of using the native, easier-to-use, built-in Windows features.

Infrared wireless connections

Infrared (IR) technology works by creating a direct signal, via a light beam, between computers. The connection is much slower than Ethernet, but it's more secure than RF technology. Also, before you even consider an IR network, you might as well know that infrared connectors must "see" each other, which limits IR networks. IR technology doesn't travel through walls or around corners. It works only in a straight line, which means it's suitable for networks only if all the computers are in the same room. Because one computer can't make a straight-line connection with two other computers at the same time, IR devices are available that collect and bounce the IR signals around the room. This enables you to build a network of multiple computers.

Most laptops have an IR connector built in — look for a small glass square on the back of the computer. The same thing is true for many printers, especially laser printers, which are equipped with that same glass square on the front of the unit. Aiming the back of the laptop at the front of the printer creates an infrared communication channel.

The connection is efficient and easy to work with, as I once learned accidentally. I was visiting a friend at his home office, and he was sitting in his office chair with his new laptop on his lap. His office, like mine, has multiple tables in a U-shape design, holding computers, monitors, keyboards, mice, and printers. He was showing me something on one of his desktop computers, and then turned his chair around to talk to me. Suddenly his laptop popped into action, launching the Add Printer wizard, which opened by telling him that the Plug and Play feature had found a new printer and was automatically installing it. What had happened, of course, is that the IR connector on his laptop had connected with the IR connector on his laser printer as he swung past it. In the split second that the two devices connected, Plug and Play took over. We both thought this demonstration of IR technology was pretty nifty.

For desktop computers, which usually don't have IR ports built in, you can buy IR network interface devices, most of which attach to your USB port.

One problem I've encountered during my tests of IR connections is that bright sunlight interferes with the signal. You need opaque window coverings if you want to go with IR connections.

Saving Time, Trouble, and Money When You Buy Hardware

A slew of manufacturers make the equipment that you need to build your network, and you should make your purchasing decisions with an eye on both reliability and price.

I'm going to mention some places to go for general research as you do your homework and also some places to buy equipment that I think provide good prices and service. None of these outlets know that I'm telling you about this, so they aren't paying me any commission or giving me special treatment in exchange for telling you about them. I'm just one of those people that can't resist giving specific advice (which, as all parents know, doesn't work well with children, but I don't expect readers to respond with, "Oh, Motherrrr," and leave the room). You may learn about resources that I don't mention here, and my omission isn't significant. It just means I didn't know about (or knew but didn't remember) that resource.

Doing your homework: Just like being in school

Making decisions about hardware, cable types, and other networking gizmos without doing some homework first is foolish. You're going to live with your decisions for a long time. In fact, everybody in the household will have to live with your decisions, so to avoid listening to gripes later, get everyone to help in the decision making. Home networking is a hot topic, and computer experts have been testing technologies and reporting their findings. Use their expertise to gain knowledge and then discuss your findings with the rest of the family. You can find reviews of the pros and cons of networking schemes in lots of places:

- **Start with any friends, relatives, or neighbors who are computer geeks.** All computer geeks are used to this treatment; people ask us for free advice at dinner parties, while we're in line at the movie theater, and almost anywhere else. Do what most people do — call the geek and pretend it's a social call. Then, after you ask, "How are you?" and before the geek has a chance to answer that question, ask your technical questions. (This is how most people interact with their computer-savvy friends.)

- **Paw through news stands, especially those in bookstores.** You can find an enormous array of computer magazines on the shelves. Look for magazines that fit your situation. For example, a computer magazine named *Programming Tricks for C++* is probably less suitable than *Home PC Magazine.* Look for *PC World, PC Magazine, FamilyPC,* and other similar publications. If the current issue doesn't have an article on home networking, check the masthead (the page where all the editors are listed) to see where you can call or write to ask for specific issues.

- **Search the Internet for articles and advice.** Type **home networking** into any search box, and you'll probably find that the number of results is overwhelming. If that approach seems onerous, try some of these popular sites that surely have the information you're seeking: www.pcworld.com, www.zdnet.com, or www.cnet.com. These sites all have search features, so you can find information easily. They also have reviews, technical advice, and "best buy" lists.

Plunking down the money: Tips for buying

After you make your decision about the type of hardware and cabling you want to use for your home network, you need to buy the stuff. You can buy kits or individual components, and many people buy both. Your cost should be less than $100 per computer to create your network.

Most manufacturers offer kits, which is a way to buy everything you need at once. Here are some things to keep in mind before you buy a kit:

- ✔ **Most kits are designed for a two-computer network.** If you have a third computer, you just buy the additional components individually. Some manufacturers make four-computer and five-computer kits.

- ✔ **Kits work only if every computer on your network needs the same hardware.** For example, if you've decided to install an Ethernet network, the kit has two NICs, two pieces of Ethernet cable, and one concentrator. However, both NICs are the same bus type. If one of your computers has only an empty ISA bus, and the other computer has an empty PCI bus, you can't buy a kit.

- ✔ **Kits aren't necessary if one of your computers has a built-in network adapter.** Many computer manufacturers are selling computers already set up with network hardware (commonly telephone line or Ethernet hardware).

In Table 1-1, I list reliable manufacturers of products for the different types of network connections. Note that, because electrical connections aren't popular, your options are limited. Also, consumer interest in IR networking is minimal, so you'll mostly find RF wireless kits.

Table 1-1	Network Connection Manufacturers	
Manufacturer	*Network Connection*	*Web Site*
3Com	Ethernet, telephone line, wireless	www.3com.com
Diamond HomeFree	telephone line	www.homefree-networks.com
D-Link	Ethernet, telephone line, wireless	www.dlink.com
Intel	Telephone line, wireless	www.intel.com
Intellon	Check to see if electrical kits are now available	www.intellon.com
Intelogis	Electrical wire	www.intelogis.com
Linksys	Ethernet, telephone line	www.linksys.com
NETGEAR	Ethernet	www.netgear.com

Even if you buy a kit, you may also have to buy individual components. Perhaps you have three computers, or perhaps one of the Ethernet cables in the kit isn't long enough to reach the computer on the second floor. After you measure the distances, figure out where the available ports are, and do all the rest of your research, you may find that individual components are the only approach you can take. A plan that doesn't match a kit isn't uncommon, and kits are really a convenience, not a money-saver. Most people find that buying individual components costs about the same as buying kits.

Every retail computer store sells individual hardware components for all types of network connections. Many large office supply retail outlets also carry these products. On the Internet, check www.cdw.com and www.buy.com.

Be sure you know an online merchant's return policy before you purchase a networking kit.

Chapter 2

Installing Network Adapters

*A*fter you decide what type of connection to use (I'm rooting for Ethernet; I don't see any reason to compromise on hardware performance), you need to install the hardware that enables the network connection. This task must be performed on every computer on the network.

If you chose Ethernet or a phone line connection, you'll probably have to open all the computers on your network. If the connection type you select involves a USB port or a parallel port, you'll be able to install the hardware without taking your computers apart.

In this chapter, I discuss the installation of these technical doo-dads. But don't worry, I don't leave you high and dry — if you don't know your computer's chassis from the chassis of a 1967 T-bird (my all-time favorite car, and I'm old enough to remember riding in one), I walk you through the basics.

Before You Get Started

You need to make sure you have the right equipment to do the job. Lucky for you, the necessities are pretty low-tech. You need

- ✔ A work table (the kitchen table will do fine)
- ✔ A medium-sized Phillips screwdriver
- ✔ A small-sized Phillips screwdriver
- ✔ Sticky tape (duct tape, cellophane tape, Band-Aids, whatever — this is for pasting labels on ports and cables)

✔ A very long pair of tweezers (if you have one — if not, don't worry; I like to use them for fishing out screws that you may drop into the chassis — something I invariably do)

✔ A felt tip pen

✔ Small self-stick labels or small pieces of paper

You're almost ready to install the necessary hardware for your home network, but before you open your computer, make sure that you follow these safety tips:

✔ **Don't use a magnetic screwdriver.** Magnets and disk drives do not peacefully coexist — magnetic attraction can delete data.

✔ **Discharge any static electricity in your body before you touch anything inside the computer.** You can get rid of static electricity by touching a metal object.

✔ **Remove any metal jewelry, especially rings.** Gold in particular conducts electricity, including static electricity.

Putting a NIC on the Bus

If you opt to use a standard network interface card (NIC), you must open your computer to install it. This type of adapter is the hardware that enables PCs in your home network to recognize each other. Putting the NIC in a bus (a special motherboard slot) requires several separate steps, but they're all easy. Work on one computer at a time instead of putting all the computers on your worktable. You won't mix up parts, and you'll have plenty of workspace. (For more on NICs and buses, peruse Chapter 1.)

Disassembling your computer: Open sesame

Because the NIC needs to be installed internally, you have to do a bit of disassembly work on the computers in your network. To properly disassemble a computer, follow these steps:

1. **Unplug the computer.**

   You'll find the process much easier if you yank (ahem, I mean gently pull) the plug from the back of the computer instead of pulling out the plug from the wall outlet.

2. **Disconnect the cables that are attached to the ports at the back of the computer.**

   Your keyboard, mouse, modem, printer, camera, and other peripheral devices are connected to your computer with cables.

3. **As you disconnect each cable, write the name of its peripheral device on a small piece of paper and stick the paper on the end of the cable.**

   Use the felt tip pen to mark the ports — for example, write *M* for mouse and *K* for keyboard — because you may have a hard time telling the ports apart. Do the same for the serial port (write *modem* or *camera*) and the parallel port (label it *printer*).

4. **Move the chassis to a worktable.**

   Chassis is just a fancy name for the box that holds all of your PC's gooey innards. You can use this opportunity to vacuum or sweep the area where your computer sat. I'm guessing it's probably very dusty. Don't feel guilty; computers attract dust.

5. **In addition, invest in either a can of compressed air or a computer vacuum so that you can clean out the ports from which you just disconnected cables.**

6. **Remove the exterior case of the chassis.**

   Use the medium-sized Phillips screwdriver to remove the screws that hold the exterior case onto the computer chassis. If your computer uses some sort of snap-up or pop-up closing device instead of screws, lucky you.

Removing the backplate

You have to get the bus ready to accept your NIC, which means removing the metal backplate at the end of the bus slot (at the back of the computer). Check out what one looks like in Figure 2-1. The backplate is attached to the edge of the computer with a small machine screw — use your small Phillips screwdriver to remove it. You can throw away the metal plate unless you think that you may want to remove the NIC and close up that slot again.

A *machine screw* doesn't come to a point at the end, unlike a wood screw that is pointy so it can drill itself into the wood.

Remove the screw and place it on a piece of sticky tape. Placing the screw on the tape prevents it from rolling off the table and onto the floor, where you can't possibly find it — these are very small screws — or you'll hear that little clinky noise the next time you vacuum. If you don't have a rug, the screw will bounce on your wooden or tile floor and land far from the table. Finding the screw takes a long time. Want to guess how I know these things?

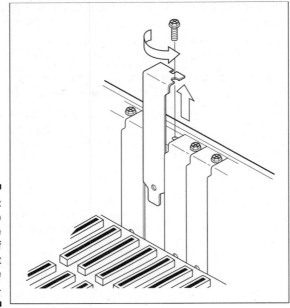

Figure 2-1:
You need to
remove the
piece of
metal that
covers the
slot.

Inserting the NIC

Now you can insert the NIC. Open the static-free bag and remove the NIC from it. Touch something metal (the computer case you removed should be handy) to discharge any static electricity in your body. Follow these steps to insert the NIC in the bus. (You won't be confused about which way it fits into the bus because the metal edge of the NIC replaces the metal plate you removed from the back of the computer, as shown in Figure 2-2.)

1. **Position the metal edge of the NIC in the open slot at the back of the computer.**

   You may have to tilt and wield the adapter a bit to line it up properly.

2. **Position the teeth on the bottom of the NIC in the bus and then push down on the NIC.**

   You may have to apply a bit of pressure, which is perfectly okay — don't worry about it. You can tell the NIC is inserted properly when you feel the metal edge fit neatly into the slot at the back of the computer.

3. **Replace the screw that you removed when you took out the metal plate.**

   Make sure the overhanging *flange* (or rim) at the top edge of the NIC nestles against the top edge of the computer frame. In fact, if everything's lined up right, you should see the screw hole because the flange has an opening for the screw.

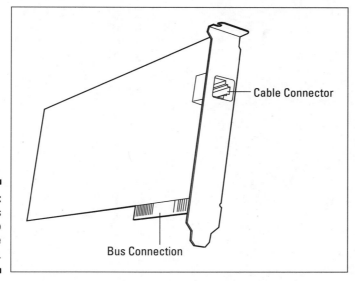

Figure 2-2:
The NIC is
shaped to
match the
bus and slot.

Cable Connector

Bus Connection

4. Put the cover back on the computer and replace the screws that you removed when you opened it.

If you drop a screw into the computer and you can't get to it, try any of the following:

- ✔ Grab it with a long pair of tweezers.
- ✔ Dangle a long piece of sticky tape to nudge the screw to a place where you can reach it.
- ✔ Turn the computer upside down over the table and let the screw drop, but beware of another possible problem — the screw landing on the floor and out of sight.

You're finished! Wasn't that easy? Now, close the computer, reconnect all the cables that you disconnected (easy if you marked everything as I suggested), and repeat these steps for every computer in your network.

Adding USB Connectors — Easy as Pie

If you purchased a kit or an individual connector that is designed to work with a universal serial bus (USB) port, installation is a snap. You don't even have to open your computer. In fact, you don't even have to turn off the computer. Just push the USB end of the cable into your USB port (see Figure 2-3). (You can find out more about USB ports in Chapter 1.)

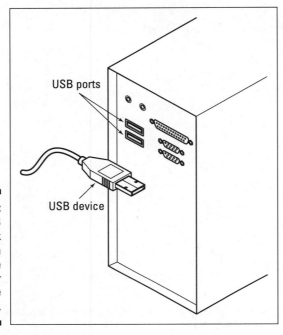

USB ports

USB device

Figure 2-3:
Your USB
network
device has a
cable
connector
for the
USB port.

You may decide to add a USB hub to your USB port, especially if you attach (or intend to attach) several peripheral devices to a computer. *USB* hubs are hardware devices that enable you to add additional USB peripherals when you run out of USB ports. Most PCs have only two USB ports, so after you have two USB peripherals (say a camera and a scanner, for example), attaching a hub to one of your USB ports enables you to expand your USB device use. The hub holds additional USB ports, and you can even use a special method of connecting a second hub (called *daisy chaining*) just in case you keep purchasing USB devices.

If your computer is running when you connect the cable to the USB port, the operating system notices what you did and immediately displays a message offering to complete the software side of the installation of your network device. That means special driver files that control your use of the device are transferred to your computer. See Chapter 5 for instructions to complete that step of the process.

Installing Parallel Port Connectors — a Piece of Cake

If your network hardware scheme involves a parallel port connection, you don't have to open your computer. However, you should unplug the computer before you begin.

Making the connection

Here's what you need to know to install the parallel port connector:

✔ The parallel port is a 25-pin female connector with one side that's slightly wider than the other side. A small threaded hole is next to each of the short sides.

✔ The parallel port network adapter is a 25-pin male connector with one side that's slightly wider than the other side. A screw with a turning device is connected to each of the short sides.

I bet you didn't even have to read the previous sentences; you just glanced at the equipment and figured it out. After you've made the connection, you're done.

Some of the parallel port network connectors provide a "replacement" port on the device or at some section of the cable to make up for the fact that you lost the ability to use your parallel port for a printer. This device is called a *printer passthrough*. However, these devices don't work terribly well (which is why not all manufacturers have adopted this scheme). For one thing, you lose some of the communication capabilities between the printer and the computer. These capabilities include the ability to send specific messages about printer problems back to the computer. For example, if you use the printer passthrough and your printer's color cartridge is out of alignment, you may see a generic message pop up that reads `Printer Error` instead of a message something like `Cartridge Needs Alignment, Please Open the Printer Tools Program`.

Additionally, using a printer passthrough imposes a performance cost. Because the printer is shared, any user on any computer can send a document to the printer. When someone uses the printer, all work slows down on the computer to which the printer is attached. The parallel port is trying to run two processes at the same time — network communication and printer communication.

You have two solutions for these problems:

- ✔ **Add another parallel port to each computer on the network that has a printer.**
- ✔ **Purchase a parallel-to-USB connector.**

  This nifty device is a printer port that you plug into a USB port — the back end looks like a parallel port, and your printers won't know the difference.

Adding another parallel port

If you use a parallel port networking scheme, you may need to add another parallel port to the computers that have printers because computers come with one parallel port. The *port* is a card, like a NIC, that you insert into a bus on the computer's motherboard. It has a parallel connector on the external side. Read about the different types of buses in Chapter 1, and follow the instructions there to determine the bus type that you need. Then follow the instructions for adding a parallel port earlier in this chapter in the section, "Putting a NIC on the Bus."

If the parallel port card you add to your PC is for an Industry Standard Architecture (ISA) bus instead of a Peripheral Component Interconnect (PCI) bus, the manufacturer may have some instructions about setting jumpers on the card. A *jumper* is a small connector that enables users to set hardware configuration options. The manufacturer provides clear instructions and illustrations for performing these tasks.

When you have a network, anybody using any computer has access to all the printers. If you are planning on sharing one printer across the network, you only have to add a parallel port to the computer that's going to provide the network printer.

Installing Laptop Adapters

Why should desktop computers have all the fun? Laptop adapters enable you to add your laptop computer to your home network too. Laptop adapters come in the form of a PCMCIA card. (*PCMCIA* stands for Personal Computer Memory Card Interface Adapter.) A PCMCIA card is about the size of a credit card. (These days, some manufacturers are calling these devices *PC cards*.)

One end of the card is the *external* side. That side has a device that provides a connection for the network, which means it accepts just about every networking solution, including cable (Ethernet or telephone) and wireless devices. You can also buy PCMCIA cards that have a USB port on the external side, if your laptop doesn't come equipped with a USB port.

The other end of the card, the *internal* side, has a row of 68 teeny holes. By a fortunate coincidence, the back of the PCMCIA slot in the laptop has 68 teeny pins. An arrow on the card indicates which way to plug it into the PCMCIA slot so that the holes meet the pins inside the slot (see Figure 2-4).

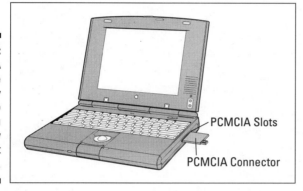

Figure 2-4: PCMCIA cards are clearly marked so that you know how to insert them.

PCMCIA Slots

PCMCIA Connector

Push the card into the slot firmly. When the card is fully engaged, a little button next to the slot pops out — you press the button when you want to eject the card. Your laptop probably has two PCMCIA slots, one on top of the other. The slots are usually on the side of the computer, hidden behind a flip-down cover that protects both slots.

Unless the documentation for your laptop has instructions to the contrary, it doesn't matter which slot you use for your connector. Be sure to check the documentation. If you're using an infrared (IR) wireless solution for your network, your laptop probably has an IR port. If not, you can buy PCMCIA cards for IR technology.

If you're using parallel port connectors for your network, your laptop has the same equipment as a desktop computer and requires no special handling — just follow the instructions for parallel port connectors earlier in this chapter.

Tricks and tips for road warriors

A road warrior is an employee who works off-site (usually visiting customers) and communicates with his employer via a laptop computer. Using the laptop, road warriors can collect their e-mail, dial in to company inventory records and credit records, or access other company databases.

If you have a road warrior in the house, he or she will love the ability to plug into either network at will. To help your road warrior out, you should install an Ethernet network in your home. Why? You can save money. The road warrior in your household probably already has a PCMCIA Ethernet connector (purchased by his or her company). The PCMCIA Ethernet connector is an expensive device (they can be three or four times as expensive as desktop NICs).

If your home network doesn't use an Ethernet network connection and you've purchased a separate PCMCIA card for your road warrior's use at home, you can keep *both* the PCMCIA Ethernet card that your road warrior uses at work *and* the non-Ethernet PCMCIA card used for the home network. All you have to do is keep one card in each of the laptop's two PCMCIA slots.

Alternatively, you can switch them before you turn on the laptop and connect to the network. Either way, you need to tell Windows which card to use when this PC is logged on to the network. To do so, you create separate hardware profiles for the laptop: one for the Ethernet PCMCIA card and one for the other PCMCIA card. (You may already be using hardware profiles to tell your laptop whether you're running in stand-alone mode or connecting to a docking station.)

You create hardware profiles in the System applet in the Control Panel. The specific steps vary, depending on the operating system on your laptop, and plenty of help is available as you use the hardware profile feature. The process is always the same — you enable and disable hardware devices for each profile. After you create hardware profiles, your laptop asks you to select the appropriate profile during bootup.

For more about hardware profiles, check out *Windows 98 For Dummies, Microsoft Windows Me Millennium Edition For Dummies, and Windows 2000 Professional For Dummies*.

Chapter 3

Installing Ethernet Cable

In This Chapter

▶ Planning the cable runs

▶ Deciding on the location of the concentrator

▶ Running cable around the house

*I*nstalling Ethernet network interface cards (NICs) inside your computers provides only half of the connections needed for computer-to-computer communication. Now you need to let the NICs communicate with each other. You accomplish this connection via Ethernet cable. In this chapter, I tell you everything you need to know to connect NICs using 10Base-T Ethernet cable.

Knowing the Lay of the LAN

The way cable is strung through a building is called a *run,* and your plan for running the cable depends on how easily you can string the cable between the computers and the concentrator. Your run is actually a series of runs because each computer must be individually attached to the concentrator (the hub that holds all the connections and provides the conversation pit for your computers).

Regarding 10Base-T cable

Ethernet cable comes in many forms, but today's standard cable (and the only form that I cover in this book) is 10Base-T cable. This cable is also known as *twisted pair cable* because the cable's wires are twisted along the length of the cable (see Figure 3-1).

Twisted-pair cable comes in two types:

✔ Unshielded twisted pair (UTP)

✔ Shielded twisted pair (STP)

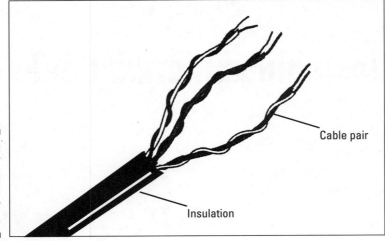

Cable pair

Insulation

The difference between the two types is pretty obvious — shielded twisted-pair cable has a shield. The shield is made of metal and encases the wires, lessening the possibility of interference from other electrical devices: radar, radio waves, and so on. However, I'm not aware of a great difference in performance between UTP and STP. UTP is less expensive, and almost all the 10Base-T cable in use is UTP. Both UTP and STP cable are available in fixed lengths, or *patches*. At either end of the cable is a connector called an *RJ-45 connector,* which you use to connect the computers in your network to the *concentrator,* or hub, of the home network.

Networking consultants buy big rolls of cable, cut each run to the appropriate length, and make their own connectors. That's a lot of work (and the tool for making the connector — called a crimper — is expensive). But you can buy cable of at fixed lengths that has a connector attached to each end called — this much more convenient option is called *patch cable.*

Concerning the concentrator

All the lengths of cable share the same home base, called a *concentrator* (also known as a *hub*). Each cable run goes from the concentrator to a computer (or from a computer to concentrator, depending on how you like to envision it).

At each end of a length of cable is a connector called an *RJ-45 connector.* One connector attaches to the concentrator, and the other connector attaches to the NIC in a computer.

One of the ports on the concentrator differs from the others, although it looks the same. That port is an *uplink port,* and you don't use it to connect a computer to the concentrator. Instead, this port has a special use (see the section, "Curing Your Network's Growing Pains," later in this chapter). Look for an icon or label to identify the uplink port or read the documentation that came with the concentrator so that you know which port to avoid.

The network arrangement shown in Figure 3-2 is called a *star topology,* although I'm not sure how that name was developed. Personally, I think the resemblance to a star is a little obscure. Perhaps *wheel spokes* is a more accurate description — which would explain why concentrator is often called a hub (as in the hub of a wheel).

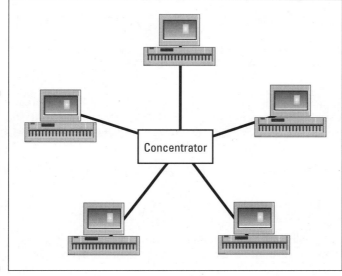

Figure 3-2:
Notice the multiple cable runs from the concentrator to each computer in a 10Base-T network.

Deciding Where to Put the Concentrator

The concentrator is the core of the network; everything travels to it (and flows from it). You should place the concentrator in a location that reduces the amount of cable you need to schlep through the house. For example, a reasonably logical person can count on the following scenarios:

  ✔ If you have two computers on the second floor and one on the first floor, putting the concentrator on the second floor means you'll have only one long cable run.

  ✔ If all your computers are on one floor, the logical place for the concentrator is at a midpoint between all the computers.

  ✔ If the same number of computers are on the first floor as are on the second floor, find a location that's as close as possible to being equidistant from each computer.

Where you decide to locate the concentrator requires a couple of other important considerations, so logical thinking doesn't always work (much like applying logical thinking to politics, or economic theories, or to guessing what "that look" on your spouse's face really means). The following sections help you work through the not-so logical considerations you need to take into account.

Concentrators are environmentally fussy

Concentrators have some environmental requirements, and if you don't cater to them, your concentrator will probably get sick and may even die. To ensure that your concentrators are in the correct environment, do the following:

  ✔ **Provide good air quality.** After you connect the cables, you don't have to manage the concentrator — no babysitting is required. That means you can tuck the concentrator away somewhere, but you must provide a dry (not humid), dust-free environment.

  ✔ **Avoid covering the concentrator.** Don't place it in a drawer and don't wrap it in plastic to avoid dust — it needs circulating air to prevent overheating.

  ✔ **Avoid excessive heat.** Keep the concentrator away from direct sunlight, radiators, heaters, and any other heat sources.

  ✔ **Avoid proximity to other electrical devices.** Don't put the concentrator next to fluorescent lights, radios, or transmitting equipment.

Concentrators are innately powerless

Ethernet concentrators require electrical power, so they must be located next to an electrical outlet. Unless you want to do some fancy electrical work (or you don't mind the cable keeping you from closing the closet door all the way), a closet — which otherwise would be a great location to hide a hub — won't work because there is no electrical outlet nearby.

Keep your concentrator plugged into a surge protector. Plug the surge protector into a wall outlet, and then plug the concentrator into the surge protector. Surges travel rapidly through cable, and when they do, they zap everything in the cable's path. A good surge can take out every NIC on the network. A *really*

strong surge can push the damage past the NIC and fry the motherboard (remember, every NIC is connected to the connector, and every NIC is also connected to its motherboard).

Distance Depends on What You Choose to Measure

Your cable run has to connect every computer to the concentrator, but you can only buy patch cable in specific lengths. The longer the cable, the more you pay. Ethernet networking kits have one piece of cable for each connector in the kit, and each piece of cable is the same length (usually 20 or 25 feet). Given these facts, the word *epicenter* becomes meaningless. For example, if the midpoint between two computers is a distance of 28 feet and you have two 25-foot lengths of cable, put the concentrator within 25 feet of one computer so that you only have to buy one longer cable.

Cable doesn't run from the concentrator to a computer in a straight line. It runs along baseboards, through walls, across ceilings, and sometimes even runs along *all* of these conduits. You can't really measure the amount of cable you'll need between the concentrator and a computer with an "as the crow flies" mentality. The only way to measure properly (and therefore buy the right cable lengths) is to read the sections on running cable later in this chapter. Then, depending on the way you run your cable, you'll have an idea of the length of cable you'll need to connect each computer to the concentrator.

You may have to account for traveling up walls, as well as across walls, ceilings, or floors. And of course, don't make your measurements too fine — you need to account for some slack. After all, why would you want the cable to come out of the wall in a straight line to the computer? You'd have to leap over the cable to cross the room.

In the end, what you're looking for is a location for the concentrator that requires as few very long cable lengths as possible. Make these considerations:

- ✔ You're more likely than not going to end up with a concentrator that is very near two computers while very far from the third computer. In the long run (yeah, the pun was intended), you'll end up saving money, time, and hassle if you accept this fact right now.

- ✔ Find a way to position the concentrator near the conduit you're using for the cable run (you may decide to run cable through a wall, a ceiling, or along baseboards). If your cables come out of a wall, put the concentrator very close to the wall to avoid the need for longer cable. Some concentrators come with devices that permit wall mounting so that the concentrator doesn't take up table or shelf space.

Handling Cable Correctly

Be careful about the way you handle cable as you run it through the chase. (A *chase* is the opening through which you place the cable, like inside a wall, in a hollow space above the ceiling, or along the baseboards of a room.) Keep the following tips in mind:

- **The bigger the hole (within reason), the better.** When you drill holes to run cable between rooms or floors, make the holes slightly larger than the connector at the end of the cable. Connectors are delicate, so you don't want to force-feed them through small openings.

- **Keep everything neat, just like your mother taught you.** When you run cable from the entry point in the room (the entrance hole) to the computer, snake it along the baseboard or the top of the quarter round until you're close to the computer. Keeping the cable tucked off to the side helps to ensure that no one trips over the cable.

- **Be nice to the cable.** Avoid bending cable at a sharp angle. If you have to run the cable around a corner, don't pull it taut.

- **When in doubt, staple like a madman.** You can use U-shaped nails that act like staples to attach cable to a surface. Use nails large enough to surround the cable — do not insert them into the cable.

- **Use an artist's touch.** You can paint the cable to match your baseboard or wall, but don't paint the connector.

Connecting two patch cables

You can connect two pieces of assembled cable with a coupler. A *coupler* is a small plastic device with two receptacles (one at each end) that accept RJ-45 connectors — you end a cable run in one receptacle and begin the next piece of cable in the other receptacle. Couplers work very much like an extension device for telephone lines.

Couplers don't have a terrific history of reliability. Frequently, when you encounter problems with computer-to-computer communication, the blame falls on these connections. Never put a coupler inside a wall or in any other location that's hard to reach, because you need easy access to the coupler if you have to check or replace the connection. The best plan is to use a coupler as a temporary solution while you wait for delivery of a custom-made patch cable that's the correct length.

Even though couplers work similarly to telephone-extension devices, do not use a telephone coupler for your computer cable.

Making your own patch cables

If you know you have a big networking job ahead of you, you can save a lot of money by making your own patch cables. You can make your own by taking 10Base-T cable, cutting the right length, and attaching an RJ-45 connector at each end. This process is rather easy — I can barely change a light bulb, but I've been making my own cable connectors for years. To make your own patch cables, you need cable, RJ-45 connectors, a wire stripper, and a crimper to seat the connection properly.

You can buy bulk cable inexpensively — a 300-foot roll of cable costs about the same as two 50-foot patch cables. If you buy a larger roll of bulk cable, the price per foot is even less. The RJ-45 connectors cost a few pennies each, but you'll probably have to buy at least a 20-pack — I've never seen them sold individually. Buying a crimper should set you back less than $100, and a wire stripper is a few dollars.

To make a patch cable, follow these steps:

1. **Cut the length of cable you need.**

   Don't forget to account for climbing up or down walls and running along baseboards.

2. **Use the stripper to remove about half an inch of insulation from the end of the cable.**

3. **Push the wires into the holes on the RJ-45 connector.**

   You'll find they slide in easily.

4. **Position the crimper where the wires meet the connector and press firmly.**

   Most crimpers come with instructions, including illustrations, to explain exactly how to crimp the connector. Most crimpers can handle a variety of connector sizes (for example, your crimper can probably make regular telephone wire connectors, called *RJ-11* connectors), so make sure you use the position marked for RJ-45 connectors.

5. **Repeat this action for the other end of the cable.**

The Chase Is On: Running the Cable

The permutations and combinations of runs depend on the physical layout of your home, of course, but the ideal way to cable your home is to find a way to run cable in a straight line between the concentrator and each computer on the network. Sounds easy, doesn't it? Good luck! The opening through which you wind and wend the cable is called a *chase*. The chase may be inside a wall, in a hollow space above the ceiling, along the baseboards of a room, or a combination of these opportunities. If you're lucky, you can find a straight-line chase between the concentrator and each individual computer.

Cabling within a room

If you put the concentrator in the same room as one of the computers (or if all the computers on your network are in the same room), you don't need to drill holes in walls or floors. Put the concentrator next to one computer. Connect the closest computer to the concentrator with a short length of cable. Then run a longer piece of cable from the concentrator to the other computer(s). Run the cable along the baseboard, not across the floor.

Cabling between adjacent rooms

Cabling your network is easy if your computers are located in adjacent rooms on the same floor because you only have to drill one hole between the rooms. Put the concentrator in one room and run one length of cable between the concentrator and the computer. Run another section of cable through the wall to the computer in the other room. You need to drill only one hole, as shown in Figure 3-3.

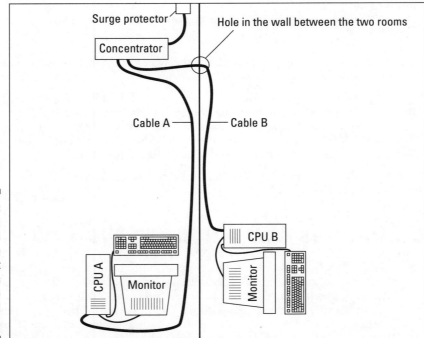

Figure 3-3:
Cabling between two adjacent rooms requires one drilled opening.

Cabling between non-adjacent rooms on the same floor

If your computers are on the same floor but aren't in adjacent rooms, you need to do a bit more work. The most direct and efficient cabling route is to find a chase along your home's beams. Most houses have beams between floors that run straight through the house, either from front to back, side to side, or both. You usually can expect a clear chase from one end to the other.

The logical way to access the chase is to drill a hole in the ceiling or floor (depending on whether the chase is above or below the level you're working on).

I hate drilling holes in the ceiling because, to say the least, the blemish looks crummy. Even if I paint the cable to match the wall, I know it's there. Instead, I use closets or walls to get to the chase.

Keeping your drill holes in the closet

Wiring through closets is a great way to hide the side effects of cabling. If you have a closet in every room that holds a computer, you're in great shape. It's less important to clean up the hole and touch up the paint when you work in a closet, unless you're some kind of decorating fanatic. If every room doesn't have a closet, don't worry — you can still confine the cabling to the corners of the room.

Drill a hole in the closet ceiling or floor of each room that holds a computer (one room also holds the concentrator). Choose between the ceiling or the floor, depending on where the chase is.

Bring the cable through the chase to each computer. You can use a *fish* (a tool specially designed for fishing cable that is sold in hardware stores) or a coat hanger you've untwisted (the hook at the end grabs the cable).

Of course, a portion of the cable has to run between the closet and the computer or concentrator. If you have enough clearance under the closet door, run the cable under the door and then attach it to the baseboard with U-shaped staples as it moves toward the computers. If you have no clearance under the closet door, drill a hole in the bottom of the doorjamb to bring the cable into the room.

Cable that's all walled up

For any room that lacks a closet, bring the cable into the room from the chase at a corner. If the cable enters the room through the ceiling from the chase above, bring the cable down the seam of the walls that create the corner (and paint it to match the wall). Then run the cable along the baseboard to the computer. If the cable enters the room through the floor from the chase below, run the cable along the baseboard to the computer.

Here are a couple of other schemes to consider if all your computers are on the same floor:

- If your computers are on the second floor, run the cable across the attic floor (or crawl space above the second floor). Then you can drop the cable down a corner to each computer.

- If your computers are on the first floor, run the cable across the basement ceiling (or crawl space). Then you can snake the cable up to each computer.

Cabling between Floors

If your computers are on different floors, you have more work to do. You need additional cable because your cable length measurement must include the height of the room in addition to the horizontal length required to reach the computer. Here are some tips on what to do if you have a multilevel home network on your hands:

- **Basement/second floor room arrangement:** If you have one computer in the basement and another on the second floor, you need sufficient cable length to make the trip to the concentrator. Putting the concentrator on the first floor instead of next to one computer may be easier because you may have a problem finding cable that's long enough.

- **Stacked room arrangement:** If the rooms are stacked one above the other, you can run the cable through the inside of the walls, near a corner. Make sure to use the opening around accessible radiators and pipes, and use stacked closets when you can. If the stacked rooms occupy three levels, put the concentrator in the middle level. If you're moving between two floors, put the concentrator on either floor.

- **Kitty-corner room arrangement:** If the rooms are on opposite ends of the house, in addition to being on different floors (as far away from each other as humanly possible), you have to use both walls (or closets) and ceilings. For the vertical runs, use any openings around pipes that are available (houses with radiators are usually filled with pipe runs.) If no pipes are available, use the inside of the wall. For the horizontal runs, find a chase above or below the room.

Now, here are some bonus tips to help you run cable across multiple levels:

- **Use gravity to your advantage.** After you drill your holes and find the space in the wall or next to a pipe, work from the top down. Put a weight on the end of sturdy twine and drop it down to the lower floor. Then tape the cable to the weight and haul it up. This way is much easier than pushing the cable up through the walls and using a fish to grab it.

✔ **Use ducts if you can.** You can also use HVAC (heating, ventilation, and air conditioning) ducts, but you should be aware that many municipalities have strict rules about this choice. Some building codes totally forbid using HVAC ducts to run cable of any type; other building codes just set standards. The advantage of using HVAC ducts is that they go into every room, and they're usually rather wide. The disadvantage is that they rarely travel in a straight line, so you may have to run cable through several rooms to connect a computer to the concentrator. Never, ever enter the duct system by drilling a hole. You must use an existing entry and exit, usually through the grate over the point at which the duct meets the wall.

✔ **Network everything.** Haul some electrical wire and regular telephone cable through the walls when you run your network cable. Later, if you want your electrician to add outlets for all the computer peripherals you'll probably accumulate, or you want to add a phone jack, most of the work is already done. In fact, if you bring several telephone wires along, you have a head start for installing a home security system or a home intercom system.

✔ **Consider getting more than one concentrator.** If you have a large amount of space to cover, you may actually save money on cable, not to mention saving yourself some trouble, if you use more than one concentrator. And you'll have a jump-start if you decide to add computers to your home network later. See the section, "Getting into the Zone," later in this chapter, for more information.

Beauty Is in the Eye of the Decorator

After you finish all the cabling and the computers are connected to the concentrator, an interesting thing occurs in many households. The person in the household who cares most about the décor (usually Mom) walks around the house muttering sentences in which the word "ugly" occurs. Teenage daughters look at the new high-tech system you installed and react with words like, "Gross!" (teenage sons don't seem to notice).

Somebody, perhaps a guest (if not a member of the family) eventually remarks, "We have a network at work, and we don't have holes in the wall that exude cable and we don't have cable crawling along the floor or the baseboard."

Professional installers use accessories to make hardware decorator-friendly, and there's no reason you can't put the same finishing touches on your system. An added benefit is that some of the accessories also make the installation safer, removing cable from places that may cause someone to trip.

Adding cable faceplates

If you run cable through walls, you can end the cable run at the wall, using an Ethernet socket that's attached to the wall with a faceplate, as shown in Figure 3-4. Then, you just need to run a small piece of cable from the computer to the faceplate. You can buy multioutlet faceplates, which you'll need in the room that contains the concentrator.

To use a faceplate to create an Ethernet socket, pull the cable through the hole in the wall and use a cable stripper to remove about an inch of insulation from the cable. If the cable is a patch cable, cut off the connector first. Then insert the wires into the socket and push against the socket to seal the connection (these are similar to electrical connections that just snap into place). Attach the socket to the faceplate and attach the faceplate to the wall (pushing the wires back into the wall).

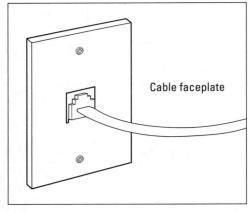

Cable faceplate

Figure 3-4:
You can
connect
computers
to a
faceplate.

Using floor cable covers

In any networking situation, a certain amount of cable is exposed because you have to run cable between the wall and the NIC in the computer. The best way to hide as much cable as possible is to put the computer desk against the wall at the point where the cable exits the wall. If that solution isn't possible, cover the cable that runs between the wall and the computer. Floor cable covers can help make your network installation less ugly and also provide safety by eliminating the chance to trip over the cable.

Floor cable covers come in two models: covers that lie atop the cable and covers that hold the cable in a channel (see Figure 3-5). Both cover types provide several advantages over loose cable:

✔ Cable covers hug the ground and don't move. You can't accidentally nudge them up into the air as you walk and then trip over the loop you created (which is what frequently happens with Ethernet cable).

✔ Cable covers are wide. And the slope to the top of the cover is very gentle, which lessens the chance that you'll trip.

✔ You can use cable covers under a rug. Don't run cable under a rug because the rubbing of the underside of the rug against the cable can weaken or break the cable's insulation jacket.

Figure 3-5:
Cable covers hide ugly cable and reduce the risk of someone tripping.

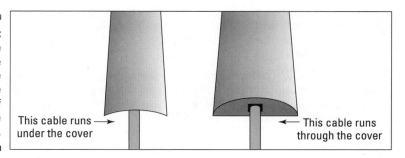

This cable runs → under the cover

← This cable runs through the cover

Most floor covers are made of plastic or rubber. You can paint the plastic covers, but I find that paint wears away quickly on rubber. If you're running the covers over a carpet, you can even glue carpet strips to the top of the cover, which may help hide the fact that your family room is crawling with cable.

Curing Your Network's Growing Pains

You can be almost certain that your home network will grow — you'll add more computers. (Read how to run cable from the new computer to the concentrator in the earlier section, "The Chase Is On: Running the Cable.") But what happens if you run out of concentrator connections? If you start your home network with a kit built for two computers, where do you plug in additional computers?

You have two solutions:

✔ Buy a larger concentrator (and sell the original concentrator to a friend who's building a home network).

✔ Buy another small concentrator and link it to the first.

You shouldn't need any instructions for carrying out the first solution.

The second solution, however, requires a little bit of homework — you need to read the instructions that came with both concentrators to understand how to link them. Every concentrator has an uplink port, which is specifically designed to connect one concentrator to another concentrator instead of connecting a computer to a concentrator. (Notice that a concentrator meant to accommodate four computers has five ports.) Before you use an uplink port, here's what you need to know:

- ✔ **Where the uplink port is:** The uplink port is always at the end of the row of ports (usually next to the place where the power cord goes).

- ✔ **What the uplink port looks like:** Notice that the uplink port is usually marked differently from the other ports, either with an icon or the word *uplink*. (If nothing is visible, check the documentation that came with the concentrator.)

- ✔ **What kind of cable you need to hook up two concentrators:** You need to use a *crossover cable* when you connect two concentrators through their uplink ports. You can buy this special cable from the same places that you can purchase regular Ethernet patch cable.

Run cable from the new computer(s) to the new concentrator and connect the old concentrator to the new one via the uplink port (or the other way around). Read the documentation for both concentrators to see whether you need to use a crossover cable and also to see whether the connection from the uplink port goes into a regular port or the other uplink port. Look at Figure 3-6 to see an illustration of a network with two concentrators.

Getting into the Zone

You can gain advantages from linked concentrators even if one concentrator has enough ports for all the computers on your network. The concept is called *zoning*, and you can zone your network to make cabling easier.

For example, say you have widely separated two computers on the first floor. One computer is in the family room at the front of the house, and the other computer is in the kitchen at the back of the house. You have two computers on the second floor, also at opposite ends of the house.

You can place a single concentrator in the family room and run cable across the first floor to the kitchen computer. Then you can run cable down the wall to the computer on the second floor at the front of the house. Finally, you can run cable down the wall and across the house to the computer on the second floor at the back of the house, but doesn't that seem like a lot of cable?

Instead, create zones for your network. For example, you can put two concentrators in the basement or in the attic. Place one near the front of the house and one near the back of the house. Drop the cables from two computers to each concentrator. Then link the concentrators to each other. Because you're using the attic or basement (where beauty doesn't count as much), you can string the cable across rafters, using hooks or duct tape. As you can see in Figure 3-7, zoning is logical, easy, and provides for network growth.

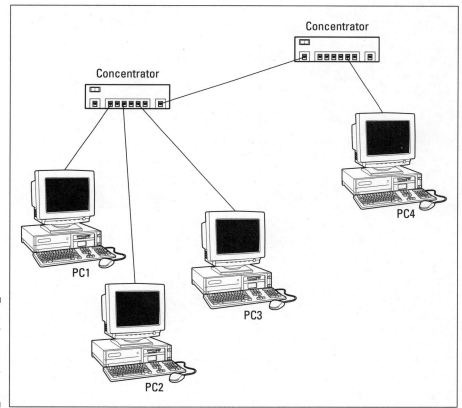

Figure 3-6: Add another concentrator when you outgrow the first one.

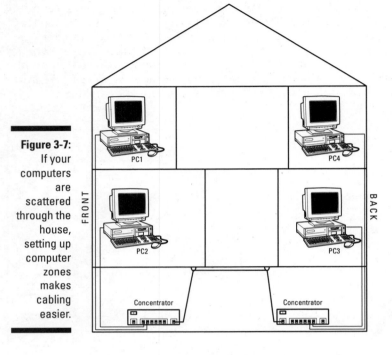

Figure 3-7:
If your computers are scattered through the house, setting up computer zones makes cabling easier.

Chapter 4

Installing Alternative Connections

*Y*ou can use several methods to set up your home networking wiring. You can use the standard utilities — phone and power lines — or you can opt for a more high-tech (high-maintenance?) wireless wiring option. If you opt to use a networking scheme other than an Ethernet networking scheme, this chapter covers the instructions that you need to connect all your computers.

I cover Ethernet wiring in detail in Chapter 3, but this chapter covers all the other types of wiring available for home networks. If you're not using Ethernet wiring, and you were thinking you could do a little mix-and-match action on your home network, think again. Your non-Ethernet hardware is probably *proprietary*. The bottom line? The stuff that came with your networking kit may not work with the stuff manufactured by another company that makes networking kits. Buy everything you need before you begin to install the network — and if you're planning to expand the network soon (or you're really nervous or a klutz), buy extra hardware to avoid a headache. You could have a real problem if the company that made your networking hardware and wiring goes belly up, or if it drops your model in favor of a newer, incompatible model.

One Standard, Indivisible, with Liberty and Networking for All

Before you start scurrying around wiring your home network, you should know that each of your wiring options (except Ethernet) has either brand-new standards or has standards that are still under construction (and consideration). (Ethernet is totally standardized. A NIC is a NIC, and it doesn't matter what company makes it — all Ethernet NICs play well with each other.)

Technical standards are usually developed by groups of manufacturers who come together to form an association specifically so that they can sit around and set standards. Eventually, if enough manufacturers adopt the standards, all the other manufacturers have no choice but to use the new standards. At that point, the proprietary technology gives way in favor of the association's technology. Here's a by-wiring option lowdown:

- Telephone line technology has been developed and adopted by the Home Phoneline Networking Alliance (www.homepna.org), and it's unlikely that any manufacturer would stray from that field.

- The Homeplug Powerline Alliance (www.homeplug.org) is trying to set standards for network devices that use household electrical wires.

- Wireless solutions are on the way to becoming standardized around technology invented by a company named Bluetooth (named for an old Viking king; www.bluetooth.org), and someday all manufacturers may adopt these settings.

  HomeRF (www.homerf.org) and the InfraRed Data Association (www.irda.org) also are working on wireless standards for PCs and other devices. You can visit association Web sites to find out which manufacturers are working with the standardization processes. Remember that part of an association's job is to accelerate demand for the technology, so be wary of the information that you see on the Web sites.

The Gang's All Here: Using Phone Lines to Connect a Network

If you've chosen to install a phone-line network, at this point you should already have installed the connectors on the computers. If you haven't installed the connectors, page back to Chapter 2 for installation instructions. (For telephone line networking, connectors are available in the form of NICs, USB connectors, or parallel port connectors).

Now it's time to connect the connectors so that they can "talk" to each other. You use your household telephone lines to accomplish this task.

To get your telephone line network up and running, just put one end of a regular telephone cable into the NIC on the computer and put the other end of the telephone cable into the wall jack. Okay, you're done. You now have a network. Well, you have to install the software drivers and take care of other software tasks (see Chapter 5), but the hardware stuff is done.

Hello? What? It's not that simple in your house? Oh, I see, you actually want to use a telephone in at least one of the rooms that has a computer. And you want to use a modem?

Don't worry. Your phone line can handle as many devices as it has frequencies. What you have to do is *gang,* or join, multiple devices so that each device is individually accessible and all devices meet at one point. That point is your telephone wall jack. I discuss some of the gadgets you can use to gang your telephone line devices in Chapter 1, and I go through the ganging options in the following sections.

Ganging the network and the telephone

You can use your wall jack for two devices at the same time by plugging a modular duplex jack (commonly called a *splitter*) into the wall receptacle. The splitter, which you can buy at the supermarket or at an office supply store, has a standard RJ-11 plug at the front, just like telephone cable. The back end has two RJ-11 receptacles, into which you can plug two devices. Use one receptacle for cable coming from the telephone and the other for cable coming from the network connector on your computer.

Ganging the network, the telephone, and an external modem

If you have an external modem and want to have a telephone near the computer that's using the wall jack for network communications, you easily can gang the three devices. All external modems have two RJ-11 receptacles. One receptacle is for the cable that goes from the modem to the wall jack, and one receptacle accepts cable from the telephone. The receptacles are marked, usually with icons (one icon looks like a wall jack, the other looks like a telephone). If your modem doesn't have icons, it has labels — *line* and *phone.*

Follow these steps to gang the network, telephone, and an external modem:

1. **Plug a splitter into the wall jack.**

2. **Connect the cable from your computer NIC into one side of the splitter.**

3. **Connect the cable from the external modem's line receptacle into the other side of the splitter.**

4. **Plug the cable from the telephone into the telephone receptacle on the modem.**

You probably figured out that this gang arrangement means that the external modem and the telephone don't have their own individual access to the wall jack. A gang arrangement isn't just sharing; it's a highly exclusive, fickle marriage. The modem and telephone are both POTS devices that can't operate simultaneously anyway.

If you pick up the telephone while you're using the modem, you will not hear a dial tone. (Picking up the phone destroys the modem communication, so hopefully you aren't downloading an important file at that moment.) Anyone calling your house hears a busy signal, so you won't hear the phone ring when you're online, either. When you're not using the modem, you can use the telephone normally, even though it isn't plugged directly into the wall. The modem's connection to the wall jack provides a pass-through connection to the telephone line.

Ganging the network, the telephone, and an internal modem

If your computer has an internal modem, the part of the modem you access at the back of your computer probably includes two receptacles — one for the telephone line and one for a telephone (just like an external modem). Follow the instructions for ganging the network, the telephone, and an external modem in the preceding section.

However, if your internal modem doesn't have a receptacle for the telephone or if you're using a PCMCIA modem on a laptop, you must arrange the gang a bit differently. In fact, you have some choices about how all the devices get to the wall jack. Here's what you do:

1. **Put a splitter in the wall jack and insert the cable from the telephone into one receptacle.**

2. **Join the cables coming out of the NIC and the internal modem.**

   You can choose one of the following methods, which also are shown in Figure 4-1:

   A. Use a Y-connector (conveniently, it looks like a capital Y), which accepts both RJ-11 connectors (from the modem and the NIC) on one end. Insert the RJ-11 connector (at the other end of the Y-connector) into the empty side of the splitter.

   B. Use a splitter to accept both RJ-11 connections and then plug the splitter into the empty side of the splitter that's in the wall jack.

   C. Use a splitter to accept both RJ-11 connections and then plug the splitter into a length of telephone cable that has a receptacle at one end and a RJ-11 connection at the other end.

   D. Use a splitter to accept both RJ-11 connections and then plug the splitter into a connector, which has a receptacle at each end. Then run cable between the connector and the splitter in the wall jack.

If you're using a USB or parallel port network connector, the principle is the same — just substitute your port for the NIC shown in Figure 4-1.

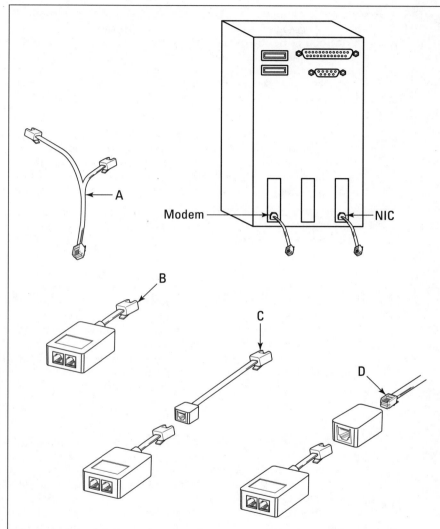

Figure 4-1:
Gang the internal modem and the NIC and then send both devices to the wall jack as one connection.

Powering Up Your Network with the Electric Company

If you choose a networking scheme that uses your home's power lines, you don't need to run cable through the walls, floors, or anywhere. Each network connector you purchase plugs into the power outlet on the wall.

To keep an electric-wire network safe, keep these points in mind:

✓ **Connectors need special help getting over their inherent problems.** If your computer and monitor occupy the nearest electrical outlet, leaving no empty outlet for the network connector, you can't plug the power line connectors into a standard surge protector or power strip — you must purchase a special strip from the company that supplied your network devices.

You need special equipment because electrical power network connectors have to overcome many inherent problems that come with transmitting data signals over power lines, and all the equipment you use must contain the electronics designed to make the system work. Overcoming those problems accounts for the lack of speed in data transmission.

✓ **Stormy weather is a harbinger of computer doom.** Be extremely sensitive to electrical problems, such as lightning storms and brownouts. Unplug your computers and network connectors at the first sign of a problem.

Wireless Technology: Look Ma, No Cable

If you opt to use wireless technology, you don't have any cables to run through the walls, the floors, or even from the computer to an outlet. Your network connectors provide the communication technology without needing help. The only detail you have to worry about is the location of your computers, and I provide those details in the following sections.

Radio frequency: Hello, den? Kitchen here

Radio frequency (RF) communication isn't new technology; it's just new to computer networking. The computers on the network communicate via radio waves sent through the air. Attached to the network connector you installed on each computer (a NIC, a USB connector, or a parallel port connector) is a device called a *transceiver*. As its name implies, a transceiver both transmits and receives radio waves. The transceiver itself is a small antenna that's capable of transmitting radio waves to a distance of about 150 feet.

Radio waves travel freely in the air until they run up against metal. Metal stops them in their tracks. (So does a large body of water, but that's probably not a problem in your house unless you plan to store your computer under a waterbed.) As a result, you can't put your computer under a metal desk or in a room with walls that are filled with plumbing pipes (unless you replace all the intake and drainpipes with PVC pipes).

Whose line is it, anyway?

The telephone lines that run through your walls have a great deal more power than you need for plain old telephone service, or POTS. The multiple wires that are inside telephone cables all don't use the same frequency. The wires that provide POTS have one frequency, but other wires use other frequencies. The technical terminology for this is *Frequency Division Multiplexing* (FDM). Here's the lowdown on some of the different frequencies:

✔ The POTS frequency services telephones, fax machines, and modems. Because all these devices share the same frequency, you can't receive telephone calls when you're connected to the Internet via a modem.

✔ A different frequency is available for special devices that provide high-speed Internet access, such as DSL and ISDN devices,

enabling you to use a high-speed device and a POTS device simultaneously.

✔ The hardware in your telephone line network uses *still another* frequency to communicate among all the computers on your network. POTS and high-speed Internet connection devices continue to operate on their own frequencies and are therefore available to you.

You don't have to worry about which frequency any service or device is using; the network devices and telephone wires automatically know which frequency to use. The only thing you have to do to ensure that your home network operates properly is to connect all the computers to the same telephone number (which isn't a problem unless you have two or more telephone numbers in your home).

The transceiver sends radio waves in a wide arc; it isn't point-and-aim technology. Each computer is unaware of the location of the other computer(s) and spins its radio waves up, down, and around, in the hope of finding a soul mate to talk to. You shouldn't place the computer near a metal filing cabinet, metal door, or any other glob of metal that can narrow the scope of its signal.

After you finish installing all the drivers and software (see Chapter 5), if any computer is missing from your network, move it. It may be out of range from the other computers, or running into an obstacle.

Here are a few additional points to keep in mind about RF communication:

✔ **If you have a laptop equipped for RF communication, you can take it outside on a nice day and still maintain your participation in the network.** The signals pass easily through windows and walls. In fact, you can take your desktop computer outside, but that's quite a bit of schlepping.

✔ **Anyone with an RF connector on a computer can lurk outside your house and join your network — ewww, creepy!** The interloper can copy or delete your files as easily as you can. For that reason, make sure that the manufacturer of your RF connectors utilizes multiple channels and spread-spectrum frequency hopping. This feature changes the frequency that the network uses automatically and often.

In addition, just in case a malicious visitor also employs frequency hopping, make sure that your RF manufacturer provides a firewall to protect your network. See Chapter 12 to find out more about firewalls.

✔ **Even if your computers remain inside, you may use some frequencies that are also in use by other devices, including outside devices.** RF-equipped garage doors are an example, and opening or closing the garage may occasionally cause interference with network communications. Or, you can impress your friends by magically opening the garage door while copying a file between computers.

In the not-so-distant future, you may find that you install additional RF-controlled devices in your home, as manufacturers begin offering appliances that can receive commands from your computer. Open the garage door before you leave the house, start the oven or the microwave, turn lights on or off — the list of possibilities is endless.

Infrared — ready, aim, communicate

Infrared (IR) connections are based on the direct interchange of visual signals. Your television remote-control device (in my house we call it the *clicker*) works with IR communication. The IR ports in your computers are transceivers, handling both the send and receive sides of computer communication. If you have an IR-based network, all the computers must be in the same room because they have to see each other.

Direct IR: Seeing 1 to 1

Basic IR communication, or *direct IR*, operates in port-to-port mode — point-and-send and point-and-receive. The ports must be close together and facing each other. The allowable distance varies by manufacturer, but if you have the two devices within a few feet of each other you shouldn't encounter a problem.

You may have to wiggle the computers around a bit, adjusting them to make sure that the IR ports have a direct line of sight. While the computers are communicating, you can't interfere with the line of sight.

Glare from sunlight or a strong lamp distorts and interferes with the signals, and you need opaque window coverings if any computer is positioned where sunlight glares against the port. However, communication proceeds just fine in a dark room (I guess that's not very helpful, huh?).

Diffuse IR: Bouncing off the walls

If you have more than two computers or if you want to add a printer to your two-computer network, direct IR doesn't work. (Well, you can make it work by physically turning the computers so that the appropriate two ports aim at each other, but that's not an attractive alternative.)

Diffuse IR doesn't require direct line of sight. In fact, positioning your computers for port-to-port eyeballing interferes with the efficiency of diffuse IR. Place your computers so that the ports are facing a wall. The technology bounces signals against the wall and disburses the signals all over the room. The receiver side of each IR port picks up the signals (and the transmit side of the port can continue to send data).

Part II
Setting Up the Computers

The 5th Wave   By Rich Tennant

"IT WAS CLASHING WITH THE SOUTHWESTERN MOTIF."

In this part . . .

After you've installed all the hardware and connected all the computers, you have to perform a few software-based chores. You can put away your tools because you do the rest of the setup stuff at the computer. The only tools you need are keyboards and mice.

The chapters in this part of the book walk you through the tasks required for setting up the software side of networking. None of the tasks are complicated, and many of them are automated, or semi-automated (the computer does all or most of the work for you, which is what computers are supposed to be all about).

Some of the stuff you have to do is routine technical stuff, like installing *drivers* (software files that control devices like NICs or network connectors attached to ports). You also find how to set up each computer so it's willing to share its contents with the rest of the network.

The information in the chapters in this part goes beyond simple networking procedures, because you also find how to share your Internet connection among your network users. Installing shared Internet access probably cures more family problems than an expensive therapist. You don't have to set rules about time limits, and you won't hear the whines and yells that echoed through the house when somebody stayed online too long.

Chapter 5

Installing Networking Software

● ●

In This Chapter

▶ Installing drivers — the software that drives the hardware

▶ Configuring services — the settings that control communication

▶ The Windows Me wizard — automating all the tasks

▶ Letting your Macintosh join the party

● ●

*S*imply connecting cable to your home computers doesn't create a network. It's like attaching a VCR to your TV set: After the cable is connected you still have to set up the system before you can do anything with it, such as record programs. On a computer network, you have to set everything up by installing the software that controls the communication features. This chapter shows you how.

Installing Drivers

Your network connectors (NICs, USB connectors, parallel port connectors, and so on) are hardware devices, and every hardware device on a computer needs a *driver*. Drivers are files that the operating system uses to communicate with the hardware, telling the connector what to do, when to do it, and how to do it.

After you install the network connector (see Chapter 2), Windows should discover it automatically the next time you start your computer. The Windows Plug and Play feature goes to work while the operating system is starting up and begins installing the software drivers immediately. If Windows doesn't automatically find the hardware and offer to install the software, your hardware is not Plug and Play compliant, and you have to install the driver software manually. The following sections detail how to install drivers for either scenario.

The Plug and Play way

The Plug and Play feature is like a little elf that looks at all the hardware in your computer during startup, and when a new Plug and Play hardware component is detected, he notifies Windows. As soon as Windows hears about the new hardware, it wants to begin installing the software drivers immediately.

Windows sends a message to your screen to tell you that it has found the new hardware you added, and asks if you want to install it. Say Yes to begin the installation, which is accomplished via a Windows wizard named, appropriately enough, the Add New Hardware Wizard.

If your network connector is a USB device, and you installed it while your computer was running, the Windows Plug and Play elf was watching and offered to install the software as soon as you installed the connector — you didn't have to restart the computer.

When you tell Windows you want to install the network hardware that the Plug and Play feature discovered, the Add New Hardware Wizard shows up to walk you through each step of the process. Figure 5-1 shows the first window of the wizard, but the graphics and text you see may differ, depending on the version of Windows you're using. However, the graphics and text are just the glitzy stuff, and the wizard's behavior is the same across all versions of Windows.

Figure 5-1:
It's easier
to install
drivers
when a
wizard
shows up to
hold your
hand.

The wizard works by asking questions and offering choices. As you complete each step, click the Next button to move to the next wizard window. You can also click the Back button if you want to return to a previous window and change your answers.

For this particular task (installing drivers for your network hardware), the wizard has only a few questions. Essentially, the wizard is trying to figure out where to find the files it needs. You have a crib sheet you can check before you give the wizard any answers. The documentation that accompanied your network hardware has all the information you need.

Luckily, this stuff isn't overly complicated, because you have only three choices:

✔ **Drivers supplied on your Windows CD.**

Windows has built-in drivers for lots of models from lots of manufacturers. The list of built-in drivers varies among the versions of Windows (for example, Windows 2000 Professional has more choices than Windows 98 Second Edition). If Plug and Play found your hardware, your version of Windows has the drivers you need.

If you purchased your computer from a manufacturer that preinstalled Windows, you may not have a Windows CD with drivers. However, the manufacturer installed all those files on your hard drive.

✔ **Drivers provided by the hardware manufacturer.**

Many manufacturers provide their own drivers, enclosing a CD or a floppy disk in the packaging. They do this either because they know that Windows doesn't provide the drivers (which means Plug and Play doesn't work and you have to install the drivers yourself), or they think their own drivers work better than the Windows-supplied drivers.

✔ **Drivers you downloaded from the Web.**

If your version of Windows doesn't have the latest set of hardware drivers, you can download drivers from the Microsoft Web site. In fact, even if you just purchased the latest and greatest version of Windows, you should check Microsoft's Web site to see if it has a latest and greatest version of the drivers. Open your browser and go to `www.microsoft.com/windows/default.asp`. Click the link to your version of Windows and then follow the links to download network hardware drivers.

Manufacturers also update drivers periodically and you can find their Web site information in the documentation that came with the hardware.

The following three sections offer further details on how to complete the Add New Hardware Wizard, based on the drivers you're using.

Using the Windows drivers

The wizard offers to search for the best driver for your hardware and displays a note that says this is the recommended option. If the documentation for your NIC (or other type of network connector) indicates that you can (or should) use Windows drivers, let the wizard do the searching for you.

You need to have your Windows CD in the CD-ROM drive. If your Windows operating system was installed by the computer manufacturer, the files you need are probably on your hard drive, and no CD exists for you to worry about (don't worry, the wizard knows where to look for driver files).

Hold down the Shift key when you insert the CD to prevent the disk from starting its AutoRun program.

Using the manufacturer's drivers

If the documentation for the NIC indicates that you should use the drivers supplied by the manufacturer, insert the disk that came with your NIC. Depending on the version of Windows you're using, the wizard options for using the manufacturer's drivers vary. In some versions of Windows, the wizard offers an option to display a list of drivers in a specific location. In other versions of Windows, the wizard offers a Have Disk button. Both options get you to the same place — a wizard window that asks where the drivers are.

In the window that asks for the location, type the drive letter for the disk that holds the software drivers. For a floppy disk, type **A:**. For a CD, enter the drive letter assigned to your CD-ROM drive (usually **D:**).

Using downloaded drivers

If you want to use drivers you downloaded, the process is the same as using the manufacturer's drivers. Select the option to search a specific location, or click the Have Disk button. Then enter the location where you saved the files on your hard drive. If you don't remember the name of the folder, click the Browse button and select the right drive and folder, as shown in Figure 5-2.

Figure 5-2:
Select the drive and folder in which you saved your downloaded drivers.

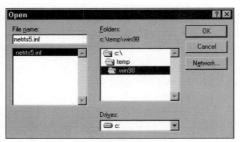

After the files are transferred to your hard drive, Windows displays a message telling you to restart your computer in order to have the new settings take effect. Click Yes to restart Windows.

Doing it yourself

If your network hardware isn't Plug and Play, or if Windows fails to detect it during startup, you need to install the drivers manually. Relax, it's easy. In fact, you're performing the same tasks that the Add New Hardware Wizard performs, except that you actually have to make some decisions instead of letting the wizard roll along on automatic pilot.

Windows might not detect a Plug and Play hardware device because of the absence of Windows drivers. If your version of Windows doesn't have a driver for the hardware in its driver's database, Plug and Play won't detect it.

Manual installation of hardware starts with the Add New Hardware Wizard, but instead of running on automatic pilot, the wizard expects you to point the way. You can use this method to install Windows drivers, manufacturer's drivers, or drivers you downloaded from a Web site. Here's how:

1. **Choose Start⇨Settings⇨Control Panel.**

   The Control Panel window opens.

2. **Double-click the Add New Hardware icon.**

   The Add New Hardware Wizard window opens.

3. **Click Next to begin.**

   The wizard tells you it's going to look for new Plug and Play devices. It doesn't matter that you know it's probably not going to work — if your new device were Plug and Play, it would have been detected when you started your computer. However, this wizard is obstinate and offers no option named "don't bother."

4. **Click Next to start the search for Plug and Play hardware.**

   Wait for the wizard to give up. After the fruitless search ends, the wizard offers to search for hardware that isn't Plug and Play. This search is a silly waste of time, because you know exactly what hardware you want to install.

5. **Select the No, I Want to Select the Hardware from a List option and click Next.**

   The Hardware Types list appears.

6. **Select Network Adapters and click Next.**

   The Select Device dialog box opens to display a list of manufacturers and models, as shown in Figure 5-3.

7. **If your network adapter is listed and you're planning to install drivers from the Windows CD, select the adapter's listing and click Next.**

   Windows finds the drivers on your Windows CD-ROM and copies the files to your hard drive.

8. **If you have drivers from the manufacturer or from a Web site, click Have Disk.**

   The Install From Disk dialog box appears, as shown in Figure 5-4. Enter the drive letter for the location of the manufacturer's disk, or click Browse to find downloaded drivers on your hard drive.

9. Follow the wizard's instructions to finish installing the drivers.

After the files are copied to your hard drive, the System Settings Change dialog box appears, informing you that you must restart the operating system to have the new settings take effect. Click Yes to restart the operating system.

Figure 5-3: Choose the manufacturer and model of your network adapter, or opt to install your own drivers.

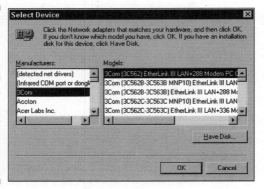

Figure 5-4: Direct the wizard to the drive that holds the files.

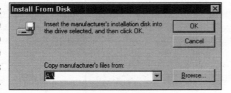

Special tasks for installing ISA NICs

If you purchased a NIC for an ISA bus, you may have to do some extra work in order to install the NIC properly. The manufacturer should have included instructions for performing these tasks, but frequently they're not very clear. This section presents an overview of the chores you face.

If your NIC is installed on a PCI bus, the bus and the operating system take care of setup chores automatically. See Chapter 1 for a discussion of ISA and PCI bus types.

Some NICs have software programs that establish the settings you need; other NICs have jumpers that you must arrange. Many NIC setup programs run in an MS-DOS session, and the documentation instructs you to choose Start➪Run and then type a command in the Open text box of the Run dialog box.

Most of the time, the setup program can determine which settings are available for the NIC. These settings involve an IRQ level and an I/O address, which are technical specifications that guarantee your NIC has a unique position in the technical scheme of things for your computer. (I won't bother you with all the technical explanations, because it's only important to know that they're unique to this piece of hardware.)

You can use the setup program that comes with the NIC to specify a particular IRQ level and I/O address. Some NICs don't use software to configure the settings. Instead, they use jumpers. A *jumper* is a small piece of plastic that "jumps" across pins, and whether or not pins are "jumpered" determines the settings. The NIC comes with documentation that explains all the possible settings and how to position the jumpers to create the setting you need.

Sometimes you need to wait until you've finished the installation (with incorrect specifications) and then correct the specifications, such as when the default settings for the NIC conflict with the settings for another device on your computer.

Determining which settings are available

Determining the unused IRQ and I/O settings before installation is faster and more efficient than waiting until later. You can determine the unused IRQ and I/O by following these steps:

1. **Right-click on the My Computer icon on the desktop and choose Properties from the shortcut menu that appears.**

   The System Properties dialog box opens.

2. **Click the Device Manager tab.**

   A list of all the devices in your computer appears.

3. **Click Print.**

   The Print dialog box for Device Manager opens.

4. **Select System Summary and then click OK.**

   A summary report of the resources in your computer prints. These reports are usually about three pages long.

The IRQ Summary section of the report lists all the IRQs currently in use, and any missing number is available (numbers range from 0–15).

The I/O Port Summary section of the report lists all the I/O addresses currently in use. When your NIC setup program presents possible I/O addresses, select one that isn't being used by another device. Then follow the instructions that came with your NIC to set the IRQ and I/O specifications.

Checking the installation settings

During the installation of the drivers, Windows determines the settings of your NIC. The determination may or may not be accurate. After installation, you need to check the settings attached to the NIC to make sure that they're accurate, which you can do by following these steps:

1. **Right-click on the My Computer icon on the desktop and choose Properties from the shortcut menu that appears.**

   The System Properties dialog box opens.

2. **Click the Device Manager tab.**

3. **Click the plus sign next to the listing for Network Adapters.**

   Windows reveals the specific entry for your NIC when the Network Adapters category expands.

4. **Select your NIC and click Properties.**

   The Properties dialog box for your NIC opens, with the General tab in the foreground.

If everything is fine, the Device Status section of the dialog box displays a message that says the device is working properly. If a problem exists, the message warns you that the device is not working properly.

If a problem exists with the NIC settings, the Network Adapters listing is probably already expanded when you select the Device Manager tab. The listing for your NIC probably has a symbol over its icon, either an exclamation point or an *X.* The symbol indicates that a problem with the settings for the NIC exists.

In either case, you should check the specific settings. Click the Resources tab to see the settings (see Figure 5-5). If the dialog box indicates there's a problem, see the next section, "Changing the NIC settings."

Changing the NIC settings

You may need to change the NIC settings if you couldn't successfully install the NIC or if Windows couldn't correctly identify the NIC, the IRQ level, and the I/O address.

If everything didn't work properly and the settings are incorrect, you must correct them. This process is sometimes complicated and sometimes easy. Sorry, but I can't be more specific than that. Follow along to see which set of circumstances matches your situation.

When IRQ and I/O settings don't match the NIC settings

You know what the IRQ and I/O settings are either from the documentation that came with the NIC, or from the preinstallation setup program that you ran. To set the IRQ and I/O settings to match the NIC settings, follow these steps:

1. **Select the incorrect setting.**

   If both the IRQ and I/O settings are wrong, select each one, one at a time.

2. **Click the Change Setting button.**

   The Edit Interrupt Request dialog box or the Edit Input/Output Range dialog box opens.

3. **Change the setting to match the physical setting of the NIC.**

   Type the correct number or use the arrows to select a new setting.

4. **Click OK three times to close all the open dialog boxes.**

   You'll probably be told to restart the computer to have your changes take effect.

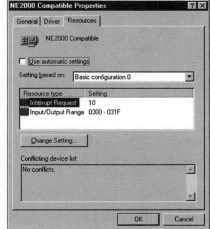

Figure 5-5:
The Resources tab of the Properties dialog box enumerates the current settings.

When the settings match but have a conflict

If the settings that appear match the settings you configured for the NIC but the installation still isn't working properly, you may have a conflict with another device. You need to rerun the preinstallation program for your NIC to change the setting that has a conflict.

Don't rerun the preinstallation program for your NIC blindly. You could spend half your life guessing the settings. Refer to the section "Determining which settings are available," earlier in this chapter, to make sure you know which IRQ or I/O settings are available and are not being used by another device.

Installing Network Protocols and Services

If you're running Windows Me on any computer, you can automate all the steps in this section for every computer on the network (except Windows 2000 Professional). This magic is accomplished with the Windows Me Home Networking Wizard. See the section "Using the Windows Me Home Networking Wizard," later in this chapter.

Computers that are connected in a network have to talk to each other. That's how they find each other and exchange files. In order to talk to each other, all the computers must speak the same language. The computer jargon for the language that computers use to communicate is called *networking protocol*. You need to install at least one networking protocol on each computer on your network.

The "mouthpiece" for communications between computers is the network adapter. The process of connecting the language to the mouthpiece (the protocol to the adapter) is called *binding*. After the protocol is bound to the NIC, your computers can talk to each other.

Once the computers can communicate, you can do stuff between computers. Each task you want to perform is a *service*. Services include sharing files, sharing printers, and logging on to the network.

Deciding on a protocol

Windows provides a number of protocols, including these two commonly used protocols:

- **NetBIOS Extended User Interface (NetBEUI):** This protocol is a simple, efficient one that works on peer-to-peer networks and Windows NT client/server networks. See Chapter 1 to find out about the different types of networks.

- **Transmission Control Protocol/Internet Protocol (TCP/IP):** This protocol is the one used on the Internet and is also used by many companies for running large networks. Mobile users find it especially useful for dialing in to network servers.

When you install a NIC, as described in the previous sections, Windows may automatically install another protocol, IPX/SPX (Internetwork Packet Exchange). Novell developed this protocol for its NetWare network operating system. Microsoft also has its own flavor of IPX/SPX, and for some reason, it's part of the installation of a NIC for some versions of Windows. Unless you have a NetWare server on your home network (which would certainly be surprising), you won't be using this protocol.

Making a decision about which protocol to use for your home network isn't always easy. The two choices to consider, NetBEUI and TCP/IP, each have pros and cons. Sometimes, the devices and operating system on your network help by forcing a decision. For example, sharing an Internet connection is probably easier with TCP/IP if you're using a DSL device or a cable modem. Check the instructions from your provider to see if TCP/IP is required.

For a regular modem, you can share an Internet connection with NetBEUI, and the Internet Sharing feature takes care of the details (see Chapter 6). NetBEUI is easier to install, because TCP/IP requires some extra steps. It does no harm to install both protocols, because the amount of extra work the computer has to do is barely noticeable to either you or the computer.

Unless TCP/IP is required, it's usually best to opt for NetBEUI, which is less complicated to install and easier to manage.

Adding a protocol

You need the Windows CD in order to access the files for the protocol you're installing, so put it in the CD-ROM drive (unless your Windows files were pre-installed on your hard drive, in which case the installation program finds them automatically). Then follow these steps:

1. **Choose Start⇨Settings⇨Control Panel.**

   The Control Panel window opens.

2. **Double-click the Network icon.**

   The Network dialog box opens, with the Configuration tab in the foreground.

   In Windows 2000 Professional, the icon is named Network and Dial-up Connections. When you double-click the icon, a new window opens. Double-click the Local Area Connection icon and then click the Properties button.

3. **Click Add.**

   The Select Network Component Type dialog box opens. The items listed in the dialog box differ, depending on the version of Windows you're running. However, all versions of Windows display the protocol choice.

   In Windows 2000 Professional, click Install (there's no button labeled Add).

4. **Select Protocol and then click Add.**

   The Select Network Protocol dialog box opens. If you're running Windows 95 or Windows 98, select Microsoft from the Manufacturer list. Windows Me and Windows 2000 Professional don't offer any choices except Microsoft.

5. **Choose NetBEUI or TCP/IP from the Network Protocols list.**

6. **Click OK.**

   You return to the Network dialog box.

7. **Click OK in the Network dialog box.**

   The necessary files are transferred to your hard drive. The Systems Settings Change dialog box opens and prompts you to restart your computer.

8. **Restart your computer.**

If you want to install both protocols, repeat Steps 3 through 5 for the second protocol.

Configuring TCP/IP

If you install TCP/IP, you have to do some additional setup work. The TCP/IP protocol requires each computer on the network to have its own address, called an *IP address*. An IP address is a string of numbers that identifies the computer. No two computers on your network can have the same IP address. (The same thing is true on the Internet, where every Web site you visit is on a computer with a unique IP address.)

If you're going to set up a shared Internet connection by using the program supplied in Windows 98, Windows Me, or Windows 2000 Professional, follow these steps:

1. **Open the Network icon in Control Panel as described in the preceding section.**

2. **In the Components list, select TCP/IP and click Properties**

   Don't select the TCP/IP-Dial-up Adapter listing (if one exists). Instead, select the TCP/IP listing that's linked to the name of your network adapter. Doing so opens the TCP/IP Properties dialog box.

3. **Select the Obtain an IP Address Automatically option.**

   The option may already be selected.

4. **Click OK.**

If you're using a cable modem or a DSL device, and you're required to set your own IP addresses, follow the instructions from the service provider.

Adding network services

The first service that you probably want to add is File and Printer Sharing for Microsoft Networks so that you can share your files and your printer with users on the other computers. Then, if you want to log on to your network with a user name, you can add one of the client services. I discuss these options in this section.

You need to have your Windows files available, so make sure the Windows CD is in the CD-ROM drive before you begin.

Adding the file and printer sharing service

Because the file and printer sharing service is so common, you don't have to go through the Add Services dialog box to install it — Microsoft provides a button for quick access to the installation of this service. Follow these steps to add the file and printer sharing service to your system:

1. **Choose Start➪Settings➪Control Panel.**

   The Control Panel window opens.

2. **Double-click the Network icon.**

   The Network dialog box opens, with the Configuration tab in the foreground.

3. **Click the File and Print Sharing button.**

   The File and Print Sharing dialog box opens (see Figure 5-6).

4. **Select the resources you want to share and click OK.**

Figure 5-6:
Tell
Windows
that you
want to
share your
files and
your printer
(if you have
a printer
attached to
your
computer).

Adding network client services

Client services are added to networks in order to provide a way for individuals to log on to the network. In a client/server network (where all the computers on the network are connected to one server computer), the server authenticates the logon name and password. In a peer-to-peer network (where all the computers on the network can access all the other computers), the logon provides a method of keeping track of users and their preferences. See Chapter 8 for more information about logon names and individual user preferences.

When you double-click the Network icon, as described in the following steps, you may see that Client for Microsoft Networks is already installed. If that's the case, you don't have to install it again (in fact, Windows won't let you install it again).

To add client services to your network configuration, follow these steps:

1. **Choose Start⇨Settings⇨Control Panel.**

   The Control Panel window opens.

2. **Double-click the Network icon in the Control Panel.**

   The Network dialog box opens, with the Configuration tab in the foreground.

3. **Choose Add.**

   The Select Network Component Type dialog box opens.

4. **Choose Client and then click Add.**

   The Select Network Client dialog box opens. In Windows 95, 98, and 98SE, select Microsoft in the Manufacturer's list. Windows Me and Windows 2000 Professional offer no manufacturers except Microsoft.

5. **Choose a client service from the right pane.**

   Choose Client for Microsoft Networks to log on to the network with your user name. Choose Microsoft Family Logon to select your name from a list of users. (Read Chapter 8 to find out more about logging on.) Windows 2000 Professional doesn't offer the Family Logon option.

6. **Click OK.**

   The necessary files are transferred to your hard drive, and you return to the Network dialog box.

7. **Click OK in the Network dialog box.**

   The Systems Settings Change dialog box opens, prompting you to restart the computer.

8. **Restart your computer.**

Naming computers and workgroups

The Microsoft networking system is fussy about keeping things straight. The networking services want to know who's who, who's where, and what's what. Because of this compulsive attitude, you must give each computer on your network a unique name. In addition, you must name the group that exists when all the computers that are linked on the network get together.

For all versions of Windows except Windows 2000 Professional (which is covered in the sidebar "Windows 2000 Professional computer names"), follow these steps:

1. **Choose Start⇨Settings⇨Control Panel.**

   The Control Panel window opens.

2. **Double-click the Network icon.**

   The Network dialog box opens.

3. **Click the Identification tab (see Figure 5-7).**

4. **Enter a unique name for this computer.**

   You can use up to 15 characters for the name, but the name cannot include any of the following characters: / \ * , . @ space.

5. **Enter a Workgroup name.**

   The *workgroup name* is the name you use for the group of computers that comprise your home network. You can use the default name of *Workgroup* or invent a different name. Make sure that all the computers on the network use the same workgroup name.

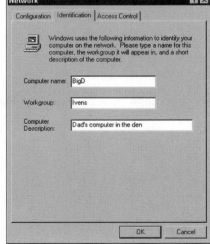

Figure 5-7:
Use the Identification tab to identify each computer on the network.

6. **Optionally, enter a Computer Description.**

   Other viewers can view the description you enter if they use the Details view in Network Neighborhood (covered in Chapter 10).

7. **Choose OK.**

   Your computer is ready to participate in the network.

   The Systems Settings Change dialog box opens, prompting you to restart your computer.

8. **Restart your computer.**

9. **Repeat these steps for each computer on the network.**

Using the Windows Me Home Networking Wizard

The Windows Me Home Networking Wizard does the entire network setup work for you and also sets up a shared Internet connection. Just to keep things simple and organized, in this chapter I'm only going to discuss the steps you go through to set up the network. I cover the Internet connection sharing options in Chapter 6. However, you may want to read Chapter 6 now, and do everything at once.

The Windows Me wizard doesn't get along with Windows 2000 Professional. If you have a Windows 2000 Professional computer on the network — along with a Windows Me computer — after you finish with the wizard, use the manual steps described in the previous section on adding protocols to configure Windows 2000 Professional.

To launch the wizard, double-click the My Network Places icon on your desktop and then double-click the Home Networking Wizard icon. The first wizard window is a welcoming message that requires no action on your part, except clicking Next to get started on the real work. The next window sets up Internet connection sharing, which I discuss in Chapter 6.

The following few sections lead you through the remaining windows of the wizard.

Choosing names

Click Next to move through the wizard to the Computer and Workgroup Names window, shown in Figure 5-8.

Enter a name for this computer, and enter a name for the workgroup. The computer name must be unique for the network, but all the computers on the network use the same workgroup name. The wizard preselects the name *MSHOME* for the workgroup, and indicates that's the recommended name for your network. That recommendation isn't made for any particular reason, and you can select the option to give the workgroup a name of your own choosing.

Share and share alike: Setting up file and printer sharing services

The next wizard window (see Figure 5-9) sets up file and printer sharing services. When you share a folder, it means network users can get to any file in that folder, using any computer on the network. When you share a printer, everyone can use it, from any computer on the network.

Your wizard window may display an additional folder, named Shared Documents. This folder doesn't exist if you upgraded to Windows Me from Windows 98 or Windows 95. However, if Windows Me was installed on a blank hard drive (usually by the computer manufacturer), the Shared Documents folder exists. The purpose of this folder is to hold documents that were created specifically for sharing, but it's not particularly useful. First of all, the Shared Documents folder does not have an icon on the desktop, and it's not all that easy to locate if you want to put documents in it. Depending on your system configuration (or perhaps it's just the wizard's mood of the moment), this folder is either a subfolder in the My Documents folder or a subfolder in the \Windows\All Users folder.

Windows 2000 Professional computer names

Windows 2000 Professional handles computer names and workgroups a bit differently. The computer name and the workgroup are set up when you install the operating system. However, if the name or workgroup you selected during installation doesn't match the network configuration you're setting up, you can change either or both settings. Just follow these steps:

1. **Right-click on My Computer and choose Properties from the shortcut menu.**

   The System Properties dialog box opens.

2. **On the Network Identification tab, click the Properties button.**

   The Identification Changes dialog box opens.

3. **Enter a computer name and workgroup name as needed.**

   Be sure you select the Workgroup option to avoid having the computer try to log in to an authenticating domain.

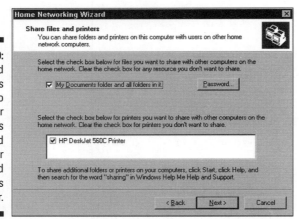

Figure 5-9:
The wizard assumes you want to share your documents folder and any printer connected to this computer.

You don't have to share the folders that the wizard lists if you don't want to, and failing to share them doesn't interfere with the wizard's tasks — your network configuration proceeds just the same. After the network is configured, you can share any folder on any computer manually, including these folders, so you don't have to make the decision now. (I discuss creating shared folders in Chapter 7.)

The Password button next to the folder name exists so you can create a password for each folder. This action limits other users' access to the folders because anyone who doesn't know the password isn't permitted to open the folder from a remote computer. Chapter 7 offers detailed instructions for creating password protection for shared folders.

If you select the option to share the folders and you also decide to skip the password option, when you click the Next button, Windows Me displays a message urging you to enter a password. Click OK to make the message go away — you can password-protect any folder at any time, and you don't have to complete this task now.

Creating a networking setup disk for all the other computers

The next wizard window asks whether you want to create a home networking setup disk for the other computers on your network. The wizard will transfer files to a floppy disk that you can take to the other computers on your network in order to configure them for network services (including the shared Internet connection feature). You should take advantage of the disk, because if you don't run the wizard on your other computers, you have to set up those computers manually, using the steps in the previous section of this chapter.

Click Next after you select the option to create the floppy disk and put a blank formatted floppy disk in the floppy drive. Click Next again to create the disk, which takes only a moment or two. Then remove the floppy disk from the drive and put a label on it that indicates it's your networking setup disk.

Click Finish in the wizard window — you're done. Windows Me transfers all the files required to run networking services to your hard drive (you may be asked to put the Windows Me CD in the CD-ROM drive if it isn't already inserted). You must restart your computer to put the network settings into effect. When your computer reboots, it's part of a working network!

Using the networking setup disk on all the other computers

The floppy disk you created is an easy-to-use tool for configuring the other computers on your network. Go to each computer and insert the floppy disk in the floppy drive. Then open the My Computer icon on the desktop. Double-click the floppy drive icon, and double-click the file named Setup.exe.

The same Home Networking Wizard you used on your Windows Me computer opens and you merely walk through each window, answering questions and making selections. Give this computer a unique name and use the exact same workgroup name you entered for your Windows Me computer. Say No to the wizard's offer to create a setup disk (you don't need another one).

Select the sharing options for the folders and printers that are on this computer. You don't have to share the suggested folders — you can decide for yourself which folders you want to share (see Chapter 7). However, if this computer has a printer, share it.

Macintosh Can Join the Family, Too

If you have a Macintosh in the house, you can add it to your network, but the process is not a cakewalk. It won't work at all unless you've chosen an Ethernet solution for your home network.

New Macs (and some older Macs) have Ethernet adapters built-in. You can buy NICs for the older Macs that lack adapters, but all the NICs I've seen for Macs operate at 10 Mbps. This means your PC NICs and your concentrator must be able to handle both 10 Mbps and 100 Mbps (most of them can, check the documentation).

If you installed a NIC, use the installation CD that came with the NIC to install drivers. A simple installation program accomplishes this (follow the instructions from the manufacturer). When all the software is transferred to the Mac, you need to restart the computer.

Appletalk and Ethertalk (the protocol that runs Appletalk over an Ethernet network) are preinstalled on most Macs. Make sure that Appletalk is active — check the Active radio button in Appleshare. Also make sure that the right network connection is selected. In the Apple menu, select Control Panels and select the Network or Appletalk option. Then select the Ethernet or Ethertalk option and close the window.

MacTalk is the default networking mechanism for Mac OS machines. Unfortunately, MacTalk doesn't know about Windows; PCs don't speak MacTalk. Your challenge is to convince the Mac to communicate using Windows-compatible networking protocols. You can meet the challenge by using TCP/IP as the network protocol. In a way, you're creating an environment in which the Mac interacts with the PC as if both of them were communicating over the Internet.

Set the TCP/IP configuration in the TCP/IP Control Panel, entering a TCP/IP address for the Mac. In addition, the Mac must be configured for sharing, which is like selecting file and printer sharing in the PC. Open the Apple Menu and select Control Panels, and then double-click the Sharing Setup option. Enter your name, a password, and the name of the computer. In the File Sharing section, check the label on the File Sharing button. If the label is Start, click the button to activate file sharing. If the label is Stop, the service is already running.

If you've purchased software to assist your efforts to join a peer-to-peer network that includes Windows machines, follow the instructions to complete the installation of networking protocols provided by that software.

Chapter 6

Setting Up Shared Internet Connections

In This Chapter

▶ Taking a look at Internet connection hardware options

▶ Configuring dial-up networking connections

▶ Sharing Internet connections

▶ Examining hardware devices that provide connection sharing

▶ Using AOL with a shared connection

*T*o use the Internet, including e-mail and Web surfing, you need a hardware device that can connect to an Internet service provider (ISP), software that drives the connection to the ISP, e-mail software, and a Web browser. Wait, don't panic, everything except the hardware comes with Windows.

When you share an Internet connection around the network, the computer that contains the modem is called the *host*. All the other computers are called the *clients*. This chapter covers the steps you need to take to set up both the host and the clients.

The Internet: From Your House to the World and Back

The Internet works by using communication hardware to move data from server to server, all over the world. A hierarchy of computers operating on multiple levels accomplishes this massive feat. For you, sending and receiving data starts and ends with your hardware, which is responsible for moving data between your computer and all the other computers on the Internet.

You're not hooked up directly with the computer you want to communicate with — your data moves through a bunch of computers to get to your target. The hierarchy of computers that runs the Internet starts (or ends, depending on the way you look at it) with a group of computers called the *backbone*. Backbone servers are strategically placed throughout the world, and they communicate with the next layer of servers, all of which communicate with the next layer, and so on and so on.

As shown in Figure 6-1, you use a hardware device to communicate with an ISP, which is a company you connect to in order to move through the Internet. The ISP uses a hardware device to communicate with the next layer of servers, and each layer moves data to the next until the packet of information reaches the target server (the Web page you want to see, or the mailbox of the recipient of your e-mail message). Each time a server moves data to another server, it's called a *hop*. If you want to see how many hops it takes to get from your computer to a particular place on the Internet, check out the "Tracing the route to a Web site" sidebar.

Understanding Your Hardware Options

To reach the Internet from your home computer, you need a hardware device that can communicate with an Internet server. Depending on where you live, you have some choices about the type of hardware you can use. Your options may include

- A modem
- A cable modem
- A DSL (Digital Subscriber Line) device

Each of these connection options has its individual pros and cons — and some options aren't as widely available. Read on for more information that can help you determine which connection is the right one for your home network.

The more time you spend on the Internet, the more you realize how much speed counts. If you have to make 15 hops to get to a server with a Web site you want to view, the Web page has to make 15 hops back to you before it can display its wares. Add to that the amount of time it takes for the graphics on the Web page to unfurl on your screen, and you realize that Internet communication is largely a matter of "waiting for something to happen."

When you make your decision about Internet hardware, make speed a priority. Go for the fastest solution you can afford.

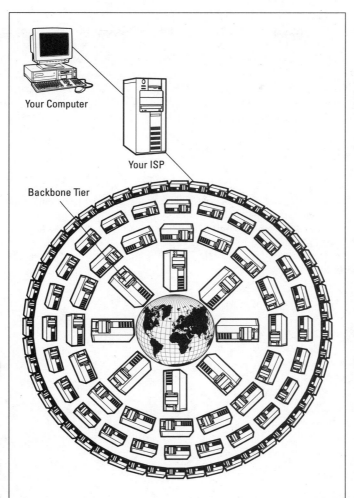

Figure 6-1:
Your data
hops from
server to
server to
reach the
right
destination.

Your Computer

Your ISP

Backbone Tier

Modems

A modem works by taking computer data (digital data) and translating it into
a form that the telephone line can handle (analog data). This process is
called *modulation*. At the receiving end of your modem transmission, another
modem receives the analog data from the phone line and translates it into
digital data that the computer can understand. This process is called *demod-
ulation*. The modulate-demodulate functions that modems provide led to the
word *modem*.

Tracing the route to a Web site

Windows has a nifty utility that lets you trace the route from your house to a Web site, and you can use it while you're connected to the Internet. It's a command line utility, so you need to open an MS-DOS command window to use it. Here's how:

- ✔ In Windows 98 and Windows 95, choose Start⇨Programs⇨MS-DOS Prompt.

- ✔ In Windows Me, choose Start⇨Programs⇨ Accessories⇨MS-DOS Prompt.

- ✔ In Windows 2000 Professional, choose Start⇨Programs⇨Accessories⇨Command Prompt.

In the command window, type **tracert *WebSite*** (substitute the name of the Web site you want to track down for *WebSite)* and press Enter. (Tracert stands for *trace route*.) The tracert utility tracks the hops between your computer and the target server. For example, I wanted to see the number of hops involved in communicating with my *For Dummies* editor. I traced the route from my house to IDG.com, the parent company of Hungry Minds, Inc. (the publisher of this book). Here's what appeared on my screen after I entered **tracert idg.com**:

```
Tracing route to idg.com [***]
over a maximum of 30 hops:
  1     1 ms     1 ms     1 ms   ***
  2    13 ms    12 ms    13 ms   phila-dslam-routed1.voicenet.net [***]
  3    14 ms    12 ms    13 ms   phila-gw-F-0-1-100mb.voicenet.net [***]
  4    17 ms    16 ms   111 ms   harris-gw-H2-0.voicenet.net [***]
  5    25 ms    24 ms    24 ms   pitt-gw-H2-0.voicenet.net [***]
  6   153 ms   133 ms   256 ms   chicago-gw-S-0-1-0.voicenet.net [***]
  7    82 ms    82 ms    83 ms   mae-west-H3-0-0-T3.voicenet.net [***]
  8    83 ms    86 ms    86 ms   mae-west2.us.psi.net [***]
  9    85 ms    84 ms    84 ms   nw.transit.tier1.us.psi.net [***]
 10    85 ms    87 ms    85 ms   rc7.nw.us.psi.net [***]
 11   100 ms   101 ms    99 ms   ip20.ci2.sanfrancisco.ca.us.psi.net
      [***]
 12    94 ms    92 ms    93 ms   idg.com [***]
```

Trace complete.

Actually, the screen didn't show me the asterisks. I've substituted *** for IP addresses, because among them is my own IP address. Giving that out is asking for trouble (even though I run a firewall).

Note the time lapses displayed on the screen, which are calculated in milliseconds (ms). I'm using a high-speed Internet device (DSL), and if you try this with a modem, you'll probably see much larger numbers, indicating slower communication rates.

Note: Internet servers that have names starting with *mae* are part of the backbone.

A modem uses the part of the telephone line's circuitry calls POTS (plain old telephone service), which it shares with telephones and fax machines. This is analog circuitry, and the maximum speed you can attain is 56K (56 kilobytes of data is transferred per second). Therefore, the fastest modem you can buy is a 56K modem. In fact, today it's probably the only modem you can buy. Don't even accept a slower modem as a gift (from somebody who upgraded to a 56K device); it's not worth the wear and tear on your nervous system.

When you use a modem to access the Internet, you dial out to your ISP, and the ISP's servers provide you with access to the World Wide Web and also provide access to e-mail. Your e-mail address generally has the name of the ISP, à la `JohnDoe@MyISP.com`.

Here are some of the pros to using a modem for connecting to the Internet:

✔ It's the cheapest Internet connection.

✔ Dial-up access is available everywhere.

Here are some of the cons:

✔ It's slow.

✔ You have to dial out each time you want to use an Internet service. Most ISPs don't permit you to dial in and just stay online all the time, so getting a separate telephone line for the modem doesn't give you a permanent Internet connection.

✔ A modem connection ties up your existing phone line.

✔ If you want a dedicated modem line, you have the added cost of paying for a second phone line. A dedicated modem line does stop a lot of the family arguments when dad wants to make a phone call at the same time the kids are playing games on the Internet.

Cable modems

Cable modems send data over your cable television company's line. Depending on the service and equipment offered by the cable company, the device is either connected to an Ethernet concentrator or to a special NIC in a computer. The latter configuration means that one PC has two NICs — one for the cable modem and one for the network. The cable modem itself splits its connection between the PC (or network) and the television cable box. Your data goes back to your local cable TV company, where the cable company maintains a Cable Modem Termination System (CMTS) at the local office (which is called the *headend*). The CMTS is like a giant concentrator, where all the people who use this cable company's modems meet. You and your neighbors are basically participating in a computer network. The CMTS also provides the pass-through to the Internet.

Here are some of the advantages to using a cable modem:

- ✔ **Cable modems are always on, and you are always connected to the Internet.** Like any network connected by a concentrator, the cable company network is always up and running. That's certainly much easier than operating with a modem, where you have to dial out each time you want to use an Internet service. And, you're not tying up your telephone line.

- ✔ **Cable modems download data much faster than modems can.** Technically a cable modem can reach speeds of over 1 million bits per second (1 Mbps). However, the cable company's own connection to the Internet may be slower than that, so the speed of transmission you actually realize is more likely to be in the several-hundred-thousand bits per second range.

- ✔ **You don't have to perform any configuration chores to get your cable modem to connect to an ISP.** The installation process the cable company performs hooks you up with its ISP automatically.

Here are some of the cons:

- ✔ **As any network grows, each node on the network operates a little slower.** If you add ten more computers to the Ethernet concentrator of your own home network, each computer on the network operates more slowly — as the available bandwidth is shared, each participant gets a little less of it. As more and more people sign up with your cable company, each of you loses some speed.

- ✔ **Most cable companies don't provide as fast of a speed for uploads as they do for downloads.** In fact, uploading is frequently as slow as 56K, the same as a modem. However, you probably won't notice the difference between the upload and download speeds, because the only important speed is downloading. Most of the time, the only time you upload is when you send e-mail. Viewing a Web page is a download process. With a cable modem, Web pages pop up on your screen, so you don't have to watch each page unfold its graphics slowly, the way modem users do.

Digital Subscriber Line (DSL) devices

A DSL device is like a digital modem (modems are analog) that hooks into your telephone line. DSL uses a separate frequency range (one that can handle digital transmissions) in your telephone wires so you can continue to use your telephone and fax.

DSL devices connect to computers via Ethernet cable. If you've cabled your network with Ethernet, the DSL device can go right into the concentrator. Or, you can put a NIC in the computer to connect to the DSL device, which means that computer has two NICs — one for the DSL and one for the network.

More versions of DSL are available than I can keep track of, and DSL providers keep inventing new versions. For your home network, however, you're probably going to want ADSL, which stands for Asymmetric Digital Subscriber Line. Because ADSL is the most common form of DSL service, most people ignore the *A,* and when they talk about DSL, they usually mean ADSL.

Technically, ADSL can support download speeds of 8 Mbps and upload speeds of 1.5 Mbps. That's beyond blazing fast. But, don't get excited; you're not likely to meet anyone who has achieved anywhere near that technically possible level. In fact, unless you're prepared to spend a great deal of money each month, you won't operate at a fraction of the technically possible speeds.

The fact that the upload speed differs from the download speed is the reason the service is called *Asymmetric.* Symmetric DSL (SDSL) provides upload speeds that are the same as download speeds. This service is much more expensive, and it's overkill for home users. Companies that maintain busy Web sites that must constantly update the information on their sites use SDSL technology.

Here are some of the pros to using a DSL device:

- You can use your telephone and fax at the same time you use DSL.
- Like a cable modem, a DSL device provides an always-on connection with the Internet.
- Unlike a cable modem, your connection is private — you're not part of a network.
- You don't have to do anything to configure the DSL device to communicate with your ISP; it's all part of the setup performed by the technician who installs the device.

  A professional installs the DSL device, because the line has to be split to accommodate the technology. The telephone company does something technical to your line before the installer arrives, in order to make the split. However, at the time of this writing, a new DSL technology, called DSL-Lite, was being tested that will make it possible for you to install your own device.

Here are some of the cons to using a DSL device:

- **Fast speeds command high prices.** DSL services are purchased from providers on a monthly-fee basis, and the fees can be rather hefty. The higher the speed, the higher the monthly cost.
- **You must meet certain requirements.** Before you can rush to order DSL services, you have to answer Yes to both of the following statements:
  - Does your telephone company provide the technology in the lines that DSL requires?

- Do you live within 18,000 feet of a telephone company central switching office?

The central switching office for a telephone company is called the *CO* (for central office).

You don't have to get out your tape measure and walk from your house to the CO; any DSL service provider can tell you if you qualify. In fact, telephone companies are becoming direct DSL service providers, which give you one-stop shopping.

✔ **Service can be spotty.** Horror stories abound about DSL service black-outs that aren't fixed for weeks at a time. The same is true of DSL devices — if they break, some DSL providers won't send a technician for weeks. Before you sign up with a DSL provider, do some homework. Get recommendations, check reviews on the Web, and get as much as you can in writing when you sign up.

Configuring Modem Connections

If you're using a modem to connect to the Internet, you need two things:

✔ **An account with an ISP.** To find an ISP that you can trust, ask friends or check reviews in computer magazines.

✔ **A software connection to the ISP.** The software connection to the ISP is part of the Dial-Up Networking (DUN) feature that's built into Windows.

After you configure the DUN connection, your modem can dial out and con-nect to your ISP, which passes you on to the Internet. You can have as many DUN connections as you need (one for each ISP you use). Most people have only one ISP, but some families have both an ISP and an AOL account, for example. Additionally, some people have accounts through their employers.

You install a DUN connection on the computer that acts as the host or server for your modem-sharing software. Setting up a DUN connection is actually quite simple. Before you start, be sure you have the following information at your fingertips (it's all provided by your ISP):

✔ The local phone number that you dial to log in to your ISP.

✔ Your online account user name. (You choose this name yourself, and you must give it to the ISP when you sign up.)

✔ Your online account password. (Some ISPs give you a password; others let you choose the password yourself, and you must give it to the ISP when you sign up.)

✔ Any TCP/IP settings needed to communicate with your ISP's server.

Your ISP also provides information about setting up your e-mail software so you can get your messages and send messages to others.

In the following sections, I show you how to set up your DUN connection to your ISP. I'm assuming you want to share your Internet connection so everybody in the household can surf the Net simultaneously. That means you must have your modem attached to a computer that's running Windows 98 Second Edition (Windows 98SE), Windows Me, or Windows 2000 Professional. The setup is different for each operating system, so go to the appropriate section.

The following sections assume you've already installed your modem. To learn all about setting up modems, check out *Windows 98 For Dummies, Microsoft Windows Me Millennium Edition For Dummies*, or *Windows 2000 Professional For Dummies*, all written by Andy Rathbone and published by IDG Books.

Creating a DUN connection in Windows 98SE and Windows Me

With the information from your ISP at hand, follow these steps to create a Dial-Up Networking (DUN) connection in Windows 98SE or Windows Me:

1. **In Windows 98SE, double-click the My Computer icon and then double-click the Dial-Up Networking folder; in Windows Me, choose Start⇨Settings⇨Dial-Up Networking.**

   In the Dial-Up Networking folder, you should see the Make New Connection icon. If any other objects are in the folder, you have already created a Dial-Up Networking connection.

2. **Double-click the Make New Connection icon.**

   The Make New Connection wizard launches to walk you through the process of installing your Internet connection (see Figure 6-2).

Figure 6-2:
The wizard's first question is what's my name?

3. **Enter a name for this DUN connection and then click Next.**

    It's a good idea to give the connection a name that makes it easily identifiable — the name of your ISP is usually a good choice.

    This wizard screen also shows the name of your modem, which you should have installed before this. If you didn't install a modem, the wizard automatically goes into "install a modem" mode and walks you through the necessary steps.

4. **Enter the area code and phone number for your ISP and click Next.**

5. **Click Finish.**

    You return to the Dial-Up Networking window, where an icon for your new DUN appears.

Unfortunately, you're not finished. The programmers created the Finish button to amuse themselves — they apparently have weird senses of humor. You have more tasks, and these are the tasks that require the technical information you acquired from your ISP. Follow these steps to finish setting up your DUN connection:

1. **Right-click on the icon for your DUN connection and choose Properties from the shortcut menu.**

    The Properties dialog box opens.

2. **In Windows 98SE, click the Server Types tab; in Windows Me, click the Networking tab.**

    The Server tab displays the settings for your ISP's server, which should be similar to Figure 6-3.

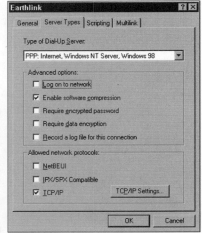

Figure 6-3:
This dialog box is where you begin to configure settings.

In Windows 98SE, your settings should be the same as those shown in Figure 6-3. If your ISP instructed you to select the encrypted password option, select that check box (this would be unusual, however). In Windows Me, the encrypted password option is on the Security tab.

3. Click the TCP/IP Settings button.

The TCP/IP Settings dialog box, shown in Figure 6-4, opens.

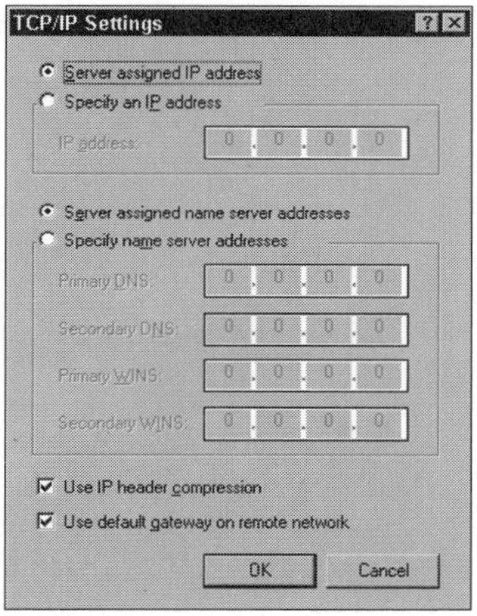

Figure 6-4:
To complete this dialog box, refer to the instructions from your ISP.

Most ISPs assign an IP address when you log on. If your ISP wants you to enter a specific IP address, follow the instructions you received to fill in the requisite fields.

4. Click OK twice to close the DUN connection dialog box.

Now you're really finished!

When you want to connect to the Internet, follow these steps:

1. Open the Dial-Up Networking window (in Windows 98SE, you must first open My Computer).

2. Double-click the icon for your DUN connection to open the Connect To dialog box, shown in Figure 6-5.

By default, Windows 98SE puts your name in the User Name field, but your ISP may have instructed you to use your e-mail address instead.

3. Enter your ISP password and then select the Save Password check box so you don't have to enter it every time you dial out.

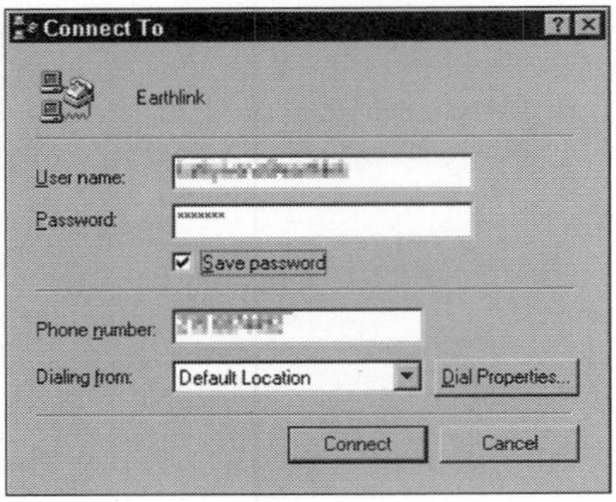

Figure 6-5:
Make sure
the dialog
box is filled
out to
match the
require-
ments of
your ISP.

4. **Click Connect.**

   Your modem dials out, and you hear some squawking noises as you
   and your ISP connect. Now you and everybody else on the network can
   open your browsers and visit Web pages, or open your e-mail software
   and correspond with the world.

> If you want to be able to connect to the Internet with a single click, instead of
> opening all those windows, right-drag the DUN icon to your Quick Launch bar
> (which is located to the right of the Start button). When you release the
> mouse button, a menu appears. Choose Create Shortcut(s) Here from the
> menu to add the DUN icon to the Quick Launch bar.

Creating a DUN connection in Windows 2000 Professional

Follow these steps to set up a DUN connection in Windows 2000 Professional:

1. **Choose Start⇨Settings⇨Network and Dial-up Connections.**

   The Network and Dial-up Connections window opens.

2. **Double-click the Make New Connection icon.**

   The Network Connection Wizard opens. Click Next to move past the
   window with the welcoming message.

3. **Select the Dial-up to the Internet option and click Next.**

   The other options appear because Windows 2000 Professional uses the
   same wizard for all types of connections, including network connections.

4. **Select the option to set up your connection manually and then
   click Next.**

5. **Select the option to connect to the Internet through a phone line and a modem, and then click Next.**

6. **Enter the phone number to dial in order to reach your ISP and then click Next.**

7. **Enter the user name and password you registered with your ISP and then click Next.**

8. **Enter a name for this DUN connection and click Next.**

9. **If you want, select the option to set up an e-mail account.**

   If you opt for e-mail setup, you're off and running on a configuration process for Outlook Express. If you were going to use Outlook Express as your e-mail software anyway, you may want to do it now. Or, you may want to worry about all that work later and just get your DUN out of the way for now.

   For this discussion, I'm choosing not to set up e-mail.

10. **Click Finish.**

   If your ISP instructed you to enter an IP address instead of obtaining an IP address from the server, deselect the option to connect to the Internet immediately before you click the Finish button. Then right-click on your DUN connection icon and choose Properties from the shortcut menu. Go to the Networking tab and fill in the IP address information according to the instructions from your ISP.

To connect to the Internet, choose Start⇨Settings⇨Network and Dial-up Connections. Double-click your DUN connection and choose Dial.

If you want to be able to connect to the Internet with a single click, right-drag the DUN icon to your Quick Launch bar. When you release the mouse button, a menu appears. Choose Create Shortcut(s) Here from the menu to add the DUN icon to your Quick Launch bar.

Sharing an Internet Connection

After you have a communications line to an Internet service provider, you have to share the line with all the other computers on the network. This process requires each computer to attach itself to an IP address, which in turn requires TCP/IP (see the "Understanding TCP/IP" sidebar). If you chose NetBEUI as your network protocol, now you have two protocols — the process of setting up your modem, cable modem, or DSL device automatically added TCP/IP to your network protocols. (See Chapter 5 for more on protocols.)

Understanding TCP/IP

Although TCP/IP is the acronym for Transmission Control Protocol/Internet Protocol, you may find a number of folks who claim it really stands for Terribly Confusing Proposition/Irritating and Perplexing. I say pay them no mind. They're just a little cranky because they haven't yet found a simple, straightforward explanation of TCP/IP. To ensure that you don't join their ranks, let me quickly explain what TCP/IP is.

Think about the fact that you can send a letter to someone in Paris, London, Tokyo, or Sydney and be reasonably sure that he or she will get it (as long as you address the letter properly). That's actually a pretty amazing feat when you realize that each country has its own language, its own customs, and its own unique postal system. The reason your letter makes it to its destination is simply because of the existence of a standardized set of rules for the manner in which mail is transmitted.

That, in a nutshell, is what TCP/IP is — a set of standardized rules for transmitting information. In the case of TCP/IP, the information is in electronic rather than paper form. TCP/IP enables computers to communicate with one another by using each computer's address, which is called an *IP address.*

E-mail, Web pages, files, and other data are transmitted over the Internet in *packets,* which are nothing more than small electronic parcels of information. The computer doing the transmitting takes a large amount of information and breaks it up into small, manageable individual packets to send it across the Internet. The receiving computer collects each of the packets and puts them all back together to reconstitute the original piece of information. Both computers follow the rules built into TCP/IP to know how to break up and reconstitute the data.

Windows 98SE Internet Connection Sharing

If the host computer is running Windows 98SE, use the Internet Connection Sharing (ICS) software to set up Internet access across the network. Unfortunately, when you installed Windows 98SE on the computer, the ICS software wasn't installed by default. If you (or whoever installed the operating system) performed a custom installation, ICS may have been installed. What's neat is that the steps you take to see if ICS is already installed are the same steps needed to install it, in case it isn't there.

Installing and configuring the host computer

Before completing the following steps, make sure that you have your Windows 98SE CD on hand (unless the files were installed on your hard drive by a manufacturer who preloaded the operating system before you bought the computer).

Here's how to determine if ICS is already installed, and how to install it if it's missing:

1. **Choose Start⇨Settings⇨Control Panel.**

   The Control Panel window opens.

2. **Double-click the Add/Remove Programs icon.**

   The Add/Remove Programs Properties dialog box appears.

3. **Click the Windows Setup tab.**

   This tab displays a listing of operating system features that have been installed. The system inspects your computer to see what's what, so it may take a few seconds before the list appears.

4. **Scroll through the list and click the listing — not the check box — for Internet Tools.**

   The state of the check box can be a clue to the status of installed Internet features (see Figure 6-6):

Figure 6-6:
This computer has no Internet Tools installed.

- If the check box is blank, no Internet tools have been installed, and you have to install ICS.

- If the check box is white, with a check mark, all the Internet tools are installed, and you don't have to install ICS.

- If the check box is gray, with a check mark, some Internet tools are installed, but you don't know yet whether ICS is one of them.

5. **If the check box is blank or gray, click the Details button.**

   A list of Internet tools displays, with a check mark next to any that are already installed.

6. **Click in the Internet Connection Sharing check box to place a check mark in the box.**

   The check mark sends a signal to the operating system that you want to install ICS.

7. **Click OK to close the Internet Tools window and then click OK again to close Add/Remove Programs Properties dialog box.**

   Windows copies the ICS software files to your hard drive and then launches the Internet Connection Sharing Wizard.

8. **Click Next to move past the Welcome window.**

9. **Tell the wizard whether you're using a modem or a high-speed connection, and then click Next.**

10. **Click Next to create the client software.**

    Put a blank floppy disk in your floppy drive. You'll use this disk to install the client software on all the other computers. When Windows finishes copying files to the floppy disk, a message appears to tell you to remove the disk and click OK.

11. **Click Finish.**

    A message appears to tell you that you must restart your computer. Click Yes to have Windows restart.

Setting up the client computers

You can use the client software on any Windows 98 or Windows 95 computer. To set up the client computers, follow these steps:

1. **Insert the floppy disk you made into the floppy drive of a client computer.**

2. **Choose Start⇨Programs⇨Windows Explorer.**

   The Windows Explorer window opens.

3. **Select the floppy drive in the left pane.**

   The right pane displays the contents of the floppy disk.

4. **Double-click `icslet.exe`.**

   The Connection Setup Wizard opens, with a welcome message. Click Next to move to the next wizard window, which explains that when you click Next again, the wizard makes the appropriate changes to your setting.

5. **Click Next.**

   The wizard announces that your system is configured for Internet connection sharing.

6. **Click Finish.**

   If the host computer is connected to the Internet right now, select the option to head for the Web when you click the Finish button. Or, connect to the Internet on the host computer before you click the Finish button. Or, wait until later to open the browser on the client computer and go to your favorite Web page.

Windows Me Internet Connection Sharing

If your Windows Me computer has the modem, then it's the host. You have to configure the computer for hosting, and you also have to create the software disk you'll use to configure the client computers.

Installing and configuring the host

In Chapter 5, I go over the Windows Me Home Networking Wizard, including the stuff you have to do in order to share an Internet connection — that wizard is a total solution. If you only used the wizard to set up your network, you can rerun it to set up Internet connection sharing. Here's how:

1. **Choose Start⇨Programs⇨Accessories⇨Communications⇨ Home Networking Wizard.**

   The first window of the Home Networking Wizard opens. Click Next to get started.

2. **Tell the wizard that this computer has a connection to the Internet (see Figure 6-7).**

   The wizard finds your DUN connection, if you have one. If you have a cable modem or a DSL device attached to a NIC, the wizard finds and displays the NIC. Click Next.

3. **Tell the wizard you want to share this connection with the other computers on the network.**

   The wizard finds the NIC that connects the computer to the rest of the network (see Figure 6-8).

4. **Decide on automatic connections.**

   This window (shown in Figure 6-9) appears only if your Internet connection is a dial-up affair (instead of an always-on connection). Choose Yes to automate the launching of the DUN connection whenever anyone on the network opens a browser or opens e-mail software when the connection isn't active. Selecting this option means the person working at the host computer doesn't have to launch the connection every time someone on the network wants to get to the Internet. It also means that other users don't have to come to the host computer (if no one is using it) to launch the DUN connection.

If you prefer to keep control of when the DUN connection is used, choose No.

Note the warning on this wizard window, and see the "The automatic updates feature in Windows Me" sidebar.

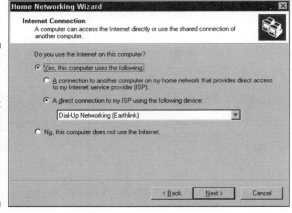

Figure 6-7: The wizard needs to know that this is the computer with a connection to the Internet.

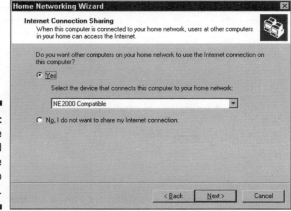

Figure 6-8: Tell the wizard you're willing to share.

5. **Go through the rest of the wizard windows, supplying the information the wizard needs.**

   The remaining windows contain the information you filled out when you set up your network with the wizard — the computer's name and your options for sharing folders and printers. The information you entered previously is still there — just check it for accuracy and click Next to keep moving.

6. **In the Setup Disk window, choose Yes to create setup disks for the other computers.**

   Put a blank floppy disk in drive A and click Next.

7. **Click Finish.**

   You may see a message telling you to restart your computer. Take the floppy disk out of the drive and click Yes to restart.

Setting up the client computers

If any client computers are also running Windows Me, you don't need to use the floppy disk you made. Just run the Home Networking Wizard on each of those computers and answer the wizard's questions appropriately. This means instead of saying "Yes, the modem is here," you say "Use the network to connect me to the modem."

For client computers that are running Windows 98 or Windows 95, use these steps to set them up for sharing the Internet connection:

1. **Insert the floppy disk you made into the floppy drive of a client computer.**

2. **Choose Start⇨Programs⇨Windows Explorer.**

   The Windows Explorer window opens.

3. **Select the floppy drive in the left pane.**

   The right pane displays the contents of the floppy disk.

4. **Double-click** `Setup.exe`.

   The Connection Setup Wizard opens, with a welcome message.

5. **Click Next.**

   The Home Networking Wizard (yep, the same one that is built into Windows Me) is installed on this computer. The wizard automatically starts the Internet connection sharing part of the program. Go through the wizard, answering questions as if you were running the wizard on a Windows Me computer.

   Remember that you're telling the wizard that the Internet connection is installed on the host computer, not the computer on which you're running the wizard.

Hardware Devices for Sharing DSL or Cable Modem Connections

If you have a DSL or cable modem connection and an Ethernet network, you can use a hardware device to share an Internet connection. A slew of hardware devices that provide this service have been introduced, and some of them provide cool extra services.

Perhaps because the technology is new, these devices don't have a generic name. Each manufacturer invents its own term, followed by the phrase "Internet sharing device." Technically, these devices are *routers*, because they route traffic between your network and the Internet. Many of them are also *firewalls*, because they have software built into them to block nefarious attempts to access your home network. (See Chapter 12 to find out about firewalls.)

To use one of these devices, you connect it to your network with Ethernet cable. Some of the devices have a single connection, which you use to join the device to your Ethernet concentrator. Other devices are concentrators, so they provide both a hub for a network and the Internet connection sharing feature.

The Internet sharing device doesn't have any buttons or screens on it, so you must install and configure it from one of the computers that it's connected to. Some of the devices have programs that you install on the computer. When you run the program, it finds the device and lets you configure it. Other devices actually have built-in Web servers. Just open the browser on your computer and type in a special address (like `http://192.168.0.1`) and then configure the Internet sharing device in your Web browser.

You must enter the same type of information as you would have entered if your DSL device or cable modem had been connected to a single computer. That means entering an IP address or telling the program to obtain an address automatically. Use the instructions from your ISP to set up the device.

Here are some of the manufacturers I've found that offer these devices:

- D-Link (`www.dlink.com`)
- WatchGuard (`www.watchguard.com`)
- LinkSys (`www.linksys.com`)
- Ramp Networks (`www.rampnet.com`)

Accessing AOL with a Shared Connection

You must have an ISP to share an Internet connection, and if AOL is the only Internet access for your household, you can't share the connection. Either everyone gets a modem (oh yeah, right, that'll work), or everyone uses the same computer to dial in to AOL.

The automatic updates feature in Windows Me

Microsoft put an automatic update feature in Windows Me. This means that periodically, when you're connected to the Internet, you're automatically connected to Microsoft's Web site, and anything that's been newly developed for Windows Me is downloaded to your computer. This all occurs automatically, and almost invisibly. After the updates are copied to your hard drive, you're asked if you want to install them. If you say no, they're not removed, they're merely hidden (taking up disk space).

You may find this feature handy, but I don't like it. Perhaps I'm just a control freak, but I don't like the idea of my computer traveling to Web sites without my knowledge, nor do I like downloading files without any notice. If new features (or fixes) are available, I prefer to go to Microsoft's Web site, read about them, and manually download them if I decide I want them. Now, I'll step down from my soapbox.

You can configure the way automatic updates work by opening the Automatic Updates icon in the Control Panel. Select automatic updating, semi-automatic updating (the computer asks before fetching the update), or forget it.

However, if you have an ISP, and one or more members of your family also want to maintain an account on AOL from a client computer, you can provide that option. You just need to tell AOL to stop trying to dial the modem. Here's how in AOL 6.0:

1. **Open the AOL software and click the Setup button.**

   The Edit America Online Setup window appears.

2. **Click the Add Modem button.**

   The Select a Connection window appears.

3. **Select the TCP/IP: LAN or ISP (Internet Service Provider) option and click the Next button.**

   LAN stands for Local Area Network, and that's exactly what your home network is.

4. **Click the Next button again to finish.**

Unlike your more generous ISP, AOL forbids sharing. Even if your household has multiple screen names, only one person can be on AOL at one time.

Chapter 7

Share and Share Alike: Configuring and Controlling Network Shares

In This Chapter

▶ Understanding shared computer resources

▶ Creating shares on each computer

▶ Protecting shared resources with a password

*A*fter you install the network hardware, install the cable to connect the computers, and *configure* (set up) the operating system to recognize and use those items, your computers are members of the network. Each computer can *see* the other computers on your network. Well, not really *see* — and looking up from your screen and seeing another physical computer across the room doesn't count! The Network Neighborhood icon on your desktop shows you the computers that are connected to your network. Double-click the Network Neighborhood icon (the My Network Places icon in Windows Me and Windows 2000 Professional) to see your neighborhood of happy networked PCs. (My network appears in Figure 7-1.)

Figure 7-1:
All the computers I added to my network appear here — hooray!

Network Neighborhood includes the computer you're using, which of course you don't access through the Network Neighborhood window because you're already there.

Seeing a computer in Network Neighborhood means that the computer is running and has the necessary hardware and software to use network services. It doesn't mean that you can look inside the computer to see the files contained within it or that you can copy files from one computer to another. You have to set up all those features, and I cover how to do that in this chapter. Check out Chapter 10 to find out more information about how to use Network Neighborhood when you want to access another computer.

Understanding Shares: It's a Control Thing

The word *share* is used a lot in network computing:

- As a verb, share means configuring a resource on one computer so that people working on other computers can use it.
- As a noun, a share is a resource that's configured for access by users on other computers. If you configure your C drive for sharing, that drive is known as a share.

A *remote user* is someone who can access one computer while sitting in front of a different computer. If you ever use your home computer to dial into the network in your office across town, you're a remote user. When you access a remote computer, the computer that you're sitting in front of is called the *local computer*.

Having control: Setting up remote access

When you set up remote access controls (the controls that dictate who can and can't dial into your home network and access files), you can have it any way you want. For example, you can limit what remote users can do on your computer or you can provide users with the ability to read your files without giving them the capability to delete those files.

To set up sharing, you have to enable the sharing feature, which you did when you set up networking services. (Turn back to Chapter 5 for information on setting up networking services.) Then you must decide how you want to control sharing.

Controlling access to your shares means devising a scheme to control which remote users can access your computer and what they can do when they get there. You may decide that you don't want to let every user on your network use every shared resource that you create. Perhaps you want to limit access to certain users. You can prevent wholesale remote access by imposing access controls. You can use two types of access controls:

- ✔ **Share-level controls** enable you to control access on a share-by-share basis. This option is the default access control.

- ✔ **User-level controls** enable you to control access on a user-by-user basis. This control type is only available if users log on to a network server that validates user names and passwords. Having home networks configured for server validation is unusual, so you probably won't be able to use this feature.

Controls for shared resources only apply to people who access your computer from a *remote* computer. Anyone who uses your computer directly can access a folder without being hampered by the controls that you set.

You configure the specific controls for each share when you create it (see the section "Sharing Drives and Folders across the Network 'Hood," later in this chapter). Right now, you just have to tell Windows whether you're planning to use share-level controls or user-level controls. Follow these steps to specify your control method:

1. **Choose Start➪Settings➪Control Panel.**

   The Control Panel window opens.

2. **Double-click the Network icon.**

   The Network Properties dialog box appears.

3. **Click the Access Control tab.**

   The Access Control dialog box displays.

4. **Select Share-level Access Control.**

   The share-level option is preselected for you. If you're using a server for logons in your network, see the "User-level controls" sidebar before deciding whether you want to take advantage of that option.

5. **Click OK.**

Controlling user actions on the network

As you set up and configure each shared resource on your computer (covered in the "Using passwords to control user access" section), you're asked about the controls that you want to impose on that share. Every time you create a share, you have three choices of access types for that share. The following controls describe what you can do to limit the number of users on your network:

- ✔ **Read-Only.** Remote users can open and copy documents from your hard drive but can't make changes to them or delete them. If you choose this option, you can either require a password to admit only certain users to the share, or you can give read-only access to every remote user.

- ✔ **Full.** Remote users can manipulate and use folders and files on your hard drive as though they were working directly at your computer. If you choose this option, you can either require a password or let all remote users have full access to your hard drive.

- ✔ **Depends on Password.** The passwords that you create contain one of the access rights. As a result, the actions that users can perform depend on the passwords they use. If you choose this option, you must create a password for each type of access.

Using passwords to control user access

You can protect your shared resources by attaching a password to each share that you create. Then you give that password only to certain users. For example, you may decide to create a shared resource for the folder that contains the files for your household budget. You probably want to give the password for that folder to your spouse and not to your kids. If you don't want anyone to use a share, invent a password and don't tell anybody what the word is.

Remember that if you want to work on your own files from another computer, you're a remote user just like any other remote user. You have to know the password to get into your own files.

User-level controls

The User-Level Access Control option is available only if users log on to a server that authenticates their user names and passwords. To perform those authentication services, the server maintains a list of users.

If you select the User-Level Access Control option, you can list the users who can access each shared resource you establish. You must select names from the list maintained by the server.

With user-level controls in place, nobody needs a password to access your shared resources because they typed their passwords during logon. If they're on the list, they're in. You type the names of the favored users when you create the shared resource.

Sharing Drives and Folders across the Network 'Hood

After you enable sharing on your computer, you can create the resources that you want to share with remote users. The most common shares are hard drives and folders, because those are the containers for files. However, you can also share peripheral devices, such as CD-ROM, Jaz, Zip, and floppy drives.

Every share you create shows up in Network Neighborhood (or My Network Places for Windows Me and Windows 2000 Professional). You can also expand the Network Neighborhood listing in Windows Explorer to see all the shares.

Understanding hierarchy: Shares have parents and children

There's a pecking order for shares. Shares are made up of *parent shares* and *child shares*.

In the normal hierarchy you see in Windows Explorer on your computer, a parent is *any* container that can contain another container. Having trouble? Think of the way the filing cabinet in your home office holds all your tax files or a manila envelope in your filing cabinet holds all the tax information for last year — both the filing cabinet and the manila envelope are parents, although the filing cabinet could be considered more of a grandparent. The bottom line is that there are parents at every level of the hierarchy. You can remember this pretty easily if you figure that the youngest generation is the one least likely to have children of its own.

Figure 7-2 describes the order in which containers and contained items are stored on your computer. This ordered pattern is called the *hierarchy*.

Drives are the top of the hierarchy and may contain folders or files or both. Folders can contain other folders or files, or both.

When it comes to shares, however, the parent-child relationship begins on the level at which you create a share. For example, say you want to allow all the users in your home network to be able to share a drive. The drive that's being shared is a parent share. The same goes if you decide that every user can share a folder — the folder is a parent share. Memorize this rule, because it's important to the way you maintain control over shares: *Every child in a parent share is automatically shared.*

(C:) This parent contains folders and subfolders

Parent container (Folder)   File

```
Exploring - C:\                                      _ □ ×
 File  Edit  View  Go  Favorites  Tools  Help
  ↩        ⇨         ⬆        ✂          ✂       ✂      □       □        »
 Back   Forward     Up   Map Drive Disconnect  Cut    Copy    Paste
 Address  C:\                                                    ▼
 Folders                        × │ Tools_95            1999bs.xls
 ⊟  [C:]                          │ WB                  2amy.jpg
  ⊟   Kathy                       │ WINDOWS             ad911.gif
   ⊟   Kathy-correspondence       │ Windows Update Setup Files  Admin 9112.jpg
        Household Stuff           │ WinZip              ADMIN911 Logo.jpg
        Personal-keep out        │ xHP1120C            ADMIN911 Logo2.jpg
      Kathy-ExpenseAcctRecords    │ 0387.doc           AUTOEXEC.001
  ⊞   mas90                       │ 193.JPG            AUTOEXEC.BAK
 ◄                             ►│◄
 109 object(s)            12.7MB (Disk free spac  My Computer
```

Figure 7-2:
The
hierarchy of
computer
components.

Child containers (Subfolders)

If you decide that every computer on the network can share a drive, every folder on that drive is also automatically shared. And when you share a folder, you automatically share every subfolder and file it contains.

In a parent-child relationship, the child inherits all the characteristics of the parent. If you create a certain type of access (such as read-only access) for a parent, then a remote user who successfully accesses a parent has the same type of access to the children.

You can interrupt the inheritance factor by changing the configuration of any folder child. Say you decide to give full access to your hard drive to every remote user, but you want to protect a particular folder from being accessed. You can either change the one folder's security by allowing access only to users who know a password or you can provide a different type of access to the folder. Or you can use both options.

The point of home networking is to provide access to files and PC components from anywhere in the network, so it makes sense that you make widely sought after files and folders easy to get to. If remote users frequently need to use a folder or a subfolder, you may want to configure the folder to be shared. For example, you may have subfolders under the My Documents folder to hold special files that are popular with all family members. A subfolder for the family's favorite recipes comes in handy for the person preparing dinner tonight. A subfolder for names and addresses of friends and relatives may also be in constant demand. Read "Sharing a hard drive" to find out more about sharing common files.

Share and care alike: Saving remote users extra clicks

Every shared resource is individually visible in Network Neighborhood and Windows Explorer. For example, if the only shared resource in the network is one shared hard drive, then the drive appears in the Network Neighborhood window. If you share a drive and also share a folder in that drive, both objects are represented in the window.

You may not think that's such a big deal, but the upshot is that you can use a share to save remote users the trouble of navigating through the hierarchy (clicking a parent share and then clicking the subfolder to find the child share) to get what they need. Instead, users can just point and click once!

Sharing a hard drive

Home networks commonly share all the folders and files on the hard drives of every computer. Sharing is a convenient way to make sure that you can find and use files no matter which computer you're using.

For example, suppose that you began working on a document last week while you were sitting at the computer in the den. Today, you have time to do more work on that document, but another family member is using the computer in the den. The computer in the kitchen is free, so you can work there. You don't have to ask the person using the computer in the den to stop and copy your file to a floppy disk and then carry that floppy disk to the kitchen. (This method of sharing files is known as *sneakernet*.) Instead, you can access the file you need from the den PC's hard drive — directly from the computer in the kitchen. This advantage is one of the coolest benefits of networking.

You don't automatically see the contents of a hard drive on another computer. First, you have to configure the hard drive for sharing, which includes naming the share, deciding what people can do with the folders and files they access on the drive, and also deciding whether you want to use passwords. Whew! Sounds like a lot of work. Don't worry, you can accomplish everything in a couple of minutes. To configure a hard drive for sharing on the network, follow these steps:

1. **On the computer you're sharing, double-click the My Computer icon.**

2. **Right-click on the hard drive you want to share (usually drive C).**

3. **Choose Sharing from the shortcut menu that appears.**

   The Properties dialog box for the drive opens, and the Sharing tab is in the foreground. The Not Shared option is selected, and all the other options in the dialog box are grayed out and inaccessible.

4. **Select Shared As.**

   The options in the dialog box are now available, as shown in Figure 7-3.

5. **Type your own name for this share (Windows automatically calls it *C*) in the Share Name text box.**

   Choose a name that describes the share. For example, for the computer in the den, DenDriveC is a good name.

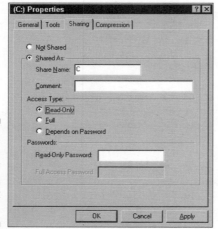

Figure 7-3:
Set the controls for this share and give it a name.

6. **If you want to provide a more complete description of the drive, you can type a descriptive phrase about this share in the Comment text box.**

   You can use the Comment text box to add more description about this share (for example, "Hard drive on the den computer"). The text in the Comment text box appears to remote users if they use the Details view of Network Neighborhood. (By default, Network Neighborhood displays an Icon view instead of the Details view.)

7. **Select an Access Type.**

   Specify the access type for this share by following the guidelines in the section "Controlling user actions on the network" earlier in this chapter. By default, Windows makes the access type Read Only, but, unless you have a good reason not to, change the access type to Full.

8. **If you want to require a password, type the password in the appropriate Password text box.**

   If you selected Depends on Password as the access type, you have no choice in the matter — you must create a password for each access type.

9. **Choose OK.**

   If you selected Depends on Password in Step 8, a Password Confirmation dialog box appears so that you can type the password again to confirm it.

10. **Confirm the password and then click OK.**

    If you don't type the password correctly in the Password Confirmation dialog box, a message that you've typed an incorrect password appears. Click OK to return to the dialog box and retype the password. If your entry is incorrect again, choose Cancel and start over with a password you can type without making typos.

You return to the My Computer window, where a hand appears under your hard drive icon. The hand indicates that the drive is a shared resource. All the shares that you create display that hand icon.

Sharing a peripheral drive

You use exactly the same steps that you used to share a drive when you want to share a peripheral drive. Peripheral drives are drives that are attached to your computer (your hard drive is internal), such as your floppy drive, a CD-ROM drive, a Zip drive, or a Jaz drive.

However, the results are a bit different because all your peripheral drives are also removable drives — the contents change depending on which disk is currently inserted in the drive. This makes it a bit more difficult to decide about access controls. Some disks may have contents that you think everybody can use, and other disks may have contents that you prefer that nobody change. (You can set read-only access to accomplish that.)

CD-ROM drives are read-only anyway. If you have a CD-R drive, never attempt to *burn,* or write to it from a remote machine. It won't work properly. Only burn CDs from the machine that holds the CD-R drive.

Trying to set access controls for peripheral drives is foolish because you spend a lot of time changing the controls, depending on the disk that's inserted at any given time. The solution is to give full access to peripheral drives and then hide any disks that you don't want other users to access.

Sharing folders

If you share a drive, you may also decide to share certain folders on that drive so that you can password-protect those folders. Or you may decide just to create folder shares so you can create an easy path to the folders for remote users. See the sidebar, "Share and care alike: Saving remote users extra clicks," for more about the appearance of shared folders in Network Neighborhood.

On the other hand, you may decide that you don't want to share your hard drive at all, even though you do want to share certain folders on the hard drive. If so, you must create a separate share for each folder you want to be accessible from other computers in the network.

You can create as many folder shares as you want by following these steps:

1. **Choose Start⇨Programs⇨Windows Explorer.**

   The Explorer window displays all the folders on your hard drive in the left pane.

2. **Right-click on the folder that you want to share and choose Sharing from the shortcut menu that appears.**

   The Properties dialog box for the folder opens. The Not Shared option is preselected, even if the folder is on a shared drive. This folder is not specifically configured as a share.

3. **Select Shared As.**

   The other options in the dialog box become accessible.

4. **Type a name in the Share Name text box.**

   Windows automatically inserts the name of the folder, which is usually a good choice. However, you can change the name if you want.

5. **If you want, you can type a description of this share in the Comment text box.**

   The description that you type in the Comment text box appears to remote users if they use the Details view of Network Neighborhood. (By default, Network Neighborhood displays icons instead of details.)

6. **Choose an Access Type and then type a password if you want to use passwords.**

   See the section "Controlling user actions on the network," earlier in this chapter, for information about access types and passwords.

7. **Choose OK.**

   You return to the Windows Explorer window, where the folder icon has a hand under it, indicating that it's a shared resource.

When a remote user looks at your computer in Network Neighborhood or Windows Explorer, the user sees no indication that a share is password-protected. The first clue comes when the user tries to open the share and sees a dialog box asking for the password. You can repeat these steps to configure any other folder or subfolder on your computer as a shared resource.

Changing passwords for shares

Sometimes a password for a share becomes so well known that even casual visitors to the household can sit in front of one computer and access shares on another computer. That's when you know that the password has outlived its usefulness. You need to create a new password and give it to a limited number of users. Changing the password for a share is easy; just follow these steps:

1. **Choose Start⇨Programs⇨Windows Explorer.**

   The Explorer window opens.

2. **Right-click on the shared resource for which you want to change the password and choose Sharing from the shortcut menu that appears.**

   The Sharing tab of the object's Properties dialog box appears.

3. **Delete the existing password.**

4. **Type a new password.**

5. **Click OK.**

   The Password Confirmation dialog box appears.

6. **Type the password again to confirm it.**

7. **Click OK.**

   The new password goes into effect immediately.

Hiding shares

Remember that shares and access controls are irrelevant when somebody is using your computer. Your hidden folder is totally accessible to anyone using your computer. A hidden share is also not hidden in Network Neighborhood if it falls victim to the rules for parent-child relationships. If your hidden share is a child of a parent share (it's a folder on a shared drive or a subfolder of a shared folder), it's going to be visible. That means that if you want hidden shares, you have to design them with a spy-like mentality. Here are some rules to help you out:

✔ If you want to hide even one folder on a drive, then you cannot share the drive on the network, because as soon as you do, every folder in the drive can be seen. Folders are children of drives, and when you share a parent, you share all its children.

✔ You cannot hide a subfolder of a folder that's shared on the network. Subfolders are children of folders, and when you share a parent, then you share all its children.

The best way to hide a folder is to make it a subfolder of a folder you're not sharing. Create a parent folder for the express purpose of creating a sub-folder that you want to hide. Give the parent folder an innocuous name so that nobody who uses your computer would be curious enough to expand the folder in Windows Explorer and find your secret. For example, create a folder on your drive and name it Tools or Maintenance. Then create a sub-folder and name it Logfiles or another name that seems equally boring or technical. In Logfiles, you can keep all your Naughty and Nice lists, and no one will suspect a thing, Machiavelli. Heh, heh, heh. You are some kind of control freak.

The best place to put your newly created private subfolder is under the Windows folder (`C:\Windows`). There's no reason to share the Windows folder because its contents are specific to the local computer. Other people who use the computer are unlikely to scroll through the subfolders in the Windows folders unless they're suspicious about your ability to be sneaky.

Creating a hidden share

To hide a folder's share, follow the steps to create a folder share that I describe in the previous section. However, when you give the share a name, make the last character of the share name a dollar sign ($). That's it, the share is hidden. Easy, huh?

Accessing a hidden share from a remote computer

When you work at a different computer and you want to get to a file that's in your hidden share, follow these steps:

1. **Choose Start⇨Run.**

   The Run dialog box opens.

2. **Type \\ComputerName\ShareName, substituting the real names.**

   For example, if you're trying to get to a hidden share named Logs$ on a computer named Den, type **\\den\logs$**. A window opens to display the contents of your hidden share, as shown in Figure 7-4.

The technical name for the format of a double backslash, followed by a com-puter name, followed by a single backslash, followed by a share name is *UNC*, which stands for Universal Naming Convention.

Figure 7-4:
Hidden
shares
display their
contents
when you
type the
correct
command.

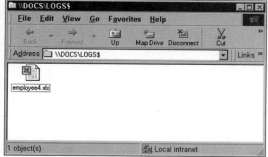

Keeping secret share access command a secret

When you use the Run command, Windows saves the command. The next time you open the Run command, the last command that you typed displays. Just click OK to run the command again. Very convenient, eh? Uh, not on a network.

Unless you do something to prevent it, the convenient and secret command that leads to your convenient and secret share will no longer be convenient *or* secret.

The only way to prevent your UNC command from being visible is to implement the user features available for networks. The Run commands are saved on a user-by-user basis, so when a user named Mom is logged on, only commands issued by Mom are visible in the list. If you use passwords to log on to computers, nobody can log on as another person even inadvertently. Flip to Chapter 8 for information about setting up user features.

Chapter 8

Setting Up User Profiles

*U*nless you've bought a computer for every member of the family (rather unlikely), people share computers in your home network. One of the nifty features that you can take advantage of when you share the same computer is a profile. Each user has his or her own *personal profile*. Profiles enable everyone who uses the computer to personalize his or her computer environment, instead of undoing the configuration efforts of the other people who use the computer.

You can make sure nobody messes with your settings by password-protecting the *logon process*. And, you can even decide which type of logon process you want to use (you have a couple of choices). The result? Whenever a computer in the network is turned on, the user has to type a password. No password, no customized features. In this chapter, I show you how to set up user and profile features.

Enabling Profiles

Windows 95, Windows 98, and Windows Me don't automatically assume that each person who uses a computer wants to create his or her own individual settings. To create the atmosphere for customized settings, you have to tell the operating system that you want each user to have a personal profile.

Windows 2000 Professional creates individual user settings by default, so you don't have to do anything to turn on this feature.

Follow these steps to turn on the profiles feature:

1. **Choose Start⇨Settings⇨Control Panel.**

   The Control Panel window opens.

2. **Double-click the Passwords icon.**

   The Passwords Properties dialog box opens.

3. **Click the User Profiles tab.**

   The options for user profiles are presented, as shown in Figure 8-1.

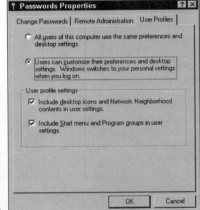

Figure 8-1:
Configure
Windows to
save each
user's
individual
preferences.

4. **Click the Users Can Customize Their Preferences and Desktop Settings radio button.**

   This option enables individual profiles.

5. **In the bottom half of the dialog box, select either or both profile options.**

   If you choose to include desktop icons and Network Neighborhood contents in user settings, Windows remembers each user's changes to those objects and setup. Be sure to select this option so that users can decorate and arrange their own desktops.

   If you choose to include the Start menu and Program groups in user settings, then as each user adds items to the Start menu (usually by installing software), the menu item appears only when that user is logged on. Selecting this option doesn't always work well because other users may occasionally need a program that another user has installed.

6. Click OK.

Now Windows is ready to keep track of all the users who work at this computer. The System Settings Change dialog box opens, prompting you to restart the computer.

7. Restart your computer.

If you select the option to include the Start menu and Program groups, don't worry that you won't be able to use software that someone else has installed because your individual Start menu doesn't contain a menu item for that software. You can put the menu item on your menu without installing the software again, but accomplishing this does require some work. See the following section, "Tweaking Profiles," in this chapter.

Adding Users to the Computer

After you tell Windows that you want to keep track of each user's settings, you have to tell Windows who those users are. Windows sets up folders for each user. Those folders hold all the information about each user's configuration settings. You can add users to the computer in one of two ways:

- ✔ You can play administrator and set up each user. If you choose this option, you don't need to know each user's password — just skip the setting passwords part (one of the things you can do when you're setting up a user). Later, each user can set up his or her own password.

- ✔ You can perform the task of adding yourself to the computer and let all the other users in the household add themselves to the computer.

Before you make any decisions about which option to use, read the section, "Changing a user's password," later in this chapter.

You don't really need a password, because Windows keeps track of your customized settings without one. A password keeps others from logging on to the computer using your name. If another user logs on with your name and makes changes to the configuration, you have to live with those changes (or take the trouble to reset everything). The password is just a way to prevent someone else from pretending he or she is you.

The technical term for no password is *null password*.

Windows provides a wizard to add users to a computer. To launch the wizard, follow these steps:

1. Choose Start➪Settings➪Control Panel.

The Control Panel window opens.

2. **Double-click the Users icon.**

   The first time you open the Users icon, the Add User wizard starts automatically. After you create the first user, double-clicking the Users icon opens the User Settings dialog box, and you have to click the New User button to launch the wizard.

3. **Read the information in the first wizard window and click Next.**

   The first window is just an introduction to the wizard, so you don't have to provide any information.

4. **In the next wizard window, type the name that you want to use when you log on in the User Name text box.**

   Most people use just a first name, unless two people in the household have the same first name. If so, you can use Mom and Sis, or Dad and Junior. Nicknames are fine, too, if you're not embarrassed by having a logon box appear that says Dogbreath or Pizzaface.

5. **Click Next.**

   The Enter New Password dialog box opens.

6. **If you want to use a password, type the password in the Password text box of the Enter New Password dialog box, which is shown in Figure 8-2. Type the same password in the Confirm Password text box and then click Next.**

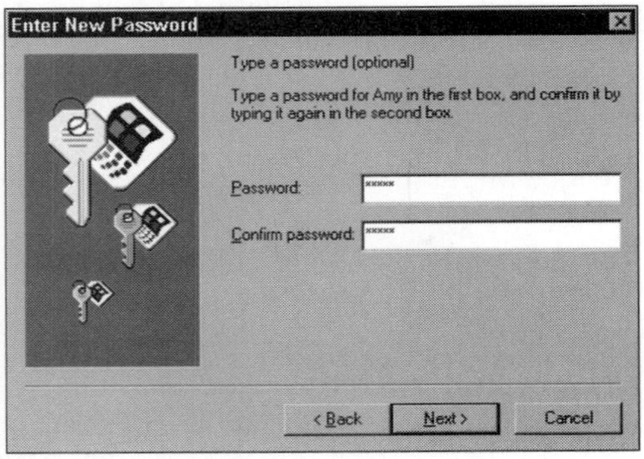

Figure 8-2:
When you
type a
password,
the
characters
turn into
asterisks so
nobody can
see what
you're
typing.

If you don't want to enter a password, click the Next button. Either way, the Personalized Items Settings dialog box opens.

If the entries in the Password text box and the Confirm Password text box don't match, the wizard asks you to type the password again. You can't see the actual characters you're typing, so use a password that's easy to type. For example, if you frequently make mistakes when you type numbers, don't use a number in your password.

7. **In the Personalized Items Settings dialog box, shown in Figure 8-3, choose the settings that you want to personalize and save in your profile. Also, choose the way that you want these items created. Then click Next.**

Figure 8-3:
Choose the
items you
want to
personalize.

You can personalize the Desktop folder, the Documents menu, the Start menu, the Favorites folder, Downloaded Web pages, and the My Documents folder.

The items you don't select remain the same as they are now. Even if you make changes while you're working on the computer, those items revert to their current state the next time you log on. See the next section, "Deciding which settings to personalize," for more information on how this works.

If you tell Windows to create copies of the current items, you're asking that the current desktop settings serve as the starting point for your configuration efforts. Everything that exists on the current desktop is automatically copied to your profile, even if you don't really need all the items (and they occupy a lot of disk space). However, if you tell Windows to create new items, the settings are saved as the user creates them.

8. **In the Ready to Finish dialog box, click Finish.**

Windows takes a few seconds to set up folders and files for a new user. (You see an animated dialog box as this activity proceeds.) Then you return to the User Settings dialog box, where the new user name is listed.

9. **In the User Settings dialog box, click New User to set up another user, or choose Close if you're finished for now.**

Every time you log on to the computer with this user name, your customization efforts are saved according to the options you set.

Deciding which settings to personalize

The Personalized Items Settings dialog box (refer to Figure 8-3) offers several choices for each user's personalization. Here are some guidelines to help you make selections:

- ✓ **Desktop folder and Documents menu.** Select this option to save your personal settings for the desktop and the Documents submenu on your Start menu.

- ✓ **Start Menu.** Select this option to save the changes that you make to the Start menu, including Program groups and items.

- ✓ **Favorites folder.** Select this option to save your settings for your Favorites folder, which holds links to your favorite Web sites as well as links to programs and documents that are on your hard drive.

- ✓ **Downloaded Web pages.** Select this option to save temporary Internet files and cookies in your own personal folders. (Temporary Internet files are called the *cache. Cookies* are pieces of data that Internet sites place on your hard drive in order to identify you when you visit those sites.)

- ✓ **My Documents folder.** Select this option to make the My Documents folder on the desktop a private folder for yourself.

Changing user options

In addition to creating users, the Users icon in the Control Panel allows you to *manage* users. Managing means that you can change the options for users, copy an existing user's setup to a new user, or delete any user names you don't need anymore.

Copying a user's settings to a new user

Say you have a user who has a really terrific configuration. The good news is that you can use that configuration to set up a new user. Usually, you find the following: a Programs menu that shows everything that's been installed, lots of handy shortcuts on the desktop, and an absolutely beautiful and highly decorative desktop. Follow these steps to clone a new user from an existing user:

1. **Choose Start➪Settings➪Control Panel.**

   The Control Panel window opens.

2. **Double-click the Users icon.**

   The User Settings dialog box opens.

3. **In the Users list box, select the user with the configuration that you want to copy.**

Chapter 8: Setting Up User Profiles

4. **Click Make a Copy to open the Add User Wizard.**

5. **Follow the instructions for adding a new user, clicking Next to move through each of the wizard's windows.**

   The wizard asks for a user name, a user password, and a confirmation of the password. Then you're asked which items you want to personalize. That's all there is to it — the new user has a terrific desktop waiting!

If you clone a user who has been working at this computer for some time, all the documents in that user's personal My Documents folder are cloned. Internet cookies are cloned. Everything that's linked to the user is cloned. To avoid that problem, remove the check mark from Favorites folder, Downloaded Web pages, and My Documents folder when you get to the Personalized Items Settings wizard window.

The best way to use the Make a Copy feature is to create a user, customize the desktop and the Start menu items, and then use that user only for copying the configuration to new users. You may want to name the user *clone* (if you think the person got all his good ideas from you) or *perfect person* (if the person *is* you).

Deleting a user

If your user list contains a name that's no longer used on this computer, get rid of the user name. You not only dump the name, but also clear out all the folders that are attached to the user, which frees up disk space. The only time you'll probably have to delete a name is if your daughter adds herself to a computer more than once. For example, she may log on as Mary Smith at the beginning of the summer and set herself up as a user. In the fall, she will most certainly return to Harvard *(Hah-vad),* where she's a straight-A student. At Thanksgiving, she may need to use the network to write her rocket science paper and decide she wants to log on as EngineerLady, or she may even forget she ever set up configuration settings as Mary Smith.

Windows won't let you delete the user who is currently logged on.

Changing a user's password

You can change passwords in the User Settings dialog box, but you have to know the current password to do so. Windows insists on making sure you know the old password before you're allowed to enter a new password. This, of course, eliminates the ability to fix things when a user forgets a password (the fix for that problem is covered later in this chapter).

You can also change passwords in the Passwords Properties dialog box in the Control Panel (shown in Figure 8-4). However, the Passwords Properties dialog box works only for the currently logged on user; the User Settings dialog box works for any user.

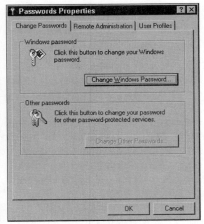

Figure 8-4:
Use the
Passwords
Properties
dialog box
to change
your
password.

Follow these steps to change the password from the User Settings dialog box:

1. **Choose Start⊅Settings⊅Control Panel.**

   The Control Panel window opens.

2. **Double-click the Users icon.**

   The User Settings dialog box opens, displaying a list of users in the Users list box.

3. **Select the appropriate user name.**

   The name you click is highlighted.

4. **Click the Set Password button.**

   The Change Windows Password dialog box opens, as shown in Figure 8-5.

5. **Type the old password in the Old Password text box.**

   If either the old password or the new password is a null password (no password at all), just make sure the appropriate box is cleared of any characters.

6. **Type the new password in the New Password text box.**

7. **Type the new password again in the Confirm New Password text box.**

   If you make a mistake, you're asked to try again.

8. **Click OK to return to the User Settings dialog box.**

   A message appears to announce that this user now has a new password.

9. **Click Close to close the User Settings dialog box.**

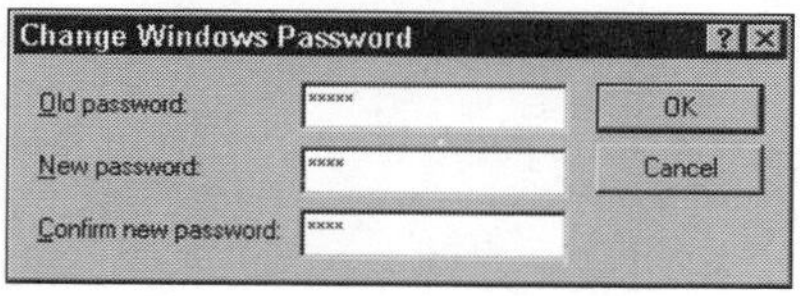

Figure 8-5:
Remember
to type
carefully,
because
you can't
see the
characters
you're
typing.

Change Windows Password

Old password:
New password:
Confirm new password:

OK
Cancel

Changing user settings

You can change the items that a user can personalize by selecting the user's name and choosing Change Settings. When the Personalized Items Settings dialog box opens, as shown in Figure 8-6, you can select or deselect items to indicate what this user can personalize. Most of the time, you make these changes for your own logon name, but if you're acting as the home network administrator, you may have reasons to work on other user names.

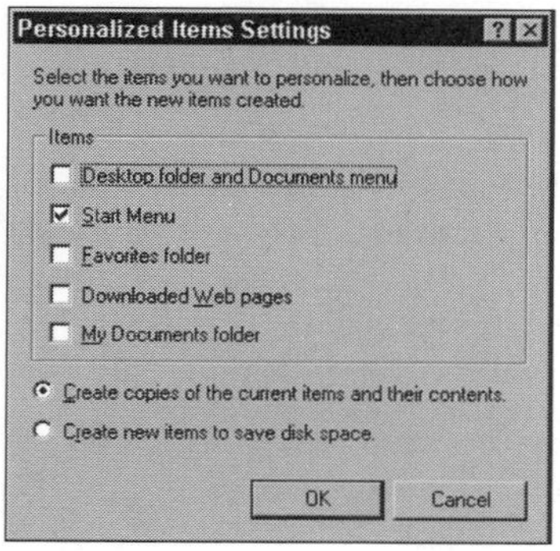

Personalized Items Settings

Select the items you want to personalize, then choose how you want the new items created.

Items
- ☐ Desktop folder and Documents menu
- ☑ Start Menu
- ☐ Favorites folder
- ☐ Downloaded Web pages
- ☐ My Documents folder

○ Create copies of the current items and their contents.
○ Create new items to save disk space.

OK   Cancel

Figure 8-6:
Some users
don't feel
the need to
personalize
every item.

Sneaking Around, Resetting Passwords, and Otherwise Foiling Windows "Security"

People forget their passwords. It's a common, frequent problem. You usually forget your password the next time you try to log on after a password change, but using a password for weeks or months and then suddenly forgetting it is not rare.

Build security by changing a user's password

Password protection is called a security wall. Unfortunately, except for Windows 2000, the wall isn't made of brick so much as it's made of straw. Straw walls can keep out those people who don't know how to get past straw. People who know their way around computers aren't intimidated by passwords, but at least you can protect the computers on your network against people who don't have computer expertise.

Windows 2000 Professional understands the meaning of the words *password* and *secret*. You cannot get past the logon screen unless you know the password. Security in Windows 2000 Professional is a brick wall.

Some people feel more secure if they change their logon password often. Frequently, these are the same people who say, "Oh, do it yourself — here's my password," when someone needs a data file from the computer. Eventually, so many other people know the password that it may as well be taped to the front of the monitor — "John's password is *gojohn*. Help yourself."

Actually, changing your password periodically is a good habit, even if you don't give out your password to everyone in the immediate five-county area. Your computer security does increase when you take this step.

To change your password, you have to know the old password. If you need a cure for a forgotten password, go to the section, "Sneaking Around, Resetting Passwords, and Otherwise Foiling Windows 'Security'," later in this chapter.

In Windows 98, Windows 95, and Windows Me, you can change your password in either of two places: the Passwords Properties dialog box or the User Settings dialog box (covered in the previous section). Use the Passwords Properties dialog box to change the password of the user who is currently logged on.

After you complete the steps in "Changing a user's password," earlier in this chapter, you see a message telling you that the password was successfully changed. Here are some tips to help you if you receive an error message:

- If you made a mistake when you typed the old password, the error message tells you that the Windows password is incorrect. Click OK and type the old password again.

- If you continue to fail when entering the old password, check the Log Off item on the Start menu to make sure that you are the current logged on user. If the user name isn't yours, choose Log Off, click Yes when Windows asked if you're sure you want to log off, and then log yourself on.

- If you're logged on correctly and still continue to fail, you've probably forgotten your password. See the section "Sneaking Around, Resetting Passwords, and Otherwise Foiling Windows 'Security'" later in this chapter.

- If you made a mistake when you repeated the password in the Confirm New Password text box, the error message tells you that the new and confirmed passwords don't match. Click OK and type the password again in the confirmation box.

- If you fail more than once when you're trying to confirm a new password, you may have chosen a string of characters that invites typos. Start again with a password that's easier to type.

Windows 2000 doesn't ask you to type the old password in order to prove you are who you say you are; the logon security is so good that you can't sneak past it.

Recognizing the symptoms of a user who forgets a password is easy. When the logon dialog box opens, the user stares at it for a moment and then shrieks or moans, "Oh no." The user usually is frozen in front of the computer for several seconds and then experiences a panic attack. (The symptoms vary according to the way that person handles panic.) However, the problem of a forgotten password is easy to solve, so the user has no reason to panic. The way to solve the problem of a forgotten password is to delete the Windows file that holds the password. That file is checked against your password entry whenever you log on. In fact, sometimes users don't really forget their passwords. The problem may be with the user's password file. If a password file becomes corrupted, or someone inadvertently deletes the file, the password won't work.

Remember that you cannot issue a new password by changing the current password, because you have to know the old password to make the change.

In this section, I go over the steps for the solution, which illustrates why I say that Windows 98, Windows 95, and Windows Me are operating systems devoid of security.

Get sneaky: Bypassing the logon process

To delete your password file, you must log on to the computer. But how do you log on if you don't have your password? Fortunately (or unfortunately, depending on how you feel about security), logging on to the network and getting around this Catch-22 without a password is as easy as pie. (Don't try this solution on Windows 2000 Professional — it won't work.)

To bypass the logon, click Cancel on the Logon dialog box, or press Esc to make the Logon dialog box go away. Presto, you're on the computer and you can do whatever you want.

You have a couple of choices about what to do next. You can either choose to continue clicking Cancel every time you log on (thereby negating the usefulness of the scant security you already have), or you can find the faulty password file and zap it into oblivion. To search and destroy, read on.

Seek and destroy: Finding, removing, and resetting a password file

If you've managed to bypass the heavy-duty logon security but still have no idea what your password is, you can solve the problem by finding the password file associated with your user name and deleting it so that you can reset the password. Follow these steps to find the file and remove it:

1. **Open Windows Explorer and select the folder that holds your Windows files (usually named Windows).**

2. **Press F3 to open the Find dialog box.**

   You want to find files with the extension .pwl, which is the extension that Windows assigns to password files. The Find dialog box should indicate that it is searching your Windows folder, as shown in Figure 8-7.

Figure 8-7:
Search the
Windows
folder for
your
password
file.

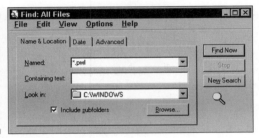

3. **In the Named text box, type pwl or *.pwl and click Find Now.**

   The Find dialog box shows a list of all the files that your computer found with the .pwl extension.

4. **Select your password file from the list that appears in the Find dialog box.**

   You can recognize your password file because it has the first eight letters of your logon name, followed by the extension .pwl. If your logon name has a space in it, the space is ignored in the password file name.

5. **Press Del to delete the file.**

   Windows asks you to confirm the fact that you want to delete the file.

6. **Click Yes to confirm that you want to delete the file.**

Your computer no longer has any record of your password. You are password-less. Is that anything like being speechless?

After you've deleted your password file, your computer has no record of a password for you. This is the same as having a null password. In fact, if you don't want to have a password any more, you don't have to do anything — just log on without a password.

Back to the drawing board: Creating a new password

If you do want a password, you have two options for resetting your password: You can create a new password immediately after deleting the old one, or you can wait to create a new password until the next time you log on.

Creating a new password before the next logon

If you want to create a new password before you log on again, you can't use the Passwords icon in the Control Panel because it's connected to the current logged-on user, and you didn't log on as yourself because you forgot your password. Here's how to create a new password and a new password file at the same time:

1. **Double-click the Users icon in the Control Panel and select your logon name.**

2. **Click Set Password.**

3. **Skip the Old password text box, and type a new password in the New Password text box.**

   Windows doesn't find an old password because you wiped out the password file.

4. **Type the new password again in the Confirm Password text box.**

5. **Click OK and then click Close to close the User Settings dialog box.**

   Windows creates a new password file.

6. **Choose Log Off from the Start menu, confirm the logoff procedure, and then log on again as yourself.**

Creating a new password at the next logon

If you want, you can wait until the next time you log on to create a new password. Just filling out the Password box in the Logon dialog box determines your new password. To log on again right away, click Start and choose Log Off. That Log Off command has no user name, because technically, nobody is logged on, as a result of your bypassing the Logon dialog box. Then click Yes when Windows asks if you're sure you want to log off.

When the Logon dialog box appears again, it contains the name of the last logged on user (probably you). You can do one of the following things:

✔ If you want to keep the null password, type your logon name, skip the password text box, and click OK. Your password file is recreated with a null password.

- If you want to create a new password, type a new password in the Password text box of the Logon dialog box. When you click OK, you're asked to confirm the password by typing it again. A new password file is created for you, and the password you entered is saved as your new password.

- If you're using Family Logon, your name appears on the list of users for this computer, but the Password text box is grayed out and inaccessible. Click OK to log on with a null password, because you have no choice. Then use either the Passwords or Users applet in the Control Panel to give yourself a new password (when you're asked to type the old password, remember to leave the box blank because you got rid of the old password).

If you once again forget the password, find and remove your password file all over again, but this time, don't create any passwords anywhere. Obviously, you're meant to have a null password.

Logging On

In Windows 98, Windows 95, and Windows Me, when profiles are enabled, a Logon dialog box appears every time you start Windows. In Windows 2000 Professional, a Logon dialog box always appears, because there's no such thing as enabling profiles. The logon process is for security.

Switching to another user

Okay, you powered up your computer and logged on. You balanced your checkbook, sent a letter to Mom, and played a game. Now somebody else wants to use the computer. If the new user just sits down in front of the computer, he's looking at your desktop decor and preference settings. In addition, he's using your My Documents folder, which doesn't make either of you very comfortable.

Actually, logging off the computer is a good idea, even if nobody else is standing over your shoulder waiting to use the computer. Logging off saves any changes you've made to your personal configuration settings. Logging off also puts a Logon dialog box on the screen so every time a user wants to use the computer, he or she will have to log on. This prevents anyone from accidentally using your profile and making changes.

Luckily, you don't have to shut down the computer to enable the next user to log on and load his or her personalized desktop. (I say "luckily" because the shutdown process is time consuming, and the startup process can seem endless.) You can just use the Log Off command by choosing Start⇨Log Off *Yourname.* (Your logon name appears instead of the word *Yourname.*) Click Yes when Windows asks if you're sure you want to log off. The Logon dialog box opens within seconds so that the next user can log on.

When the logon dialog box returns, the name of the last user who logged on appears in the User Name text box. The new user must remove that name and replace it with his logon name and password (if he has one).

Getting to know the default desktop

You can bypass the logon process by clicking Cancel on the Logon dialog box, or by pressing Esc to make the Logon dialog box go away. The most common reason for users to bypass the logon is because they don't know the password required for a successful logon — not always a sign of some sinister intent. Being human, users sometimes just forget their own passwords.

When you bypass the logon, the desktop that appears is the desktop that was in effect when profiles were enabled on the computer. Call it the default desktop. If you turned on the profile feature immediately after installing Windows, the default desktop is quite sparse. The only desktop icons are those that appear as a result of installation choices. The Programs menu has only a few items (also the result of installation choices) such as Windows Explorer, the MS-DOS Command Prompt, and the Accessories you installed. You may also find a Startup folder, but it's probably empty. If you have been using the computer for a while — installing software, creating desktop shortcuts, and so on — before you enabled the profiles feature, the default desktop offers those elements.

Anyone who uses the default desktop can make changes to it. A new default desktop results from saving those changes. The default desktop has two uses:

- ✔ It's the desktop for users who skip the logon procedure.
- ✔ It's the desktop that's used when you create a new user.

You can deliberately skip the logon just for the purpose of making changes to the default desktop. Then, from this desktop, create a new user. You preset the basic settings for that user with this desktop.

Using the Family Logon feature

So you can't believe that users frequently forget their passwords? Wait till you hear that users also fail to recall their names (okay, not their real names, their logon names). Most of us use nicknames or first names or some cute appellation for a logon name. Most folks don't choose to log on as Bentley T. Backstroke, Jr. The more likely logon choice is Bentley, Bent, or Junior.

Forgetting your logon name is not all that unusual, and I've found that it's a far more common event for people who have strange and esoteric logon names at work. If your company assigns you a logon name of 77645G567 (some companies use names like that) and you decide to use Sammy on your home computer, you can expect a brain fog to settle in when you look at that home-based Logon dialog box. You're sure that you're not supposed to use that weird logon from work, but you're not really certain what you entered when you set yourself up as a user on your home computer. Was it Sam? Sam Smith? Ssmith? Sam S?

You can bypass the logon (see the previous section, cleverly titled "Get sneaky: Bypassing the logon process") and use the default desktop to open the Users list in the Control Panel, where you find your name on the list. Write it down, and then log on again.

One way to make sure nobody forgets his or her logon name is to use a clever logon device called Family Logon. With this feature enabled, the Family Logon dialog box — rather than a traditional logon dialog box — opens when the operating system starts up. The Family Logon dialog box lists all the users registered on this computer, as shown in Figure 8-8. You just have to select your name, type your password (if you have one), click OK, and you're in!

Figure 8-8:
With Family
Logon,
you don't
have to
remember
your own
name.

Family Logon is available if your computer is running Windows 98, Windows 95, or Windows Me. Windows 2000 Professional, which is designed as a business operating system, doesn't understand the notion of a family.

Installing the Family Logon feature is easy. Before you begin, however, your Windows files must be available so that the appropriate files can be transferred to your hard drive. Put the Windows CD in the CD-ROM drive. If the manufacturer preinstalled Windows, the files are probably on the hard drive, and the documentation that came with the computer explains where they are.

Hold down the Shift key when you insert a CD to prevent the CD's program from opening automatically.

Follow these steps to install the Family Logon feature:

1. **Choose Start⇨Settings⇨Control Panel.**

   The Control Panel window opens.

2. **Double-click the Network icon in the Control Panel.**

   The Network dialog box opens, with the Configuration tab in the foreground.

3. **Click Add.**

   The Select Network Component Type dialog box opens.

4. **Choose Client and click Add.**

   The Select Network Client dialog box opens.

5. **In the Select Network Client dialog box, shown in Figure 8-9, choose Microsoft from the Manufacturers pane on the left.**

   Windows Me shows only Microsoft on the left pane.

6. **Choose Microsoft Family Logon from the Network Clients pane on the right.**

7. **Click OK.**

   You're back at the Network dialog box, and the necessary files are copied to your hard drive.

8. **In the Primary Network Logon text box, choose Microsoft Family Logon from the drop-down list.**

9. **Click OK.**

   The Systems Settings Change dialog box opens to tell you that these settings take effect after you restart your operating system.

10. **Click Yes to restart the system.**

    When Windows restarts, the Family Logon dialog box opens so that you can select your user name and type your password if you have one.

If you're not using a password, the password box is grayed out when you
select your user name.

Logging Off

After you finish working on the computer — and nobody's standing over your
shoulders waiting impatiently to be the next in line — play it safe and log off.
Otherwise, the next person who sits down in front of the computer may just
start working, which can change your configuration. When the computer is
up and running, people tend to forget that they need to log off the previous
user and log themselves on. Going right to work is just too tempting.

If you don't use passwords, you may want to erase your name from the Select
User Name text box in the logon dialog box that appears after you log off. (Just
use the delete key to erase the letters.) Removing your name prevents the next
user from accidentally clicking OK or hitting the Enter key, thus getting to your
desktop. Such a move happens more often than you may imagine, and the
result is two surprised and disappointed users. Your desktop is different the
next time you log on, and the user who changed your desktop is annoyed when
he logs on properly and the changes he made aren't on his desktop.

When you log off, any open software windows are closed for you. Before the
logoff procedure starts, you're given an opportunity to save any data that
you've changed in the software since the last time you saved your documents.

If you have an operating system window open, such as the Control Panel or
My Computer, you can expect to find it open when you log on again. The
same is true even if lots of other users log on in the meantime; the window
just waits for you to return. Another user can't see the open window on the
desktop (unless she left the same window open when she logged off).

Tweaking Profiles

Your personal profile is a collection of the configuration options you set for
yourself. Every time you make changes to the desktop or install software, the
results are stored in your profile. When you log on to Windows with your own
user name, your own user profile is loaded when Windows starts.

What's in my profile?

You can see the elements in your profile by looking in the folders that contain
your profile information. When you know how to find and identify profile
elements, you can take advantage of the tricks and tips available for changing

your profile easily. To see the elements in your profile, follow these steps in Windows 98, Windows 95, and Windows Me (instructions for Windows 2000 Professional appear later in this section):

1. **Choose Start⇨Programs⇨Windows Explorer.**

   The Explorer window opens.

2. **Click the plus sign to the left of the folder in which your Windows software is stored (usually named Windows).**

   In Windows Me, first expand My Computer, and then expand the C drive to get to the Windows folder. The subfolders under your Windows folder are displayed in the left Explorer pane.

3. **Click the plus sign to the left of the subfolder named Profiles.**

   Folders for each user on the computer are displayed in the left Explorer pane.

4. **Click the plus sign to the left of the subfolder for your logon name.**

   You can see the subfolders for your own personal profile in the left Explorer pane, as shown in Figure 8-10.

Figure 8-10: Your profile folders store all the objects that make up your personal configuration settings.

Where your desktop really lives

Click the Desktop folder to check out the subfolders and shortcuts it contains. The objects that you see in the folder represent the objects that you find on your desktop when you log on to Windows. You can have both folders and shortcuts on your desktop.

Here are some tidbits of information to note when you view your profile's Desktop folder:

- The default desktop icons aren't represented in your profile Desktop folder. Those icons include My Computer, Network Neighborhood, the Recycle Bin, and the My Documents folder.
- The objects in the profile Desktop folder are linked to your real desktop. If you delete or add an object in either place, the change is made in both places.

Viewing your Start Menu folder

You can view and manipulate the items that appear on your personal Start menu within your personal profile folders. Click the plus sign next to the Start Menu folder to expand it. Then select the Programs subfolder, and also click its plus sign to expand it.

The left pane displays the subfolders on your Programs menu, and the right pane shows the listings that appear on your Programs menu, as shown in Figure 8-11.

Subfolders under the Programs folder represent program groups that appear on your Programs menu. These are the listings on your Programs menu that have right-facing arrows to indicate a submenu. A folder represents a menu listing, and clicking on the folder in the left pane displays the items on the submenu in the right pane.

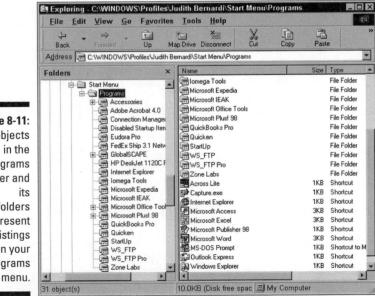

Figure 8-11: The objects in the Programs folder and its subfolders represent the listings on your Programs menu.

You can use the objects in these folders to change the way your Programs menu presents items. Common manipulations include the following:

✔ **Create folders to hold groups of program items.** You can create a new subfolder in the Programs folder and then move related program items into that folder. This action is useful if your Programs menu is very long.

✔ **Move items from a subfolder to the Programs folder.** This is a handy trick if you use a particular item from the Accessories submenu frequently. Rather than moving down another level to open a menu item, you can put it on the main Programs menu.

Finding your profile in Windows 2000 Professional

By default, Windows 2000 Professional doesn't set up a profiles subfolder in the folder that holds the Windows files. Instead, it uses a folder named Documents and Settings. A subfolder for each user exists under that folder. You can perform the same actions to manipulate your profile; you just do everything from the Documents and Settings parent folder.

However, sometimes, if you install Windows 2000 Professional as an upgrade, over a previous version of Windows, the system keeps the Profiles folder in the folder that holds the Windows software. In Windows 2000 Professional, that folder isn't named Windows, it's named WINNT.

Adding software listings to your Programs menu

Adding software to the Programs menu on a computer with profiles enabled creates an interesting problem. If you configured profiles settings to include the Start menu, the changes that one user makes to the Programs menu aren't reflected on the Programs menus for the other users.

For example, if your spouse logs on and installs a bookkeeping program, he or she can start the program from the Programs menu. If you want to use the program, however, you can't choose the listing from your own Programs menu because the listing isn't there. You have to put it there yourself! Don't install the software again to accomplish that; use the Profile folders.

You can add a listing for any program installed on the computer to your Programs menu. The listings in the Programs menu are nothing more than shortcuts that have been placed in the Programs folder in your personal profile. You only have to copy the shortcut into your own Programs folder.

Because many programs install groups of listings, copying the shortcut is the only way to ensure that you have all the choices. Follow these steps to copy a program listing from one user's Programs menu to your own Programs menu:

1. **Click the plus sign to the left of the user profile that has the Programs menu listing that you want to add.**

   All the subfolders for this user's profile are displayed in the left Explorer pane.

2. **Click the plus sign to the left of the Start menu folder to reveal the Programs folder, and then click the Programs folder.**

   All the folders (groups) and individual items on the Programs menu are displayed in the right Explorer pane.

3. **Right-click on the program item that you want to add to your own Programs menu and choose Copy from the shortcut menu that appears.**

4. **Click the plus sign to the left of your own profile folder.**

   All the subfolders for your profile are displayed in the left Explorer pane.

5. **Click the plus sign to the left of your Start menu folder to reveal your Programs folder.**

6. **Right-click on your Programs folder and choose Paste from the shortcut menu that appears.**

   The program listing is copied to your own Programs menu.

Part III
Communicating Across the Network

"I think Doreen is trying to send me a message. She set up the vacuum cleaner for sharing."

In this part . . .

Now for the fun stuff — actually using your network for communicating from computer to computer, printing, exchanging files, and generally getting all the benefits of network computing.

In this part of the book, I walk you through the tasks required for setting up shared printing. You find out how to install and use printers that are attached to your own computer and remote computers.

You also find out how to get files from any computer on the network, and how to send files from your computer to another computer. And, for real convenience, this chapter also explains how to open software and then load a file that's on another computer.

Chapter 9

Printing Across the Network

*O*ne terrific side effect of installing a computer network in your home is the ability to share a printer. Households without networks face some difficulties when it comes to printing. Network-deficient households (that seems to be a politically correct term, don't you think?) have had to rely on some less-than-perfect solutions.

One solution is to buy a printer every time you buy a computer. I can think of lots of other ways to spend that money, and I bet you can, too.

Another solution is to buy one printer and attach the printer to only one of the computers in your home network. Anyone who uses a computer that doesn't have a printer has to copy files to a floppy disk, go to the computer that has a printer, load the same software that created the files (the same software has to be installed on both computers), open each file from the floppy disk, and print. I guess all this walking comes under the heading of "healthy exercise," especially if the computers are on different floors of the house, but this setup isn't exactly a model of efficiency.

Neither of these scenarios is acceptable after you understand how easy it is to share printers over a network.

Setting Up Shared Printers

If you want all the computers on your network to be able to access a single printer, you have to set up the Windows printer-sharing feature. Then you have to set up the printer for sharing. You perform these tasks at the computer to which the printer is connected.

The most difficult part of setting up network printing is deciding which computer gets the printer. Here are some common guidelines:

- ✔ **Location.** If you have room for a table at the computer location (and storage space for paper), that's the computer to choose.

- ✔ **Usage patterns.** If one computer on the network is used far more often than any other computer, that's the computer to select.

Some households have more than one printer. You may have a black and white printer and also a color printer. When you enable printer sharing, each user can choose a printer every time he or she wants to print.

You can attach two printers to one computer if that's more convenient, but you have to add a second printer port to the computer. Printer ports are inexpensive (usually less than $10) and are easy to install. (Just read the directions that come with the hardware.) The *port* is a card that fits in a slot on the computer's motherboard. In Chapter 1, I tell you how to buy the right type of card for your computer.

Enabling printer sharing

The first thing you have to do is tell Windows that the printer attached to the computer should be shared with other users on the network. If you didn't set up printer sharing when you originally set up your network (see Chapter 5), follow these steps to accomplish this simple task:

1. **Choose Start⇨Settings⇨Control Panel.**

   The Control Panel window opens.

2. **Double-click the Network icon in the Control Panel.**

   The Network dialog box opens.

3. **Click the File and Print Sharing button.**

   The File and Print Sharing dialog box opens. (See Figure 9-1.)

Figure 9-1:
A simple click of the mouse turns your computer into a network print server.

4. **Click the I Want to Be Able to Allow Others to Print to My Printer(s) check box.**

5. **Click OK.**

   You return to the Network dialog box.

6. **Click OK again.**

Windows displays the Systems Settings Change dialog box, which informs you that you must restart the computer in order to put your new setting into effect. Click Yes to restart the system now.

Installing a printer

You have to *install* a printer, which means setting up the files Windows needs to communicate with the printer. Those files are called *printer drivers*. Well, of course, *installing* also means the physical installation of the printer, but that's quite simple and the documentation that comes with your printer explains all the steps.

Then you must tell Windows that this printer is going to be shared with other users on the network. When you have a printer on a computer, and you share that printer, your computer becomes a *print server*.

If you already installed a printer on this computer, including the drivers, you can skip this task and move ahead to the section "Sharing a printer," later in this chapter.

Using Windows files to install a printer

You need your Windows CD to install a printer because the printer driver files are on the disk. If your printer came with its own CD or floppy disk, read the section "Using manufacturer disks to install a printer," later in this chapter.

Put the Windows CD in the CD-ROM drive. Hold the Shift key so that the CD doesn't open automatically. If it does open, just click the X in the upper-right corner of the window to close it. Then follow these steps to install your printer:

1. **Choose Start⇨Settings⇨Printers.**

   The Printers window opens. If this is the first printer you're installing on this computer, the only icon in the folder is the one named Add Printer. (If you installed faxing services, you also have an icon for Microsoft Fax.)

2. **Double-click the Add Printer icon.**

   The Add Printer Wizard window opens. The first window explains that the wizard helps install a printer. Click Next.

3. **Select Local Printer and then click Next.**

The wizard wants to know whether this printer is a *local printer* (attached to the computer) or a *network printer* (attached to another computer). Information on installing a network printer is in the section "Installing a Network Printer," later in this chapter.

4. **Select the manufacturer and model for the printer.**

Scroll through the Manufacturers list in the left pane (see Figure 9-2) to find the company that made your printer. When you select it, the Printers pane on the right displays all the printers from that manufacturer. Scroll through the list to find the right printer model. Then click Next.

Figure 9-2:
The wizard
lists a
slew of
manufac-
turers and
models,
so you
shouldn't
have a
problem
finding your
printer.

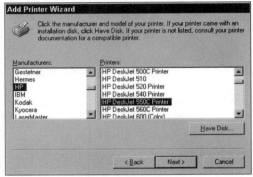

If you can't find the exact printer model, read the documentation that came with your printer. Look for the section on printer emulation to find out which model matches your printer.

5. **Select the port to which you've attached your printer.**

It's probably LPT1, but if this printer is the second printer you're attaching to this computer and you've installed another printer port, choose LPT2, which doesn't appear unless you have installed a second printer port. Click Next after you select the port.

6. **Name the printer and specify whether it is the default printer.**

Type a name for this printer in the Printer Name text box. By default, the wizard inserts the model name for the printer, which is usually perfectly acceptable as a name.

You also have to tell Windows whether or not this printer is the default printer for Windows software. Select Yes if you expect to use this printer when you print from your software programs. Of course, if this is the first printer you're installing, it has to be the default printer.

The default printer is the printer that is automatically selected when you print from software. If you have other printers, you can use the software Print dialog box to change to another printer. More important, for those occasions when you don't have a choice of printers, the default printer delivers your print job. Examples of not having a choice include printing by clicking the Print icon on a toolbar, printing from Notepad, and printing from many DOS programs.

Click Next to move on.

7. Select Yes to print a test page.

The wizard gives you a choice, but it's foolish not to test the printer.

Click Finish because you've reached the last wizard window, although you're not quite done.

The files that Windows needs are transferred from the CD to your hard drive. Then the test page is sent to the printer. Look at the test page. (It congratulates you on setting up a printer successfully and prints all sorts of technical information about the printer drivers that were installed.)

8. Tell Windows whether the test page printed correctly.

If the test page printed successfully, you're finished. If not, Windows opens a Print Troubleshooter. (See Figure 9-3.)

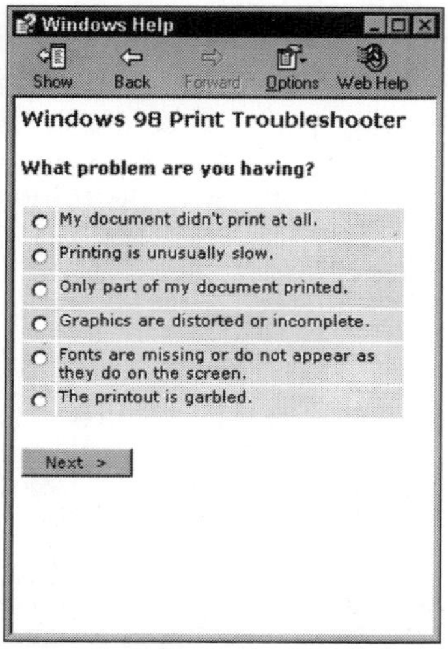

Figure 9-3:
This Print Trouble-shooter is from Windows 98SE — the Print Trouble-shooters in Windows Me and Windows 2000 Professional offer slightly different choices.

Select the appropriate choices, and the troubleshooter makes suggestions. Keep going until you solve the problem. If the problem isn't solved by the time the troubleshooter runs out of suggestions, you're advised to call the printer manufacturer for more help.

Using manufacturer disks to install a printer

Windows supports most printers, which means that the printer drivers are on your Windows CD. However, Windows doesn't support some printers, in which case you must use the drivers supplied by the manufacturer. Those drivers probably came with the printer (on a CD or floppy disk), but if not, you can call the company or visit its Web site to get the files.

In addition, some printers come with software that works with the manufacturer's drivers to enhance your ability to control and manipulate the printer's features.

If you are using the manufacturer's disks, read the directions to find out which of the following two methods you should use:

- ✔ Use a setup program on the disk to install the software.
- ✔ Use the Printer Wizard and choose Have Disk when the wizard presents a window listing printer manufacturers and models.

If you're instructed to use a setup program, the software can usually be launched automatically by placing the CD in the CD-ROM drive. If the CD-ROM doesn't start, follow these steps to begin setup manually:

1. **Double-click the My Computer icon.**

   The My Computer window opens, displaying the drives on the computer.

2. **Double-click the CD-ROM drive icon.**

   The opening window of the CD-ROM drive varies, depending on the manufacturer. Usually a menu appears, sometimes in icon form. Choose the installation item. If the installation procedure isn't evident on the opening screen, read the documentation that came with the printer to find out how to install the software.

If you're instructed to use the Windows Printer Wizard, follow these steps to install the printer:

1. **Follow the first three steps in the "Using Windows files to install a printer" section.**

2. **At Step 4, choose Have Disk instead of choosing a manufacturer and model.**

3. **Supply any information and follow any instructions that appear on your screen.**

Sharing a printer

After your printer is installed, you can begin using it on your computer. But the household members who are using the other computer(s) on your network want to print, too. You have to share this printer with them. If you don't, they'll just keep bothering you to insert a floppy disk, load software, and print the documents they've created. To save yourself all that aggravation, follow these steps to share the printer with the rest of the network:

1. **Choose Start⇨Settings⇨Printers.**

   The Printers folder opens, displaying an icon for the printer you installed on this computer.

2. **Right-click on the icon for the printer you want to share and choose Sharing from the shortcut menu that appears.**

   The printer's Properties dialog box opens, and the Sharing tab appears in the foreground. The Not Shared option is selected, and all the other fields on the dialog box are grayed out.

3. **Select Shared As.**

   The text boxes on the dialog box are now accessible. (See Figure 9-4.)

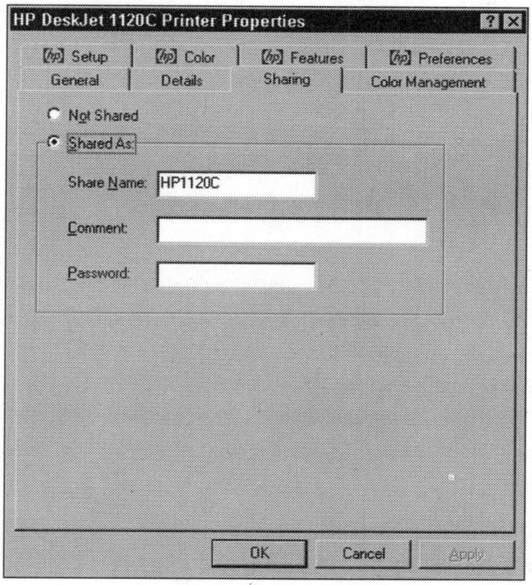

Figure 9-4:
Turn on sharing so that everybody else in the household can use this printer.

4. **Type a name for the printer in the Share Name text box.**

   You can accept the name Windows automatically enters, which is usually a shortened form of the printer model. Or you can use a name of your own choice.

5. **Optionally, type a description in the Comment text box.**

   Large companies with large networks and lots of printers use the Comments text box to help users identify the printers. For example, "laser printer next to the cafeteria" may be a good identifier for a corporate printer, while "Den printer" may work well for home use. Users only see the comment text if they select the Details view in Network Neighborhood when they double-click the icon for the computer that is directly connected to the printer.

6. **Optionally, type a password for the printer.**

   If you choose to require a password, users who don't have the password won't be able to use the printer. On a home network, there's rarely a reason to use this option. Companies with printers that hold checks use passwords for those printers. If you do type a password, you're asked to confirm the password by typing it again. You won't see the actual password as you're typing because Windows substitutes asterisks for your characters.

7. **Click OK.**

   You return to the Printers folder, and your printer icon has a hand under it, indicating that this printer is a shared resource. This computer is now a print server.

If you performed the installation process on a computer running Windows 2000 Professional, you can take additional steps to make it easier for other users on other computers to use this print server. See the section "Using Windows 2000 Professional as a print server" later in this chapter.

Installing a Network Printer

Put on your running shoes! After you configure a printer for sharing, it's time to run to the other computers on the network and install that same printer.

Of course, you're not going to perform a physical installation; the printer is staying right where it is. Installing a printer on a computer that has no physically attached printer means that you're installing a *network printer*.

Choosing an installation method

Two approaches are available to you for installing a network printer:

- ✔ **Use Network Neighborhood.** Double-click the Network Neighborhood icon. In the Network Neighborhood window, double-click the icon for the computer that has the printer. Right-click on the printer icon and choose Install from the shortcut menu that appears.

- ✔ **Use the Printers Folder.** Choose Start⇨Settings⇨Printers to open the Printers folder and then double-click the Add Printer icon.

Both methods launch the Add Printer Wizard. Both methods require the installation of software drivers for the printer, so you need to have your Windows CD or disks from the printer manufacturer.

If the printer you're installing for remote printing is on a computer running Windows 2000 Professional, the process is different — and much easier. See the section "Using Windows 2000 Professional as a print server," later in this chapter.

Running the installation procedure

For this example, I use the Add Printer icon in the Printers folder, instead of finding the printer in Network Neighborhood. This method makes the example slightly longer, but it provides a complete explanation for installing network printers. (My job is to be as thorough as possible.) If you use the printer icon in Network Neighborhood, you can jump to Step 4, where you can find the information about the printer location already filled in.

Be sure that the printer driver's software CD or disk is in the appropriate drive and then follow these steps:

1. **Choose Start⇨Settings⇨Printers.**

   The Printers folder opens.

2. **Double-click the Add Printer icon.**

   The Add Printer Wizard opens with a welcoming message.

3. **Click Next to start.**

4. **Select Network Printer and click Next.**

5. **Click the Browse button to search the network for shared printers.**

   This wizard window has two parts: the location of the network printer and a question about printing from MS-DOS software.

   Clicking the Browse button opens a window in which you can search the network, but if you know the location of the network printer, you can type it directly in the Network Path or Queue Name text box. The location is a UNC (Universal Naming Convention) statement in the form of \\computername\printername. For example, the location might be \\DenComputer\DeskJet540C. Find out about using UNC statements in Chapter 10.

6. **When the Browse for Printer dialog box opens (see Figure 9-5), click the plus sign next to the computer that has the printer.**

   The listing in the Browse for Printer dialog box expands to display any shared printers that are connected to that computer.

If you opt for a network cabling system that uses direct connections for printers (such as household electrical wires), the printer is cabled just like the computers. The printer appears as a stand-alone component on the network, and you don't have to expand a computer's listing to see it.

Figure 9-5:
Expand a
computer's
icon to see
the printer
attached
to it.

7. **Select the printer and click OK.**

   The printer's location (in the form of a UNC statement) is entered in the Network Path or Queue Name text box.

8. **Specify whether you print from MS-DOS-based programs. Then choose Next.**

   MS-DOS software can't handle network printing, so Windows uses a special feature called *capture*. The print job is captured when it's sent to the printer port and is then redirected to the network printer. The software thinks that the printer is connected to your computer.

   If you say Yes to MS-DOS printing, the next window explains that your software needs to have a port associated with the printer. Click the Capture Printer Port button, select LPT1 as the device, and click OK. You return to the previous wizard window.

   Click Next.

9. **Select Yes to send a test page to the remote printer and then click Finish.**

   The printer files are copied to your hard drive, and a test page is sent to the printer. Of course, because the printer is on a remote computer, you have to walk to the printer to see the document. Or yell to whoever is in the room where the printer is and ask that person to check the printout. If the test page prints correctly, select Yes in the dialog box that asks about the test. If the test page does not print properly or doesn't print at all, select No. Then use the printer troubleshooter to try to resolve the problem. See the section "Installing a Network Printer," earlier in this chapter, for information about the Print Troubleshooter.

An icon for the printer appears in your Printers folder. Whenever you print, the print job is sent to this remote printer.

Using Windows 2000 Professional as a print server

Windows 2000 is an operating system that's built from the ground up to service business needs. One nifty side effect is that a computer running this operating system is designed to be a print server.

If you use your Windows 2000 Professional machine as a print server on your home network, when you install the network (remote) printers on the other computers, you can let Windows 2000 Professional install drivers automatically the first time each computer accesses the printer.

To take advantage of this efficiency, install the printer on the Windows 2000 Professional computer by using the instructions presented earlier in this chapter. Then set up sharing using these steps:

1. **Right-click on the printer icon in the Printers folder and choose Sharing from the shortcut menu.**

   The Sharing tab of the printer's Properties dialog box appears.

2. **Select the Shared As option and type a name for the share.**

3. **Click the button labeled Additional Drivers.**

4. **Select the option named Windows 98 or Windows 95 and click OK.**

   Windows 2000 Professional requests the CD with the drivers. If you have a copy of the Windows 2000 Server CD, it contains Windows drivers that work for Windows 98, Windows 95, and Windows Me for most printers.

   If you don't have a Server CD or if the CD doesn't have drivers for the printer you installed, use the CD or floppy disk you would have used to install the printer on one of your Windows 98, Windows 95, or Windows Me computers.

5. **Click OK to close the printer's Properties dialog box.**

   The files are copied to the hard drive of the Windows 2000 Professional computer. You don't have to restart the computer.

   Unlike other versions of Windows, with Windows 2000, you almost never have to restart a Windows 2000 computer after you install software or drivers.

Now you don't have to travel from computer to computer to install printer drivers. On each computer, open Network Neighborhood and double-click the icon for the Windows 2000 Professional computer. Double-click the printer icon and watch everything happen automatically. This is so cool!

Renaming network printers

After you install a remote printer, you can change its name to something that reminds you where it is or what it does. Doing so changes the printer name only on your computer; it doesn't change anything on the computer to which the printer is attached. Follow these steps to give the network printer a personalized name:

1. **Choose Start⇨Settings⇨Printers.**

   The Printers folder opens.

2. **Right-click on the icon for the network printer and choose Rename from the shortcut menu that appears (or select the icon and press F2).**

   The icon title is selected (highlighted), which means you're in edit mode.

3. **Type a new name and press Enter.**

   Choose a name that describes the printer for you. For example, HP in Den is a good descriptive name, and will be easier to remember than Printer Numero Uno or Clive.

Using both local and network printers

If you have two printers in the house, you can attach them to separate computers. Just follow the steps explained earlier in this chapter for installing local printers and then follow the steps to install each printer as a remote printer.

You can switch between printers when you want to print by using the Print feature of your Windows software. All Windows software works in the same fashion, so you can count on being able to use these steps to switch printers:

1. **Choose File⇨Print from the menu bar of your software program.**

   The Print dialog box opens. The appearance of this dialog box differs depending on the particular software you're using, but the essential features are the same.

2. **Click the arrow to the right of the printer Name text box.**

   A list of installed printers (both local and network) appears in the drop-down list, as shown in Figure 9-6.

If you click the Print button on the toolbar of your Windows software or you print from Notepad, the currently selected printer receives the print job. No dialog box opens to afford you the chance to choose a printer.

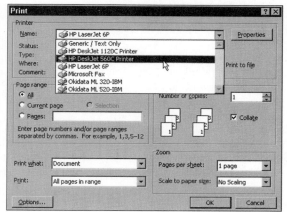

Figure 9-6:
The Print
dialog box in
a Windows
software
program
has a drop-
down list
of all the
printers
you've
installed,
whether
local or
network.

Using password-protected printers

It's highly unusual to password-protect printers in a home network environment, but you may have a reason to do so. For example, if you've loaded special paper in the printer (for example, checks, or photographic paper), you
may want to password-protect the printer and not let anyone know the password. When you put the regular paper back into the printer tray, remove the
password. When you want to use a remote printer that's password-protected,
you're asked to supply the password. (See Figure 9-7.)

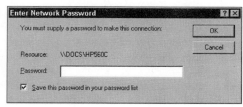

Figure 9-7:
If you don't
know the
password,
the printer
won't take
your
document.

The first time you use the printer, select Save This Password in Your Password
List. You won't have to type the password again (unless it changes).

Devising schemes for using multiple printers

You can design all sorts of arrangements to take advantage of having multiple printers on your network, with each printer attached to a different computer. When you devise a method to manage your printers, your decisions should be based on the types of printers you own. Here are some suggestions:

- ✔ **Make the local printer the default printer.** This option works well if all the printers are the same type, or at least similar — for example, they're all monochrome inkjet printers (print in black and shades of gray), laser printers, or color inkjet printers.

  With this scheme, you don't need the network printer unless something happens to the local printer. If the local printer stops working or the cartridge goes dry and you don't have a spare handy (or you're in a hurry and decide to worry about replacing the cartridge later), you can switch to the network printer quickly. Using the local printer for most print jobs saves you the annoyance of getting up and walking to the network printer every time you print. (If you need the exercise, you can always reverse the scheme.)

- ✔ **Configure the printers for different features.** If your printers have the capability of holding different paper sizes, you can make one of them the letter-size printer and make the other the legal-size printer. Or put inexpensive paper in one printer and good bond in the other. Then just use the appropriate printer for each printing project.

- ✔ **Use each printer for its best feature.** For example, if you have a dot-matrix printer and an inkjet or laser printer, use the inkjet or laser printer for stuff that has to look good (for example, your resume or a letter to your senator). Use the dot-matrix printer for everything else. Or, if one printer is an inkjet and one is a laser printer, use the laser for multiple page print jobs (lasers usually print faster) or for print jobs with a lot of graphics (most laser printers have more memory than most inkjet printers).

Some of these printer set-up schemes are important for more than convenience; they actually lower the cost of using printers. The business term for getting the most out of your printers (or any other piece of machinery) is *TCO* (total cost of ownership), and it's a significant consideration when you buy and use any type of equipment.

After you design your scheme, you have to do two things to make sure that the plan is implemented successfully:

- ✔ Rename the printers with names that reflect their intended uses. Follow the instructions in the section "Renaming network printers," earlier in this chapter to find out about renaming networked printers.

Renaming the local shared printer can be complicated. If you rename the icon, Windows doesn't change the name of the shared resource. In fact, if you rename the icon, the printer is no longer shared. Windows considers the printer to be a new and different printer after a name change. Be sure to follow the steps that show you how to create a shared printer in "Renaming network printers" (again) if you rename a local shared printer.

✔ Explain the plan to all the members of the household. This part works best if you use a threatening tone or some other means of making everyone take you seriously. Try tapping the flat of your left hand with a rolling pin and sneering.

Managing Network Printing

Keeping the printing process on an error-free, even keel is slightly more complicated with network printing than it is for a one-computer, one-printer environment. However, it's not overly complex, and printer problems aren't all that common.

Understanding the spooler

When you send a file to a printer, Windows does some work on the file with the help of those files (drivers) you copied to your hard drive when you installed the printer. Windows checks the file to make sure that everything is sent to the printer in a format the printer understands. The work that Windows performs is saved in a file, and that file, called a *spool file.* This process is called *spooling,* and happens, unbeknownst to you, in the background. In addition to the spool file, Windows creates a second file, called a *shadow file,* which contains the name of the user who sent the job to the printer, the data format type of the print job, and other technical information.

The two files sit in the spooler, waiting for their turn at the printer. Documents are sent to the printer in a first-come, first-served order (unless you interrupt that order using a process I discuss in the section, "Manipulating print jobs," later in this chapter). This lineup of documents waiting to go to the printer is called the *queue.* After the print job is done, the spool file is deleted automatically. The shadow file hangs out until the next time you restart the computer, even though it's of no possible use to you. Of course, the shadow file doesn't do any harm — unless you print a lot of documents and you don't reboot your computer every day, because you end up with a lot of shadow files taking up disk space.

The best way to clear the spooler is to restart the computer, but if you like doing things the hard way, you can locate the folder \Windows\Spool\ Printers and delete all the files with an extension of .shd.

Manipulating print jobs

You can control individual print jobs that are sent to the printer, but you have to move fast, because everything happens very rapidly.

Printing controls are available in the printer's dialog box, which you can open with these steps:

1. **Choose Start⇨Settings⇨Printers.**

   The Printers folder opens.

2. **Double-click the icon for the printer.**

   The printer's dialog box opens, displaying any print jobs that are currently in the queue.

You can pause, delete, and move the print jobs that are in the queue, but which print jobs you see depends upon these factors:

✔ If you open the dialog box for a remote printer, you see the jobs that you sent to the printer.

✔ If you open the dialog box for a local printer, you see all the jobs that the local and remote users have sent to that printer. (See Figure 9-8.)

Figure 9-8:
The printer attached to this computer has jobs from three different users on three different computers.

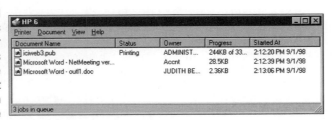

You can manipulate each job, or the printer itself, with the commands available in this dialog box. You can change the way that documents print in the following ways:

✔ **Pause a print job.** Right-click on the listing for the print job and choose Pause Printing from the shortcut menu that appears.

A check mark appears next to the Pause Printing command to indicate that the job status has changed to paused. The print job is temporarily stopped, and the next job in line starts printing.

Pausing a print job is a quick way to let an important print job jump ahead of the job in front of it.

✔ **Resume a print job.** Right-click on a paused print job and choose Pause Printing again from the shortcut menu that appears to remove the check mark.

The job status changes to Printing.

✔ **Pause the printer.** Choose Printer⇨Pause Printing from the menu bar in the Printer dialog box.

All the print jobs are paused. Most of the time you use this command to clear a paper jam in the printer or to change paper.

✔ **Cancel a print job.** Right-click on a print job listing and choose Cancel Printing from the shortcut menu that appears.

The document will not print.

✔ **Cancel all the print jobs.** Choose Printer⇨Purge Print Documents from the menu bar of the printer dialog box.

All print jobs are cancelled.

When you pause or cancel a print job, the printer usually keeps printing. It does so because any data that has been sent to the printer is in the printer's memory and continues to print.

You can also drag print jobs around to change the order of printing. Select the job you want to move and drag it up higher in the queue if it's important or down to the bottom of the queue if it's unimportant. However, dragging print jobs does have two restrictions:

✔ You can't move any print job ahead of the job that is currently printing.

✔ You can't move the job that is currently printing — it's too late.

Printing Tricks and Tips

Very little goes wrong with the printing processes in Windows, even across a network. However, knowing a few tricks makes network printing easier. This section covers those tips.

Troubleshooting remote printing

Sometimes when you're printing to a remote printer, you see an error message telling you that there was a problem printing to the port. (The *port* is the path to the remote computer that has the printer attached.) Before you panic, thinking that something awful has happened to your network printing services, check the condition of all the hardware.

Check the print server

Computers that have printers attached (called *print servers*) have to be turned on if you want to print from a remote computer. If the computer is turned off, turn it on.

It doesn't matter whether you know the logon password for the user name that appears during the logon process because you don't have to complete the logon process. Nobody has to be logged on to a computer in order to use its shared printer. The Windows operating system on that computer simply must be started. That's a really nifty way to design network printing!

Check the printer

If the computer is turned on and you still get error messages when you try to print, check the printer. Make sure that it's turned on. Check any buttons, indicator lights, or message windows that may be trying to tell you that something is amiss.

Most printers have a "ready light," a button that lights up to say that everything is cool and the printer is ready to do your bidding. If the ready light isn't on, follow the instructions in the printer manual to investigate the problem. The most common problems are that the printer is out of paper, there's a paper jam, or the cartridge is out of toner (or ink).

Check the network cable

If the computer is on and the printer is fine, check the network cable. Cable that isn't connected properly can't send data.

Using a printer shortcut on the desktop

Most of the time you print from a software program. You create a document, and then you print it. But sometimes you just need a printed copy of an existing document and you don't want to open the software, open the document, and use the commands required to print the document.

If you put a shortcut to the printer on your desktop, you can drag documents to the shortcut icon to print them effortlessly. Here's how to create a printer shortcut on your desktop:

1. **Choose Start➪Settings➪Printers.**

   The Printers folder opens.

2. **Right-drag the printer icon to the desktop.**

   When you release the right mouse button, a shortcut menu appears.

3. **Choose Create Shortcut(s) Here from the shortcut menu.**

   A printer shortcut appears on your desktop.

A good place to put the printer shortcut is on the Quick Launch toolbar. That way, an open window won't hide it.

Using the printer shortcut is easy and timesaving. You can use it whenever you have any folder or window open (such as Windows Explorer, My Computer, or My Documents) that contains document files. Just drag a document file to the printer shortcut on the desktop. That's all you have to do — Windows does the rest. You can leave the room or sit and watch as the following events take place:

1. **The software that was used to create the file opens.**

2. **The file opens in the software window.**

3. **The software sends the file to the printer.**

4. **The software closes.**

   Cool!

If you right-click on a document file instead of dragging it to a desktop shortcut, you can choose Print from the shortcut menu that appears. The same automatic printing events occur.

Using separator pages to identify users

If everyone in your household uses the printers, you are likely to experience a lot of printer traffic. Not everyone's going to run immediately to the printer to pick up print jobs. What you have after a day or so is a nice jumbled pile of papers — and no one willing to claim them. Or worse, one user (not your teenage son) may wander over to the printer to pick up his print jobs and notice several other print jobs are in the tray. This user may pick up the first piece of paper and read it — it isn't his print job so he tosses it aside (knowing him, it lands on the floor instead of on a tabletop). The user will probably continue to shuffle through the papers, taking his own documents and tossing the others helter-skelter.

It's less messy if each job comes out of the printer with a form that displays the name of the owner. Luckily, such a form exists in Windows, and it's called a separator page. A *separator page* (sometimes called a *banner*) automatically prints ahead of the first page of each document.

The down side of separator pages is that they can be a huge waste of paper. You may end up spending the money you save on ink purchasing ream after ream of paper. Also, if your teenage son is a slob, you'll just have one extra piece of paper per print job to get shuffled around in a big ugly pile.

Adding separator pages in Windows 95, 98, and Me

For a Windows 95, Windows 98, or Windows Me print server, go to the computer that has the printer attached and turn on separator pages, and follow these steps:

1. **Choose Start➪Settings➪Printers.**

   The Printers folder opens.

2. **Right-click on the appropriate printer icon and choose Properties from the shortcut menu that appears.**

   The printer Properties dialog box opens, with the General tab in the foreground.

3. **Click the arrow to the right of the Separator Page list box and choose a Separator Page type.**

   The Separator Page choices are None, Full, and Simple. Both the Full and Simple separator pages contain the document name, the user name, and the date and time that the document was printed, but the Full option uses large, bold type, while Simple uses the Courier typeface that's built into the printer.

4. **Click OK.**

Adding separator pages in Windows Professional

If you have a Windows 2000 Professional print server, follow Steps 1 and 2 in "Adding separator pages in Windows 95, 98, and Me," and then follow these steps:

1. **Click the Advanced tab.**

2. **Click the Separator Page Button**

   The Separator Page dialog box appears.

3. **Click Browse to select a separator file.**

   Separator files have the extension `.sep`. Choose `Sysprint.sep` for PostScript printers or `Pcl.sep` for non-PostScript printers.

4. **Click OK twice to close the dialog box.**

Chapter 10

Communicating Among Computers

- -

In This Chapter

▶ Visiting the network neighborhood

▶ Opening shares to see what's in them

▶ Using shortcuts to move to folders on other computers

- -

*T*o get resources from another computer, you have to access that computer across the network. Windows offers several ways to communicate with a remote computer from where you're sitting (the computer you're using is called your *local computer*). In this chapter, I show you all the ways to get to remote computers in order to view the files and folders stored on each computer.

In addition, you also find out about shortcuts that are available for working in a network environment. You can use these tricks to make accessing remote computers on your network easier and faster.

Most of the time, the reason you're accessing another computer is to fetch something, usually a file. The methods you can use to move files and folders are covered in Chapter 11.

Traveling to the Network Neighborhood

The computers on your network are gathered in a single Windows window, which makes it easier to find them. In Windows 95 and Windows 98, the computers hang out in a place called Network Neighborhood. In Windows Me and Windows 2000 Professional, the hangout is named My Network Places. An icon for the gathering place is on your desktop.

Visiting Network Neighborhood (Windows 95 and 98)

When you double-click the Network Neighborhood icon, you see all the computers on your network. Figure 10-1 shows my home network, consisting of four computers.

Figure 10-1:
Network Neighborhood shows all the computers on the network, including the one you're using.

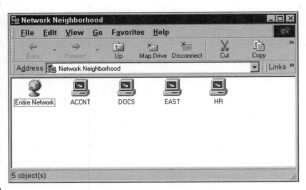

You can see the shared resources (shares) on a remote computer by double-clicking that computer's icon in Network Neighborhood. A new window opens to display the shares. When you double-click a share, yet another window opens to show you the contents of the share.

The Entire Network icon

The Network Neighborhood window includes an icon for the entire network. If you double-click that icon, you see an icon for the *workgroup* (the group that the computers on your network belongs to). If you double-click the workgroup icon, you see the individual computers in your workgroup, which are the same computers you saw in the original Network Neighborhood window. You're back where you started. The Entire Network icon is really for larger networks that may have multiple workgroups, but that's not the way home networks are configured. So don't bother with the Entire Network icon.

Calling on My Network Places (Windows 2000 and Me)

The My Network Places window works just a bit differently than the Network Neighborhood window. In Windows Me, the first time you open the window, you see three icons: Add Network Place, Home Networking Wizard, and Entire Network (see Figure 10-2). Windows 2000 Professional doesn't have an icon for the Home Networking Wizard, because that feature doesn't exist. (The Home Networking Wizard is covered in Chapter 5.)

Figure 10-2:
My Network Places doesn't display the computers on the network — you have to do a little work to see them.

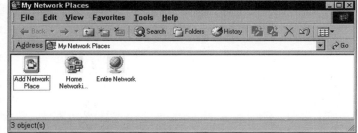

To enter the neighborhood — that is, to see all the computers on the network the way they're displayed in a Network Neighborhood window — double-click the Entire Network icon. That action opens a window in which you see an icon for your workgroup. Double-click that icon to open a window that displays all the computers on the network — finally! Double-click any computer to see its shared resources.

Adding a network place

To avoid all that mouse clicking, you can put a shared resource that's on a remote computer into the main My Network Places window with the Add Network Place Wizard (you do almost everything in Windows Me and Windows 2000 Professional with a wizard).

You can even put a Web site into My Network Places and double-click its icon to travel to that site.

To add an icon for a network place, follow these steps in the My Network Places window:

1. **Double-click the Add Network Place icon.**

   The first Add Network Place Wizard window opens, as shown in Figure 10-3.

Figure 10-3:
Enter the
address
of the
resource
you want to
add to My
Network
Places
or click
Browse to
locate it.

2. **Enter the address of the place you want to add and skip to Step 5. If you don't know the address, click the Browse button to locate the place.**

   The computers on your network are displayed in the Browse for Folder window.

   Instead of clicking the Browse button, you can type in the address of the place you want to add. For a shared resource on your network, enter the name of the computer and the name of the share, in the format `\\Computer\ShareName`. For a Web site, use the format `http://www.DomainName.com`, substituting the name of the Web page for *DomainName* (and substituting a different extension such as `.org` or `.net` if the domain name doesn't end in `.com`).

   The format of a Web page address is called a *URL* (usually pronounced "yur-el"), which stands for Uniform Resource Locator. The format for a network share is called a *UNC* (pronounced "U-N-C"), which stands for universal naming convention. You can find more information about UNCs in the section "Say UNC-le: Understanding UNCs," later in this chapter.

3. **Click the plus sign next to the computer that has the shared folder you want to get to.**

   All the shared drives and folders (called *shares*) on the selected computer are displayed in the window.

4. **Select the share you want to use and click OK.**

   If the share has a plus sign next to its icon, it means it contains folders (shared drives always fit this description). Even though those folders aren't set up as shares, you can select one and click OK. (See the discussion on parent-child relationships for shares in Chapter 7.)

After you click OK, you return to the wizard window, where the UNC for the network share you selected is in the text box.

5. **Click Next.**

6. **Enter a name for this network place.**

   This is the name that appears in the main My Network Places window. Windows automatically enters the share name, along with the name of the computer on which it resides, which is usually just fine. If you selected a subfolder of a share, Windows uses its folder name.

7. **Click Finish.**

   A window for the shared folder you selected opens, and you can choose the file you want to work with. If you're merely setting up the share as an icon in your My Network Places window, close the window for the shared folder. You return to the My Network Places window, where an icon for this share now appears.

Managing the icons in the My Network Places window

Windows also adds places to the My Network Places window. Every time you open a share and access a file, an icon for that share appears in your My Network Places window. After a while, the window can become incredibly crowded, as shown in Figure 10-4.

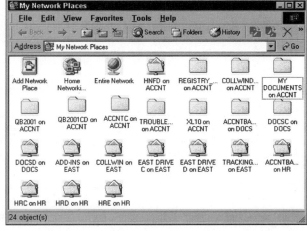

Figure 10-4: When the window is this crowded, it's hard to find the share you need.

I don't know about you, but I get both annoyed and lazy when I see a window that's this crowded. As a result, when I need to get to a share on another computer, I just double-click the Entire Network icon and find the share. Although doing that defeats the whole purpose of these handy-dandy icons, I just find it easier and less confusing.

Here are a few additional points about the icons in the My Network Places window:

- ✔ Every icon of a share that's in this window is a shortcut — just like the desktop shortcuts you create for frequently used programs. You can, therefore, delete the icons without affecting the real share.

- ✔ Every once in a while, delete all the icons except for the few you use often. Hold down the Ctrl key and click each superfluous icon. Then press the Delete key.

- ✔ Even better, delete all the icons whenever you open the My Network Places window and use mapped drives for the shares you access often. See the section "Mapping Drives," later in this chapter, to find out how to use that feature.

Viewing information about the neighborhood residents

By default, the computers in Network Neighborhood and My Network Places are displayed as icons. The name of the computer (which you entered on the Identification tab of the Network Properties dialog box in the Control Panel) is displayed under the icon (refer to Figure 10-1). Chapter 5 contains the information for setting up network properties.

When you double-click a computer's icon, the window that opens to display its shares also uses icons as the default view. Under the icon for each share is the name you assigned when you created the share (refer to Figure 10-4).

When you create a share, you have the opportunity to enter not only a name for the share but also a comment (description). If you want to see the description fields that you or other users have entered, you must change the way Network Neighborhood and My Network Places display computers and shares. The descriptions don't show in the default view (which is the Large Icons View).

To see the descriptive information about all the components on your network, change the view by choosing View➪Details from the menu bar of the window. Figure 10-5 shows the Network Neighborhood window with the Details view turned on (My Network Places works the same).

You don't have to use the View menu to change to Details view every time you open a window. Windows remembers the view you select for a window, and presents the same view every time you open that window.

Figure 10-5:
Displaying
more
information
about the
computers
on your
network
means that
users don't
have to
remember
which
computer
name
belongs to a
· specific
computer.

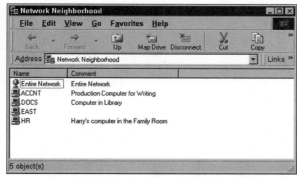

Exploring the neighborhood in Windows Explorer

You can also view Network Neighborhood or My Network Places in Windows Explorer. Scroll down the left pane to find the listing for Network Neighborhood or My Network Places, depending on your operating system. Select the listing to see all the computers in the right pane, or click the plus sign to expand the listing to display the computers in the left pane (or do both, as shown in Figure 10-6).

Figure 10-6:
You can
change the
view of
Windows
Explorer to
Details to
see the
descriptions
of
computers
and shares.

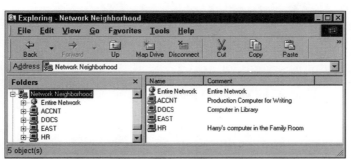

The importance of adding descriptions

Descriptions are even more important when you double-click a computer's listing to see its shares. Most of the time, the share name makes sense to the person who created the share, because he knows what's in the folder or what the printer does (for example, prints color, has a certain type of paper in the tray, and so on).

However, other household members may not understand those share names, and giving others more information is an act of kindness. The following figure shows the window that appears after double-clicking a computer to see its shares. The descriptions for the shared folders and printers are quite useful.

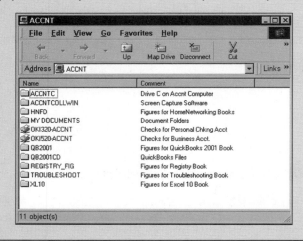

To see the shares, expand a computer's listing by clicking the plus sign. Select a share in the left pane to see its contents in the right pane.

Psst — What's the Password?

If the person who created a shared resource wants to limit access to the resource, he or she can create a password (see Chapter 7 for information about creating passwords for shared resources). If that person doesn't tell you the password, you're outta luck. Only the favored few who receive the password can open the shared resource.

Opening a password-protected share

You can't tell whether a share is password-protected until you try to access it. To access a password-protect share, follow these steps:

1. **Click the share in Windows Explorer or double-click the share in Network Neighborhood or My Network Places.**

   The Enter Network Password dialog box appears, as shown in Figure 10-7.

Figure 10-7:
Say the
magic
word!

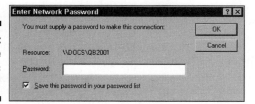

2. **Enter the password for the share in the Password text box and click OK.**

   When you enter the password, you don't see the characters that you type because they appear as asterisks. This is a security measure to prevent anyone who may be hanging around from seeing the password.

   You also have the option to select the Save This Password in Your Password List check box. If you select this check box, the local computer stores the password. Then, the next time you want to open this shared resource from this computer, the computer fetches the password from your password file and enters it automatically. You don't even see the Enter Network Password dialog box, unless the person who created the shared resource changes the password. This information is saved in your own user profile, so if any other user logs on to the same computer, the password process isn't available to that person.

If the password that you enter isn't correct, or you saved the password and the user who created the shared resource changed the password, Windows displays an error message. If you think that you may have mistyped the password, click OK and try again. If that doesn't work, click Cancel in the Enter Network Password dialog box. Then find the person who created the shared resource and either get the password or find out why you can't have it.

If you need one particular file from a password-protected folder, ask the owner of the folder to move that file to a different folder if he or she doesn't want to compromise the security of the folder.

Creating permission-level passwords

You can also configure passwords to determine what users can do with the contents of a share. The *permission level* that's set for a shared folder applies to all the files in that folder (see Chapter 7 for more information about setting up passwords and permissions on shares). The person who created the shared resource decides what type of permission level to grant:

> ✔ **Read-Only.** You can open or copy files in this folder, but you can't delete any files, change the contents of any files, or add anything (files or subfolders) to the folder.
>
> ✔ **Full.** You can add, change, or delete anything in the folder.
>
> ✔ **Depends on Password.** Your permission level is either Read-Only or Full, depending on the password that you use.

Unfortunately, you receive no message indicating your permission level for the folder that you use. After you enter the correct password, the only way to find out whether you have Read-Only permission is to do something that requires Full permission (such as saving a file to the folder or changing the name of a file) and see whether you get an error message. It's like driving in a state you're not familiar with, where you don't know if the state permits right turns on red until you see the first sign that says "No Turn on Red."

Say UNC-le: Understanding UNCs

When you access remote resources, you're using a convention called the *universal naming convention* (UNC). The format for displaying the UNC works like this: `\\computername\resourcename`.

Naming your computers and shared resources

Computers on Windows networks have names: Naming a computer is part of the configuration process when you set up the network features on your Windows computer. You can name your computers whatever you want. Some people use descriptive names (Den, Kitchen, Laptop, and so on); some people use names that reflect the owner or primary user of the computer (Dad, Sis, and so on); and others just give computers names that don't necessarily have anything to do with anything. I have a colleague who named the computers on his home network Zeke and Fred because "when I brought them home and set them up, they looked like a Zeke and a Fred." Hey, whatever works.

In addition to the computer name, you have to consider other names when you work on your network — the share names. Each shared resource has a name, because providing a name is part of setting up the share.

Share names are usually a bit more descriptive than computer names because people tend to use the name of the drive or folder that's being shared. For example, if you have a folder on your computer named Addresses, then you probably named the share Addresses when you configured the folder for sharing.

Understanding the UNC format

When you understand that a computer has a name and a shared resource has a name, using a formatted style to refer to a particular shared resource on a particular computer makes sense. Once upon a time, a computer nerd said, "Hey, let's call that the UNC." And everybody who needed to access shared resources in this way said, "Okey-dokey."

So if you're working on your network and you open a folder named Budgets on a remote computer named Bob, you're working at a UNC named \\Bob\ Budgets.

Now this format may look familiar because it's very similar to the way you enter paths when working in MS-DOS. For example, your Windows files are located at C:\Windows, which means they're on drive C in a folder named Windows. Some important operating system files are in a subfolder named System. The path to that subfolder is C:\Windows\System.

In a path, the letter (for example, *C*) followed by a colon (:) indicates the drive. In the same way, in a UNC statement, a double backslash (\\) followed by a name indicates a remote computer.

Your own computer has a name, too, because it's on a network. If your computer's name is Bigdaddy, your system files are in \\Bigdaddy\Windows\ System. Anyone working at another computer on the network uses that UNC to get to that folder. You can't use the UNC to get there when you're using the computer; you must use an MS-DOS path statement because using a UNC statement signals your computer to look to the network to find the folder. When you use the MS-DOS path format, you tell your computer that the target folder is on the local computer.

Displaying UNCs

You can see the path or UNC for any object on any computer when you're working in Windows Explorer and Network Neighborhood/My Network Places, if you configure those windows to display this information (they don't display the UNC by default). Use these steps to display path and UNC details in Windows Explorer:

1. **Open Windows Explorer or Network Neighborhood or My Network Places.**

2. **In Windows 95 or 98, choose View➪Folder Options. In Windows Me or 2000, choose Tools➪Folder Options.**

   The Folder Options dialog box opens.

3. **Click the View tab of the Folder Options dialog box.**

The View options appear, as shown in Figure 10-8.

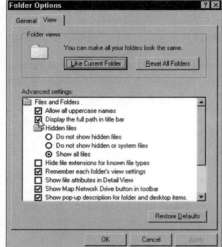

Figure 10-8:
The
advanced
settings for
Windows 95
or 98
(Windows
Me and
Windows
2000
Professional
have similar
settings).

4. **Select the Display the Full Path in Title Bar check box.**

5. **Click OK.**

Now when you select drives or folders on your own computer or on remote computers, you see the full path or UNC statement in the window.

Opening a share by typing the UNC

If you get tired of double-clicking your way through Network Neighborhood or My Network Places, you can open a share on another computer by typing the UNC:

✔ **In the Run dialog box:** Choose Start➪Run and type the UNC in the Run dialog box. After you click OK, a window opens, displaying the contents of the share.

What's nifty is that after you do this once, the UNC is saved in the Run dialog box command list. The next time you want to run a UNC, click the arrow to the right of the Open text box and select the UNC from the drop-down list.

✔ **In a Web browser:** You can use your browser to open a share and display its contents in the browser window, as shown in Figure 10-9. Just enter the UNC in the Address bar of your browser window and press Enter. As with your favorite Web sites, you can add UNCs to your Favorites list (or Bookmarks, if you're using Netscape).

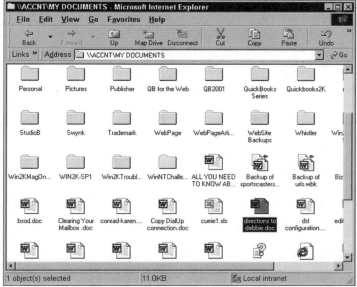

Figure 10-9:
Use your browser to access shares and add oft-used UNCs to your Favorites list.

Creating UNC shortcuts

If you access a particular UNC frequently, you can create a shortcut to the share on your desktop or your Quick Launch bar. A shortcut saves you all those mouse clicks you'd need to navigate through Network Neighborhood or My Network Places. Follow these steps to create a shortcut:

1. **Open Network Neighborhood or My Network Places.**

   Don't open the window in Full-Screen mode — you want to be able to get to the desktop.

2. **In Network Neighborhood, double-click the computer that has the share you're after. In My Network Places, double-click Entire Network, double-click the workgroup, and then double-click the computer that has the share you're after.**

   In My Network Places, don't use any of the shortcuts to shares that appear in the window (they're shortcuts, not icons).

3. **Right-drag the share to the desktop or to the Quick Launch bar.**

4. **Release the mouse button and choose Create Shortcut(s) Here from the menu that appears.**

Mapping Drives

You can use a feature called *mapping* to more easily access a shared resource on another computer. Mapping means assigning a drive letter, such as *E* or *F*, to a shared resource on another computer.

The drive letter you use becomes part of the local computer's set of drive letters, starting with the first letter available after all your local drives have been assigned. The drives you create are called *network drives*.

Understanding drive letters

The computer you use already has at least two drive letters. The floppy drive is A, and the hard drive is C. If you have a second floppy drive, it's B. If you have a CD-ROM drive, it also has a drive letter (probably D). If you have a Zip, Jaz, or other peripheral drive attached to your computer, a drive letter is assigned to that, too.

To see the drive letters that your computer is already using, open My Computer. All the devices on your computer that have drive letters are displayed in alphabetic order.

For example, say that a computer named Eve, located in the kitchen of a house that has a home network, has three drive letters that belong to local resources:

- Drive A is a floppy drive.
- Drive C is a hard drive.
- Drive D is a CD-ROM drive.

Drive C is configured as a shared resource named EveDriveC. The hard drive has many folders, of course, and some of them have been configured as shared resources that can be accessed by users on other computers. Eve's shares include the following folders:

- AddressBook, which has the share name Addresses
- FamilyBudget, which has the share name Budget

The other computer on the network is in the upstairs hallway (in a handy little nook that was just perfect for a computer console). That computer is named Adam, and it has the following resources with drive letters:

- ✔ Drive A is a floppy drive.
- ✔ Drive C is a hard drive.

The hard drive on Adam is a shared resource named AdamDriveC. It has lots of folders, too, and the following folders have been configured as shares:

- ✔ LegalPapers, which has the share name Legal
- ✔ Letters, which has the share name Letters

Of course, when Adam looks at Eve, or Eve looks at Adam, those shares are UNC statements. If Adam wants to get to a file named MyFile on Eve's hard drive, entering C:\MyFile would fail, because even though Eve's drive is named C, that drive letter designation is connected to (mapped to) Adam's local computer.

Mapping a UNC

Even if you have two floppy drives, two hard drives, a CD-ROM drive, and a Zip drive, most of the letters of the alphabet are unused. So put the alphabet to work! Turn a UNC into a drive letter. When you assign a drive letter to (or, in other words, map) a UNC, your life gets easier (well, your life as a computer user gets easier; the rest of your life is your problem, not mine). Here are some of the benefits of mapping:

- ✔ Every object on your computer that has a drive letter is displayed in Windows Explorer in a logical list, so you don't have to expand Network Neighborhood or My Network Places in Windows Explorer to find a mapped share.
- ✔ Every object on your computer that has a drive letter is displayed in My Computer. You can double-click the My Computer icon and then open a local drive or a remote share with equal ease.
- ✔ You can use an MS-DOS command session and MS-DOS commands to work with any remote storage object (drive or folder) that has a drive letter. For example, if you want to copy documents from a remote folder that you've mapped to drive G to your documents folder, you can type **copy g:*.doc c:\documents**.

When you open the hard drive of a remote computer, you can use any folder on that drive. However, if a folder isn't configured specifically as a shared resource, you can't map it. Ask the person who uses that computer to create a shared resource for that folder. Or go to the computer and do it yourself.

The easiest and fastest way to do anything with the remote computers on your network is with Network Neighborhood or My Network Places, because they're dedicated to network resources. Follow these steps to map a network drive to a UNC:

1. **Open Network Neighborhood or My Network Places.**

   A window opens to display the computers on the network.

2. **Double-click the icon for the remote computer that you want to use.**

   All the shared resources on the remote computer appear in the window (see Figure 10-10).

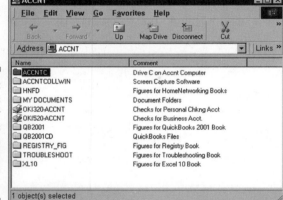

Figure 10-10:
This computer has shares for the hard drive and some folders.

3. **Right-click on the share that you want to map as a network drive.**

   The shortcut menu for the share appears.

4. **Choose Map Network Drive from the shortcut menu.**

   The Map Network Drive dialog box opens, as shown in Figure 10-11.

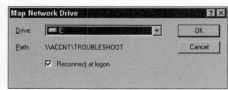

Figure 10-11:
Windows uses the next available drive letter for your first network drive.

5. **Select the Reconnect at Logon check box if you want to map this drive automatically every time you start this computer.**

   This feature can become a bit complicated; see "Reconnecting mapped drives," later in this chapter, for more information.

6. **Click OK.**

The UNC you just mapped opens in a window. You can open a file and go to work, or map another network drive by repeating these steps.

You can also map a network drive in Windows Explorer. Just click the Network Neighborhood icon in the left pane, click the icon for the appropriate computer in the right pane, right-click on the share you want to map, and choose Map Network Drive.

Viewing and using mapped drives

After you map a UNC as a drive, you can move easily to its share by using one of these techniques:

- ✔ **Double-click the My Computer icon to open the My Computer window.** All the drives on your computer, including UNCs that are mapped to a drive letter, appear in the My Computer window. Just open the drive and go to work.

- ✔ **Open Windows Explorer.** All the drives on your computer appear in the left pane, including every remote share (UNC) that is mapped to a drive letter. Click the minus sign next to drive C to get rid of the folder display so you can see all your drives more easily. Open any drive to use it.

Using the example of Eve and Adam (if you haven't yet met Eve and Adam, see "Understanding drive letters," earlier in the chapter), you can see how this works.

Adam has a computer named Adam. On the C drive of that computer is a folder named LegalPapers. He shared that folder and gave the share the name *Legal.* Eve uses files in that folder constantly, and to make life easier, she mapped drive E to the share.

- ✔ When Eve wants a file, she opens drive E, which is a virtual drive that is mapped to the UNC \\Adam\Legal.

- ✔ When Adam wants a file he opens C:\LegalPapers.

Once you've mapped a drive, like real drives, you can get to everything on that drive. For example, Adam also shared his hard drive, giving it the share name *AdamDriveC.* Eve mapped F to that drive share, and when she opens Drive F, she sees the same thing Adam sees when he expands drive C in Windows Explorer.

If Eve finds she constantly uses files that are in a folder on drive F (drive C to Adam), but that folder isn't shared, she can't map a drive to that folder. Mapping works only for shared resources. She can ask Adam to share that folder, too, so she can map it; or she can continue to expand drive F and move to that folder in the same way she moves through folders for real drives on her computer, using Windows Explorer.

Reconnecting mapped drives

When you're mapping a UNC to a drive letter, you can select the Reconnect on Logon option. This means that every time you log on, Windows verifies the network drive — or, in other words, it peers down the network cable to make sure that the shared resource that's mapped to the drive is there. This verification slows down the logon process, but you probably won't notice a big difference.

Incidentally, the reason that the option is Reconnect on Logon instead of Reconnect on Startup is that the mapped drives you create are part of your personalized profile. If multiple users share a computer, the mapped drives that appear are those created by the user who is logged on. If a user named Sandy logs on to the computer Eve uses, Eve's mapped drives don't exist. Sandy has to create her own mapped drives (which may very well duplicate the mappings created by Eve).

The jargon for mapped drives that are configured to reconnect at logon is *persistent connections*.

Remapping when reconnection fails

You can easily imagine that a problem may arise if you have two computers on your network and both have mapped network drives that are configured for reconnection on logon. The computer that runs the logon procedure first loses, and the computer that logs on second wins!

When the first computer looks for the mapped drive during logon, the second computer isn't yet up and running. The UNC isn't available so the mapping function fails. Windows displays a message telling you that the mapped drive isn't connected and asking if you want to reconnect the next time you log on. Say Yes. If your computer can't reconnect to a mapped drive at logon, it's no big deal. The logon process works, and everything's fine, except that the mapped drive doesn't appear until you map it again.

Configuring reconnection options

You can configure Windows 95 and Windows 98 to wait until you need to use the drive before the network resource is checked. If the computer that contains the shared resource isn't ready, you won't suffer any delay during the logon process (Windows keeps searching for several seconds before giving up). On the other hand, when you use the network drive, Windows checks its availability first, delaying access to the network share for a few seconds.

Here are the available configuration choices:

- ✔ **Quick Logon.** The network drives that you mapped are listed in Windows Explorer and My Computer, but during the logon process, Windows doesn't check to see if they're really available.

  Your computer doesn't try to connect until you actually try to use the drive, which is when Windows checks to make sure that the remote share is available. This speeds up the logon process by a few seconds, but it delays the connection process by the same few seconds.

- ✔ **Logon and Restore Network Connections.** Your computer connects to the remote resources for the mapped drives during the logon process. This delays the logon process, but you know immediately if a problem exists with any of your mapped drives.

Follow these steps to configure the way you want mapped drive reconnections to work:

1. **Choose Start➪Settings➪Control Panel.**

   The Control Panel window opens.

2. **Double-click the Network icon.**

   The Network dialog box opens with the Configuration tab in the foreground.

3. **Select the component named Client for Microsoft Networks to highlight it.**

4. **Click the Properties button.**

   The Client for Microsoft Networks Properties dialog box opens, as shown in Figure 10-12.

5. **Select either Quick Logon or Logon and Restore Network Connections.**

6. **Click OK twice.**

Windows displays a message telling you to restart the computer to put this change into effect. In fact, the message dialog box offers to restart Windows for you. Because you don't particularly need to make the change right now, and it's only important the next time you log on, you can just click No.

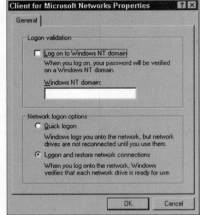

Figure 10-12:
Change the
logon
options to
suit the way
you want to
reconnect to
mapped
drives.

Working with mapped drives in Windows Explorer

The first thing you notice, when you map drives for all the network resources you use often, is that you save a whole lot of time in Windows Explorer. If you want to copy or move a file, everything you need is right in front of you in the Explorer window. The mapped drive is listed in the left pane of the Explorer window, along with all the folders on your local hard drive and all the other drives on your computer. You don't have to expand Network Neighborhood; expand the computer that has the share that you want to use and then click the share.

If you have a long list of folders on your hard drive and you have to scroll through them to see the other drives on your computer (including mapped drives), save yourself the trouble. Enter the letter of the drive that you want to access in the Windows Explorer Address bar.

Both the Address bar and the Go To dialog box also accept UNC statements. You can enter the UNC for a remote share to display its contents in Windows Explorer. This feature is handy if you haven't mapped a drive for a remote resource.

Working with mapped drives at the command line

If you're comfortable working with MS-DOS commands, you can use those commands on a mapped drive just as if you were working on a local drive.

In a couple of situations, I find that the command line is faster and easier than Windows Explorer. For example, if I need to rename a group of files that have similar filenames (all the files start with abc), I can accomplish that in one command: `ren abc*.* xyz*.*`. In Windows Explorer, I'd have to rename each file separately.

Here's how to use a mapped drive in a command prompt window:

1. **Open the command prompt window:**

   - In Windows 95 or 98, choose Start⇨Programs⇨MS-DOS Prompt.

   - In Windows Me, choose Start⇨Programs⇨Accessories⇨ MS-DOS Prompt.

   - In Windows 2000 Professional, choose Start⇨Programs⇨ Accessories⇨Command Prompt.

2. **Enter the drive letter for the mapped drive, followed by a colon (for example, E:).**

   You're now working on the remote computer, and you can perform any command line tasks.

You can even map a drive with a command prompt. Windows has a command named Net Use. The syntax for creating a mapped drive with the Net Use command is: `net use x: UNC`, where *x* is the drive letter you want to use and *UNC* is the UNC statement for the shared resource. To disconnect the mapped drive, enter **net use *x*: /delete**.

For example, if you want to map G to the shared resource named Letters on the computer named Adam, enter **net use g: \\adam\letters** and wait for the response "The Command Completed Successfully." Now drive G is mapped, and it shows up in Windows Explorer and My Computer.

I use the Net Use command as part of an MS-DOS command file (called a *batch file*) to back up files. I copy bunches of files from different folders across the network, and I do it twice: once to a shared folder on another computer and once to a shared Zip drive on another computer. If I tried to back up ten different folders to a remote share, I'd have to select each folder in Windows Explorer or My Computer, and use the Copy and Paste commands to complete the task. Because the files were backed up yesterday, I'd see messages from Windows saying the files already exist, and I'd have to notify Windows that it's okay to copy them anyway. When all the copying is finished, I'd have to go through the same routines again to make the second backup to the Zip drive.

Using the command line means the whole process is unattended: I can map the drive, control error messages, and disconnect the drive when the process finishes. I do all that work without being near the computer because the commands are on autopilot — I'm in the dining room enjoying dinner. You can find detailed information about using batch files to perform backups in Appendix A.

Chapter 11

Accessing Other Computers on the Network

*O*ne nifty advantage to a network is that you can work on any file, anywhere, at any time. Other users are creating files on other computers all the time. Occasionally, you may want to see one of those files. In fact, you may want to work on one of those files. Perhaps you want your very own copy of a file that currently resides on another computer.

If you find yourself working on different computers at different times, you probably have files of your own on all of them. That can be nerve-wracking. Imagine that you're sitting in front of the computer that you use most of the time, looking for that letter to Uncle Harry. You know you started it yesterday, and today you want to finish and mail it. But where is it? You look through all your document subfolders; you even use the Windows Find command to search for it. It's nowhere to be found. Think back — could it be that you began the letter on the computer in the den? And now you're working at the computer in the kitchen?

You don't have to get up and walk to a remote computer to use a file that's on it, whether you or another household member created the file. Let the network cable do the work by transferring the file from the other computer to the one you're using now.

Working with Remote Files

When you open remote folders to access the files within them, you can do almost anything with those files that you could do if they were on your own computer. The only hindrance that you may face is when a remote folder is configured for limited actions (see Chapter 7 to find out about setting permissions for file manipulation). For this discussion, however, I assume that you have full permission to manipulate the files on the remote folder.

Copying files between computers

You can copy a file from a remote computer to your own computer by either dragging it or using the shortcut menu.

You can use the exact same techniques to copy files in the other direction, from your computer to the remote computer. Just reverse the processes described here.

Copying by dragging files

If you drag a file from a remote computer to your own computer, you copy it, which means the original file is still on the remote computer, and a copy of that file is on your computer. This process is different from dragging a file from one folder to another on your own computer, which *moves* the file instead of copying it. That's because Windows assumes that you don't want to deprive the user of the other computer of the file. It's a good assumption.

To make dragging files from a remote computer to your own computer easier, use Windows Explorer because you can see both the remote computer and your own computer in a single window. Follow these steps to copy a file by dragging it in Windows Explorer:

1. **Open Windows Explorer.**

   In Windows 98, choose Start⇨Programs⇨Windows Explorer.

   In Windows Me and Windows 2000 Professional, choose Start⇨Programs⇨Accessories⇨Windows Explorer.

   The Explorer window appears on your desktop.

2. **Expand the network listing by clicking the plus sign.**

   In Windows 95 and 98, the listing is named Network Neighborhood.

   In Windows Me and Windows 2000 Professional, the listing is named My Network Places.

   All the computers in your network are displayed in the left pane.

3. **Click the plus key next to the remote computer that has the file you need.**

   All the shared drives and folders on that remote computer are displayed in the left pane.

4. **Click the remote folder that holds the file you want.**

   The files in the remote folder appear in the right Explorer pane. If necessary, scroll through the right pane so the file you want is visible.

5. **In the left Explorer pane, expand the drive and folder of your own computer to get to the correct folder.**

   The correct folder is the folder into which you want to copy the file. Don't select the folder; just use the plus sign to expand drives and folders until you can see the target folder in the left pane. You want the files from the remote computer to remain in the right pane.

6. **Use the scroll bar on the left pane to position the target folder near the file you want to copy.**

   This maneuver just makes it easier to drag the file — the distance is shorter.

7. **Drag the file to the local folder in the left pane.**

   When your mouse pointer is on the folder (as shown in Figure 11-1), release the mouse button.

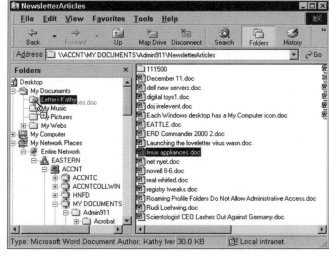

Figure 11-1:
A file from another computer is about to reach the target folder (named Letters-Kathy).

Only folders that have been configured for sharing are displayed when you look at a remote computer in Windows Explorer. If the folder that holds the file you want isn't a shared folder, click the plus sign next to that folder's parent folder, which reveals all the child folders in the left pane. Then select the folder you need.

Dragging between separate windows

Some people find it a bit difficult to drag files within the Windows Explorer window, because the objects are small, so your movements have to be rather precise. If you agree, you can drag files from one computer to another over separate windows. In fact, you have several ways to accomplish this:

1. **Double-click the Network Neighborhood or My Network Places icon on the desktop.**

2. **Double-click the computer and then the shares on the remote computer to get to the window that has the file you want.**

3. **Open My Documents and any subfolders to open the window that has the contents of the target folder. If you're not putting the file in My Documents, open My Computer instead and double-click the drive and folder(s) necessary to open the target window.**

4. **Position the windows near each other.**

   It's okay if they overlap or if they're separated — you just need to be able to get to each window.

5. **Drag the file from one window to the other, as shown in Figure 11-2.**

If you want to copy multiple files, hold down the Ctrl key and select all the files that you need. Then drag one file to the target folder, and all the other files come along for the ride.

Copying by right-dragging files

Perhaps you're not very adventurous and you're afraid that you may move the file instead of copying it. Or perhaps you can't remember whether dragging moves or copies files when you're working with multiple computers.

To play it safe, drag with the right mouse button (called *right-dragging*). When you release the mouse button, a menu appears. Choose Copy Here from the menu.

Copying with the shortcut menu

You can use the shortcut menu that appears when you right-click on an item to copy a file. This method eliminates the need for a second window. Follow these steps to copy files from a remote computer to your own computer:

1. **Open Windows Explorer.**

2. **Expand the Network Neighborhood (or My Network Places) listing, and then expand the remote computer to select the folder that holds the file you need.**

   The files in the selected folder appear in the right Explorer pane.

3. **Right-click on the file that you want to copy.**

   The shortcut menu appears. If you want to copy multiple files, hold down the Ctrl key as you click each file. Then right-click on any file to see the shortcut menu.

4. **Choose Copy from the shortcut menu.**

   The file (or group of files) is placed on the Windows Clipboard.

5. **In the left Explorer pane, right-click on the folder on your local computer into which you want to copy the file.**

6. **Choose Paste from the shortcut menu that appears.**

   The file is copied to your local folder.

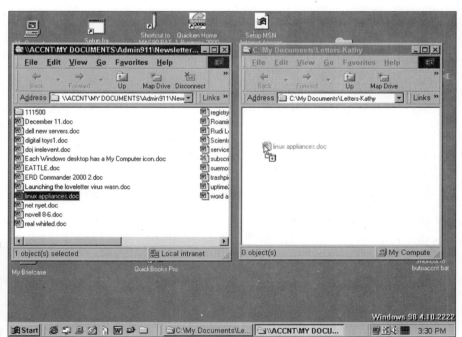

Figure 11-2:
Drag the file
from one
window to
the other.

Relocating files

Sometimes you may want to move a file; removing it from the remote computer and placing it on your local computer (or the other way around). Moving files is less common than copying files, but if you used to work on the computer in the den and have decided that you prefer the computer in the kitchen, you may want to move your files over to your new computer.

Moving by right-dragging files

You can drag files from the remote computer to your own computer with the right mouse button (called *right-dragging*). If you drag with the left mouse button, you copy the files instead of moving them.

Use the steps discussed in the section "Copying by dragging files," earlier in this chapter. You can use either Windows Explorer or two windows, depending on your comfort level. Then right-drag the file or files you need from one computer to the other. When you release the right mouse button, a menu appears. Choose Move Here from the menu. The files move from the original location to the new location.

Using the shortcut menu to move files

If you don't want to open separate windows in order to drag files, you can use the file shortcut menu to cut and paste.

Follow the steps in the earlier section "Copying with the shortcut menu" to select the file(s) you want to move. Instead of choosing Copy from the shortcut menu, choose Cut. Then choose Paste to move the files to the folder of your choice on your own computer. The files move from the original location to the new location.

Deleting files from remote computers

You can delete a file from a remote computer as easily as you can delete files from your own computer. Just select the file and press the Delete key. The same thing is true of folders. However, deleting a file from a remote computer is much more dangerous than deleting files on your own computer. The problem is that the Recycle Bin doesn't work across the network. A deleted file is really deleted, so you can't recover it from the Recycle Bin right after you say "oops."

Okay, now I hear you talking to this page. You're saying when you look at a hard drive on a remote computer, you can see the Recycle Bin, so I must be wrong. Well, double-click that Recycle Bin to open it. Now, double-click the Recycle Bin on your own desktop. Notice anything strange? The files in the two Recycle Bins are identical.

This is a cute trick that Windows plays on network users. When you open the Recycle Bin on a remote computer, instead of flashing a message that says "Access Denied" or "No Way, Go Away" and refusing to open the folder, the system acts as if you're opening a real Recycle Bin. But you're opening a copy of your own, local, Recycle Bin.

Opening Remote Files in Software Windows

You don't have to take the trouble to copy or move files to your own computer when you want to work with them in a software program. You can open and save files on remote computers right from the software. In fact, software written for Windows is designed to do this.

Both computers need to be running the same software. In other words, if you want to open a Microsoft Word document that you see on a remote computer, you must have Microsoft Word on your own computer.

This feature is handy if you don't always work at the same computer. Of course, if you have enough clout to tell whoever is working on your favorite computer to move to another machine, you don't have to worry about this eventuality. And, you should be writing books on effective family dynamics. Most of us with more users than computers in the household have to use whatever computer is available.

Opening distant files

If you work in a Windows software program and you want to work on a file that's located on a remote computer, you can accomplish that right from the software. Follow these steps to use a remote file in your software:

1. **Click the Open button on the software toolbar, or choose File⇨Open from the menu bar.**

   The Open dialog box appears. The contents of the default document folder are displayed (usually the My Documents folder on your own computer).

2. **Click the arrow to the right of the Look In box and select the network listing from the list of locations (see Figure 11-3).**

   In Windows 98, select Network Neighborhood; in Windows Me and Windows 2000 Professional, select My Network Places and then select Entire Network.

   The Open dialog box displays the computers on your network.

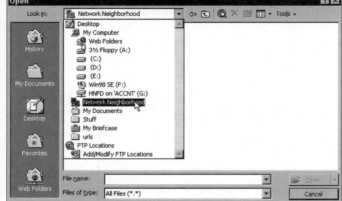

Figure 11-3:
The Open
dialog box in
any
Windows
software
can take
you to any
resource on
your
computer or
on the
network.

3. **Double-click the icon of the remote computer that you want to access.**

   Icons for the shared drives and folders on the remote computer appear in the Open dialog box.

4. **Double-click the folder that holds the file you want to use.**

   The files located in that folder are displayed in the Open dialog box.

5. **Select the file and click Open.**

   The file loads in your software window, so get to work!

If the file that you need is located in a subfolder of a shared resource, it won't appear when you double-click the computer's icon (only the *folders* that are configured for sharing show up in the display). You must open the parent folder (which is a shared folder or the hard drive) and then open the sub-folder to get to the file.

Saving remote files

If you open a file from a remote computer, saving it doesn't change its original location. Every time you click the Save button on the toolbar, or press Ctrl+S, or choose File⇨Save, you save the file in its original location on the remote computer.

The same thing is true for files that you open in software residing on your local drive — they're saved to the same location every time you click the Save button.

Suppose that you open a file that's on a remote computer and work on it in a software program, and then you decide that you want to have a copy of it on your own computer. Well, doing that is easier than you might think, because you don't have to close the software and use the copy function described earlier in this chapter. You can work on the document and copy it in one fell swoop, using the features in the software program.

The same shortcut action is available for documents that you create on your local computer, if you decide that you want to share the file with a user on another computer.

Saving a remote file to the local computer

You've opened a software program and loaded a document from another computer on the network, using the steps discussed in the "Opening distant files" section, earlier in this chapter. You work on the document, making creative changes and adding brilliant new text. Then your brain comes up with a thought that matches one of these ideas:

- ✔ The user who created the document likes it just the way it is. If you prefer the changed document, you should keep it on your own computer.

- ✔ The original document is meant to be used as a template, and you'd prefer to have your own copy of it.

- ✔ You haven't finished working on the document, and reloading it is faster if the file is in your local My Documents folder.

- ✔ You know that you want to continue working on the document and just in case the other computer isn't running the next time you need it, you don't want to climb the stairs to the den.

- ✔ You just want your own copy because you just want your own copy.

For any of those common reasons (or for some reason I didn't think of), you can save the file to your own local computer. To accomplish this, follow these steps:

1. **Choose File⇨Save As from the menu bar of your software window.**

   When the Save As dialog box opens, the saving location is the same remote folder that you opened to fetch the file.

2. **Click the arrow to the right of the Save In text box.**

3. **Choose the folder you normally use for saving files on your local computer.**

4. **Click Save.**

   You can change the name of the file before you click the Save button if you don't want both files to have the same name.

You now have a copy of the file on your local computer, and the original file remains on the remote computer.

Saving a local file to a remote computer

When you work in a software program and you create an absolutely terrific work of art, a fantastic poem, or a mathematically brilliant budget that helps your family save 20 percent of your income without any deprivation, you should show it off — er, share it. If you just created the document, you should save it to your local documents folder first, because having your own copy of a document is a good idea.

Or, in another scenario, perhaps you're working on the computer in the kitchen because somebody else is working on your favorite computer (in the den). You're sure the next time you want to use a computer, you'll be able to get to the machine in the den. Therefore, it makes sense to save the file on the den computer, where it will be handy when you want to continue working on it.

Follow these steps to save the document on another computer:

1. **Choose File⇨Save As from the software menu bar.**

   The Save As dialog box appears.

2. **Click the arrow to the right of the Save In text box and select the network from the list of locations.**

   In Windows 98, select Network Neighborhood; in Windows Me and Windows 2000 Professional, select My Network Places and then select Entire Network.

   Icons for the computers on your network appear in the Save As dialog box.

3. **Double-click the icon for the remote computer on which you want to store a copy of your document.**

   The shared folders on the selected computer appear in the dialog box.

4. **Double-click the folder into which you want to save the document.**

   If the folder you want to use is a subfolder of a shared folder, open the shared folder first and then open the subfolder.

   If the only shared resource is the hard drive, open the hard drive and then open the appropriate folder.

5. **Choose Save to copy the document to the remote location.**

   If you want, you can also change the name of the document before you save it to the remote computer.

Uh oh, two documents with the same name

If you have a document with the same name on two different computers, your life could get a bit complicated. Well, at least your life as it's related to this document (your real-life complications are probably unrelated to computer networks).

The files most certainly have different content — you opened the file from one computer, made changes, and saved it on another computer. Here's the problem: If you open the copy on your local computer and use the Save As command to save it on the remote computer, you replace the file that was on the remote computer. In fact, Windows displays a message asking you if you really want to replace that file. The same thing occurs if you do it the other way around (open the remote file and use the Save As command to save it on your local computer).

If you've been working on both files, you don't want to replace one file with the other — you'll lose your changes. The solution is to change the name, sort of. Make it a rule that every time you use the Save As command on a document that's shared between computers, you append text to the filename. The best text to append is a number. For example, if the original file had the name Budget, the first time you save it on another computer, change the filename to Budget2. Each time you use the Save As command to change the location of the file to another computer, increase the number.

When you're working locally, just keep saving the file under the same name — you don't need to use the Save As command until you want to change the computer on which you're saving the file.

Eventually, if the document is one you've worked on numerous times, you'll probably end up with several copies of the file on each computer. Perhaps the computer in the den has files named Budget2 and Budget4, while the kitchen computer has files named Budget and Budget3.

At some point, open all the copies of the file on one computer, at the same time (all Windows software lets you open multiple files at the same time). Cut, copy, and paste parts of the document into one document, in order to create one masterpiece that contains every change you want to keep. Then delete the other copies.

The same danger occurs if you copy or relocate files instead of opening them in software. Be careful not to replace one file with another if the file that's going to disappear contains data you want to keep.

Understanding documents in use

Two people can't work on the same document at the same time. When one user is using a document, no other users can access the same copy that's being used.

Loading a remote document that's being used

If you try to open a document that's already open on another computer, the software displays a message telling you the document is being used. The document may be one that lives on the local computer (the one you're working on) and has been opened remotely by a user on another computer. Or the document may live on another computer, and a user on that computer is working with it.

The software offers to make a copy of the document and to load that copy in your software window, displaying a message like the one in Figure 11-4.

Figure 11-4:
Somebody's
using this
document,
but you can
have a copy
of it.

Some Windows software has even more power and offers to load a copy and then notify you when the person using the document closes it (see Figure 11-5).

Figure 11-5:
Some
software (in
this case
Microsoft
Word 2000)
can track
what's
happening
to the
document
that's
already in
use.

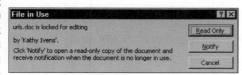

Click OK to have a copy of the document placed in your own software window. The file is in *read-only* mode, which means you can't save it back on its originating computer using the same name.

It's important to realize that the copy you see is from the hard drive of the remote computer, not the software window of the remote user. That means that you get a copy of the file the way it looked the last time the remote user saved it, which may have been three minutes ago, yesterday, or last week. That user is obviously still working on the file, but any changes or additions since the last time she saved aren't copied to your software window.

So, now you have a copy of the file in your software window. You can make all the changes and additions that you care to, just as if another user wasn't using the file. Have a ball!

Saving a document that's in use

Eventually, you're going to want to save the file, and that may present a problem. You may run into one of several possible scenarios, and each has an upside and a downside.

The first scenario is that you want to save the file, with your changes, and the first user is still working with the file. An error message appears, informing you that the file is in use. Click OK and a Save As dialog box appears so that you can save the file under a different name or in a different location. Here are your options:

- ✓ **Use a different filename and save the file in the original location on the remote computer.** For example, add your initials to the end of the existing filename.

- ✓ **Save the file to your local computer.** Click the arrow to the right of the Save In text box and select your local hard drive or the My Documents folder.

  The problem with this option is that you now have two files with the same name, but different content, on the network (albeit on two separate computers). If you think that you and the original user may want to compare and combine the two documents, save the file under a different name when you save it to your local computer.

The second scenario is that you want to save the file and the first user has finished working with the file. Of course, that user has saved the file, and the latest saved version contains all sorts of changes and additions.

When you try to save your version of the file, a message appears telling you that the file has been changed and saved by another user. Here are the options that you get in that message (shown in Figure 11-6):

- ✓ **Click Yes to save the file.** This option replaces the file that the first user saved. Now leave home because your life is in danger. This is a dirty trick, because you end up overwriting all the work saved by the first user.

- ✓ **Click No to open a Save As dialog box.** Here, you can save the file with a different filename, in a different location (remote computer or local computer), or both.

 ✔ **Click Cancel to return to the document without saving.** Have a discussion with the first user to arrive at a solution, and then return to your computer to save the file. If the first user isn't available, or you can't decide how to handle the situation, the safest route is to choose File⇨ Save As and save the file to your own computer with a different filename.

If your software offered to notify you when the first user closes the file, two events occur:

 ✔ The file is reloaded into your software window and all the changes the first user made are added to the file (you have a copy of the final saved file). Because you had to open that file as a read-only file, you didn't make any changes to it. If you saved the file under a different name (with the Save As command), you can copy and paste your changes from that file into the original file.

 ✔ The software offers to get rid of the read-only restrictions on saving the file (see Figure 11-7).

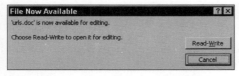

Even though all the other user's changes are included in the file you're working on, play it safe — use the Save As command to save the file with a different name. Later, you and the other user can discuss the differences and decide whether it's okay to open the file again and use the Save As command to save it with the original name.

Files that should never be opened across the network

Don't open files from software programs that automatically save data as quickly as you enter it. This is usually true of database programs. No Save or Save As command is available — as soon as you enter data and move on to the next record, the data is saved automatically. If somebody else is working on the same record, you end up with conflicting data.

Most database programs have safeguards against this behavior — for example, they don't permit you to open the database file remotely, or they don't permit you to open a database file if it's in use, or they're built for shared access. For example, you may be using accounting software that is specially designed for multi-user activities. (One example of this type of software is QuickBooks, but you must purchase the multi-user version.)

However, some older database programs may let you open a file that's in use and manipulate it. Then, when you finish entering data and the automatic save process begins, the software, unable to manage multi-user procedures, goes crazy. The software may crash or freeze, or the data may become corrupted.

Play it safe — don't share database files unless you've purchased database software that's built for multi-user access.

Licenses and other complications

Software that is multi-user enabled doesn't have to be installed on every computer on the network. It's designed to let all the users on remote computers open it on one central computer and run it from there. The computer on which it's installed is called the *server,* and the remote computers that run the software are called *clients.* Some multi-user software also requires installation of a few files on each client computer in order to use the software program on the server.

Single-user software must be fully installed on every computer before a user on that computer can run it.

When you buy software, you're actually buying a license to use the software; you're not buying the software program itself. That license has terms, and you agree to the terms when you install the software. It is almost always illegal to purchase one copy of a single-user software program and then install it on multiple computers on your network. You must buy a separate copy for each computer.

Breaking the license agreement is illegal. It's also immoral. It's no different from buying a can of vegetables at the grocery store, hiding another can in your coat pocket, and paying for only one can at the checkout counter. Just as shoplifting is illegal, so is installing software for which you didn't buy a license. Just because it's harder to catch somebody who installs software illegally than it is to catch a shoplifter, it doesn't mean the act is less illegal or immoral. When you set up a home network, your actions are visible to your children. Stealing is not the kind of example you want to set.

How About Including My Macintosh?

This is the part of the chapter in which I'm supposed to tell you how to include a Macintosh computer into the file-trading circle you've established for your PC-based network.

I tried, but I couldn't make it happen. Well, I could, but not in a manner I wanted to live with on a daily basis, and you'd agree. In fact, I wouldn't want to work this way once in a great while, much less a daily basis.

Here's the deal: The only way I could move files between a Macintosh and the PCs was by launching a browser and using the FTP feature to download and upload files. The Mac had been configured as discussed in Chapter 5.

FTP, which stands for File Transfer Protocol, is a way to transfer files between Web sites and your computer. The FTP protocol uses the Internet's TCP/IP protocol to move files. The Web site acts as a server, and your computer acts as a client. If you have the right permissions, you can also upload files from your computer to the Web site. When you're on the Internet, you don't normally have such permissions, except for your own Web site. When you set up a Macintosh, you make sure the Mac, which is the Web server, is configured to give you uploading rights. Otherwise, you would only get files from your Mac; you wouldn't send the Mac any files from your PCs.

FTP is just one of the protocols that uses the Internet's TCP/IP protocol. Other protocols you use include http (HyperText Transfer Protocol) for viewing Web pages and SMTP (Simple Mail Transfer Protocol), which moves your e-mail between your computer and the Internet.

To make it worse, after I figured out how to transfer files between a Mac and my PCs, I found out that the configuration settings, and the ability to use the Mac as a Web server, differ among different Mac models, and also among different versions of the Mac operating system.

After I returned to my chair from my "walk to the wall and bang your head against it" episode, I started contacting Mac network experts, some of whom are well-known authors of books about Macintosh computers.

"I want to network a Mac," I'd say. "Sure, easy," each replied, "install File and Print services for Macintosh on your Windows 2000 or Windows NT 4 domain and on all the servers in your network that will be responsible for Mac client/server processes."

"No, no," I'd say, "not in a business network, this is a peer-to-peer home network."

Some of them laughed. One person said, "you can't get there from here." But a few experts said I could buy software to accomplish this. You can buy software for the PCs or software for the Macintosh. You don't need both.

The following two sections discuss software that you may want to consider buying in order to include a Mac in your network.

Mac, meet Dave

For the Macintosh, buy Dave. Yep, that's the name of the software. It's from Thursby software, which you can reach at www.thursby.com/products/dave.html.

What this software does is replace AppleTalk with TCP/IP protocols that your PCs can recognize and interact with. In effect, it makes the Macintosh look like a PC to the other PCs on the network. Macintosh purists (sometimes regarded as a cult-like group) may not love that description. It even lets the Mac user log on to the network the way PC users do.

You must be using a Mac with a 68030 or higher processor, and you must have at least 16MB of RAM. The software supports Mac OS 7.6 through 9.0. You can download a free trial, which is a limited version of the software, before deciding to purchase it (the purchase price is about $150.00).

The company also has a product called MacSOHO that has fewer features, but does support file sharing between Macs and PCs. You may want to investigate it.

From a PC LAN to a PC MACLAN

Miramar Systems, at www.miramar.com, offers a product called PC MACLAN that is installed on PCs that need to interact with Macintosh computers.

PC MACLAN for Windows 95/98 uses IP addresses to let PCs running those operating systems communicate with a Mac that's configured as an AppleShare IP Server. The software should work on Windows Me, but that's my logical guess, not the company's promise.

PC MACLAN for Windows NT/2000 lets you add the Mac File services that are built into business client/server networks to your Windows 2000 Professional computer.

With PC MACLAN, your PCs can print to a Mac printer (the Mac becomes a print server), and your Mac can print to a PC printer if it's a PostScript printer (not common in home networks). To let the Mac print to a PC printer that isn't PostScript, you must use a third-party software program called Ghostscript. Miramar has included Ghostscript in its GS Director software, which is included in some versions of its PC LAN software.

The Macintosh must be running Mac OS 8 or higher.

Part IV
Network Security and Maintenance

The 5th Wave   By Rich Tennant

"If it works, it works. I've just never seen network cabling connected with Chinese handcuffs before."

In this part . . .

Securing the network is the technical terminology for keeping the bad stuff — including viruses and Internet invaders — away from all the computers on the network. You probably know what a virus is (even if you've never encountered one on your computer), but you may not know what Internet invaders are. These are malicious people who try to break into your computer while you're connected to the Internet, a feat that's amazingly easy to do if you don't take the proper precautions. In this part, you find out what steps you can take to keep the bad stuff out of your network.

Maintenance is the technical term for, well, maintenance — I guess there's no better word. Your computers and your network need maintenance to stay healthy — just like your car or your teeth. In this part, you discover techniques and tools you can use to keep things humming along.

Chapter 12

Making Your Network Safe and Secure

• •

• •

*A*s users, we make mistakes. We inadvertently delete important files (including software files) and perform other accidental actions that can totally mess up a computer.

However, some people deliberately work at the task of destroying computers, and they perform their dirty deeds by installing viruses on your computer. Other nasty folks invade your computer while you're on the Internet, and get private information from your files (or leave viruses on your computer).

This chapter discusses methods you can use to make sure the computers on your network have as much protection as possible against the misery these actions can cause. However, the most important ingredient in your scheme to protect your network is a healthy dose of paranoia. Be suspicious. Be afraid.

All About Viruses

A *virus* is programming code that is designed to cause damage and is disguised to appear to be a normal program. Most viruses are also designed to clone themselves if they find a network environment so that they can move on to the other computers.

Viruses can be transmitted in several different ways:

- ✔ As files on a diskette or CD
- ✔ As attachments to e-mail messages
- ✔ As infected program code from the Internet (which users download)

Three major classes of viruses exist, and each class has a number of subclasses, as rogue programmers devise innovative ways to ply their nefarious trade.

File infecting viruses

File infecting viruses attach themselves to program files, which are files with the filename extension `.com` or `.exe`. When the program is loaded, the virus is loaded as well, and does its work independent of the program that runs when you open the program file. The program file is just the mode of transportation — the way the virus gets itself loaded into memory. Years ago, file infecting viruses were the only viruses around.

Some file infecting viruses don't need the main executable file to infect your system. They can attach themselves to another file type, one that is loaded by the main executable file. Among the file types that programs load (and viruses can use) are filenames with the extensions `.sys`, `.ovl`, `.prg`, and `.mnu`.

There are also viruses that are programs at the same time. The filename is innocuous, and the filename extension is `.exe`. Opening the file unleashes the virus. This virus type is frequently transmitted to its victims as an e-mail attachment.

System and boot infectors

System and boot infectors infect the code that's placed in certain system areas on a drive. On a floppy disk, they attach themselves to the DOS sector. On hard drives, they attach themselves to the Master Boot Record (MBR).

This virus type doesn't launch itself into memory and go to work until you boot your computer. If you boot to a floppy disk — using the infected disk — the virus is activated. If you start your computer normally, the virus loads itself into system memory when the boot files on the MBR load.

Macro viruses

Among the most common viruses today, macro viruses are really misnamed. They should be called VB viruses. These viruses attach themselves to Visual Basic (VB) code, which some software programs use to create or run macros. (Macros are automated procedures you can use to perform tasks in software.) Almost all the software from Microsoft uses VB code, and all the software included in Microsoft Office uses VB code.

Some software programs that provide the power of macros use their own proprietary code that doesn't run separately from the program. It's much more difficult for a virus to insert itself within macro code that doesn't use VB. WordPerfect is an example of a software program that provides powerful macro abilities without using any VB.

Antivirus Programs: For Prevention and Cure

An important defense against viruses is an antivirus program. Good antivirus software performs four tasks:

- ✔ Scans your drive looking for viruses
- ✔ Checks every executable file as you open it to make sure no virus is piggybacked on it
- ✔ Checks your e-mail to find viruses as messages that are brought into your inbox
- ✔ Removes any virus code it finds (or deletes the file if it cannot remove the virus)

A number of antivirus software programs are available, and here are three that I've used and have been pleased with:

- ✔ Norton AntiVirus at `www.symantec.com`
- ✔ McAfee VirusScan at `www.mcafee.com`
- ✔ Command AntiVirus at `www.commandcom.com`

I'm sure other programs exist that are just as good as the three I've mentioned.

Most antivirus software programs offer a variety of configuration options during installation. You can make the program active all the time so it's sniffing out files constantly. You can schedule scans of your drives at regular times. Check the documentation that comes with the antivirus software you buy to see what all the bells and whistles can do.

The most important thing to know about antivirus software is that you cannot just install it and relax. New viruses are invented every minute (reliable sources put the number of new viruses at 400 per month). The cures are invented moments later (usually). The cures are put into files that you must download in order to update the antivirus software files. Check for updates at least once a week.

Common Sense: Part of Your Arsenal

If you develop an enhanced sense of suspicion, even paranoia, you're less likely to suffer a virus attack. Therefore, changing your normal friendly, naïve, personality into that of a suspicious curmudgeon makes sense.

Develop e-mail paranoia

The most common delivery method for viruses is e-mail. That's because rogue programmers have figured out that if they can invade e-mail software, they can automatically send their destructive code to lots of additional victims — they use your address book and send the virus to every e-mail address they find. This practice is why many people end up with virus infections — the virus came from somebody they know (even though that person didn't know he or she was sending the virus).

Therefore, follow these precautions when reading e-mail:

✔ Don't open any files attached to an e-mail message from somebody you know, unless you know in advance that those files are coming to you.

✔ Don't open any files that are attached to an e-mail message from somebody you don't know.

✔ Don't open any files attached to an e-mail message if the subject line is strange. In fact, don't even open a message if the subject line seems weird — some viruses are capable of launching themselves when the message is opened. Just delete the message unread.

Develop Internet download paranoia

Be incredibly careful about downloading files from the Internet. Here are specific precautions to take:

✔ If you're not absolutely sure of the source, avoid downloading the file.

✔ Make sure your antivirus program is configured to check the files on the download Web site. If your antivirus software can't do that, and you're reasonably certain the site is safe, take the precaution of downloading the file to a floppy disk. Then have your antivirus software scan that disk before you install the software.

✔ If your kids are downloading multimedia files (music and video), do whatever you need to do to make them paranoid and suspicious. Kids download many of the viruses that attack family computers.

Firewalls: Defense for Internet Attacks

Some of the people who use the Internet are annoying, or even dangerous, jerks. They're like the kids who destroy property just for the fun of it, or break into homes and steal personal items. Mostly, these jerks are kids, at least emotionally they're kids. They're the kind of kids we called "punks" in my salad days. Today, some people call these punks *hackers*, but the real root of that word isn't negative — it used to mean people who hacked away at programming code, out of curiosity. Frequently, these people improved the code. However, I'll use the current jargon and refer to this danger as *Internet hacking*.

While you're on the Internet, you're vulnerable to any malicious act that a hacker wants to perpetrate. This is especially true if you're using an always-on connection to the Internet, via a cable modem or a DSL device (see Chapter 6).

Fortunately, you can protect your network from Internet hackers by purchasing and installing a firewall. The following sections discuss firewalls in more detail.

What a firewall does

A firewall works by watching everything that happens on your computer that has anything to do with anything outside your computer. Unless you say it's okay, no action occurs between your computer and another computer. That other computer could be on the Internet or on your network.

Because the firewall stops any computer from accessing your computer, you must configure the firewall software to accept communications between your computer and the other computers on your network. Doing so frees the firewall to concentrate on communications between your computer and a computer on the Internet.

The firewall blocks communication in both directions — to and from the Internet. The software you use to access the Internet, such as your browser and e-mail program, must be given permission to do its job.

Any computer that tries to access your computer is either stopped dead in its tracks or is stopped temporarily until you tell the firewall whether to let the computer gain access (depending on the way you configure the firewall's behavior).

Examining a firewall's log file

After you install a firewall program on your network, open your firewall's *log file* (a list of all the attempts made to access your computer) and look at the information (there's a command somewhere on the menu bar of the firewall software to accomplish this). All the computers that have tried to get in to your computer are listed by their IP addresses. Go to one of the Web sites that provides reverse lookups, which means you can enter an IP address and the Web site will tell you the name of the computer. (I use `www.eons.com/iplookup.htm`.)

Sometimes the IP address belongs to an ISP, and it's part of a range of addresses assigned to that ISP. This means a customer of that ISP, who has been assigned that IP address for his Internet session, is trying to get into your computer. You probably won't be able to determine who the customer is. However, you can notify the ISP that at a certain time on a certain date, this particular IP address was trying to break in to your computer, and the ISP can determine to whom the address was assigned at that moment. Tell the ISP to let you know what it does to resolve the problem.

Sometimes the IP address is identified as belonging to a particular company. I've found a lot of marketing companies snooping around my computer. They're trying to see which Web sites I visit, and then they can sell my e-mail address to spammers who want to sell me stuff related to my interests. I usually go to the companies' Web sites and send e-mail to the highest-ranking contact I can find listed. The messages say "gotcha, cut it out."

You can't tell whether a snooper was trying to do some damage, either by leaving behind a virus or stealing personal information. You can only tell that the snooper has tried to hack your computer.

My experience with ZoneAlarm

I've tried several firewall software programs, and the one I eventually chose is ZoneAlarm, from Zone Labs (`www.zonelabs.com`). I think it's the best firewall available for a home network. By the time you read this, other software companies may have made firewalls available, and you should check computer magazines and experts to get recommendations.

Within moments of installing ZoneAlarm, a message popped up telling me that another computer was trying to access my computer over the Internet. ZoneAlarm asked if I wanted to let this computer in — it gave the IP address of the unknown computer. I clicked No, and a few minutes later another pop-up message appeared. These messages kept appearing. I was amazed and a little frightened about all the time I had operated without a firewall.

Finally, I got tired of saying No every few minutes, and configured ZoneAlarm to stop asking and just say no. I also chose to keep a log file of all the attempts. Every once in a while I open the log file, and I'm always amazed at the number of times outside computers are trying to mess around with my privacy. The log file gets very large, very fast.

Testing the security of your system

Definitely test each computer if you haven't installed a firewall, but also test it after your firewall is running. Here's a good way to test your system:

1. **Enter** www.grc.com **in your browser's address bar.**

   This is the Web site of Gibson Research, which has been around for many years. The techies at Gibson are absolute geniuses when it comes to computers.

2. **Click the Shields Up logo.**

   The Shields Up page appears.

3. **Scroll to the Shields Ups logo and click it.**

   The Shields Up program determines how vulnerable your computer is to spying, prying, and destructive hacks. Click Yes when the message about going to a secure site appears.

4. **On the next Web page, scroll to the Test My Shields logo and click it.**

   You may have to click Yes or OK to another message. Then the probe begins. The process takes a while, perhaps a full minute or so.

5. **Read the report.**

   Here's what the report tells you, depending on whether you have a firewall:

   - **If you're not running a firewall:** The first thing you see is `hello <your name>`. The test software peeked into your computer and found the file that holds your logon name. Then the real scary stuff begins, as shown in Figure 12-1.

     The stuff you see in Figure 12-1 is nothing. As I scrolled down to read the rest of the report, I found the test software was able to get into all my shared folders. It knew stuff about the technical side of my Internet connection that added up to an invitation to invade.

   - **If you're running a firewall:** You should get a report similar to the one shown in Figure 12-2.

While you're on the grc.com site, travel through its pages to learn more about the kind of spying, prying, and destructive actions that outside computers can wreak on your computers. The site also offers some interesting software for testing your computers, your ports, and controlling your network.

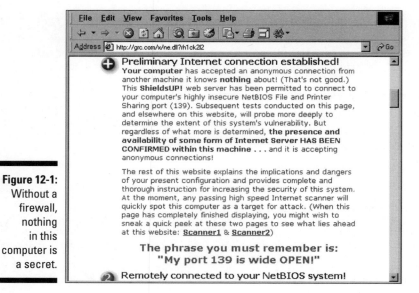

Figure 12-1:
Without a
firewall,
nothing
in this
computer is
a secret.

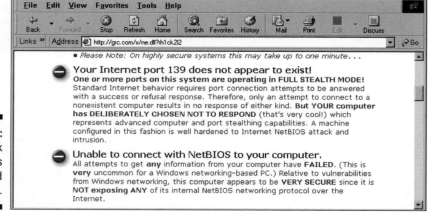

Figure 12-2:
Thank
goodness
for a good
firewall.

A case study in hinkey firewall technology

I sometimes select text from a Web page and save it, because I want to read it at my leisure or when my mood is right (it's usually very technical stuff). After I select the text from the page, I right-click on the selected text and choose Copy. Then I open a word processor and use the Paste command to save the text. ZoneAlarm asks if I want to let my word processor go out on the Internet (remember, firewalls work in both directions).

The first time this happened, I answered No, just to see what would happen. I figured the word processor (which happens to be Microsoft Word) wouldn't accept the text because it apparently had to fetch it directly from the Web page — why else would it try to go out to the Internet? As soon as I clicked No, the Paste command worked, and my text was in a Word document. I guess Word just figured, "Heck, I'll try and see what happens."

Then I configured ZoneAlarm to block Word from the Internet permanently, and I haven't had a problem since.

Chapter 13

Playing God: Damage Control Advice for the Pessimistic Network Administrator

Sometimes, things go wrong with the computer itself — the physical parts of a computer. You can avoid many problems with a little preventive maintenance.

The important consideration, now that you're a network administrator, is that you're protecting your network in addition to protecting each individual computer.

Network computers are connected — they talk to each other, and they interact with each other. Each computer on the network has a physical relationship with the other computers on the network. The computers can pass problems around the network neighborhood through the cable.

In this chapter, I tell you how to care for your hardware so you don't have an epidemic of sick computers. I also tell you how to prepare for the day that your preventive measures don't work — in the end, all hard drives *do* die.

Avoiding Zapped Computers

You know that electricity is dangerous, so you probably avoid sticking your fingers into live light bulb sockets and electrical outlets. Your computers may not have fingers, but they're sensitive to electricity, too, and it's up to you to protect them from a variety of electrical dangers.

Protecting against electrical surges

An *electrical surge* is a sudden spate of very high voltage that travels from the electric lines to your house and ultimately to your computer. Computers are particularly sensitive to surges, and a real surge can fry your computer. The chips burn up, and your computer becomes a doorstop.

Most of the time, surges occur as a result of a lightning strike, but the danger of a surge also exists if there's a brief blackout followed by a return of electricity. During the return of power, the voltage can spike. (See the section "Protecting against lightning hits," later in this chapter.)

You can safeguard against spikes by plugging your computer into a *surge protector*. The surge protectors that are commonly used look like electrical power strips, usually with four or five outlets. Read the specifications before you buy a surge protector to make sure that it's rated for real surge protection. (Voltage can rise by 10 volts or hundreds of volts, so make sure that the surge protector you buy can handle these extreme surges.)

Surge protectors work by committing suicide to protect your computer. They absorb the surge so it doesn't travel to your equipment. (Some surge protectors have reset buttons that bring the strip back to life.)

If a power surge hits any piece of equipment that is attached to your computer by cable, the surge can travel to your computer. Therefore, plugging the computer into the surge protector isn't quite enough; you also have to use the surge protector to power the accessories connected to your computer.

Because any surge received by a single computer can travel over the network cable to the other computers on your network, make sure that all the following equipment for each of your computers is plugged into surge protectors:

- ✔ Monitors
- ✔ External modems
- ✔ External removable drives
- ✔ Speakers

Notice that I didn't list a printer. Never plug a printer into the same surge protector that your computer is already plugged into. (In fact, if you have a laser printer, you should *never* plug it into the same circuit as your computer.) See the section "Protecting Printers," later in this chapter, for more information.

Protecting against telephone line surges

I've seen several large networks destroyed during a lightning storm, and in each case, the surge came through the telephone lines, not the electrical lines. Here's what happens: Lightning hits the telephone line; the surge comes through the telephone jack in the wall; it travels along the telephone cable from the wall to the modem; it travels from the modem to the computer's motherboard; it travels from the motherboard to the rest of the computer parts, including the network interface card (NIC); the NIC sends the surge out to the network cable; the cable sends the surge back to every NIC on the network; and each NIC sends the surge to its computer's motherboard. Every computer on the network is fried.

In most communities, the power company installs lightning arresters, which help diffuse the effects of a direct lightning hit on the electric lines. However, I know of no telephone company that protects its phone lines against lightning. When a lightning storm is close, unplug your modem telephone cable at the wall jack and then unplug the computers.

If your telephone company has fiber-optic lines, you don't have to worry about lightning hits because those lines don't conduct electricity. Ask your telephone company what types of lines are connected to your home.

Protecting against lightning hits

If lightning hits your power lines or your house, your surge protector may not be able to protect your equipment against the resulting surge. Thousands or tens of thousands of volts — sometimes more — result from a lightning strike. A surge protector can provide only so much protection, and a direct lightning hit exceeds that limit.

The only protection against lightning strikes is to unplug your computers and all your computer equipment. Stop working. Then walk around the house and unplug other equipment with chips that could fry during a lightning storm (like your microwave oven, VCR, and so on).

Protecting against power loss

When you're running Windows, you *can't* just turn off your computer when you don't want to use it anymore. You must initiate a shutdown procedure using the Shut Down command on the Start menu. Otherwise, you may have a problem starting your computer, or you may run into mysterious problems when you try to use software and Windows features after a power failure.

The electric company doesn't know and doesn't care about the need for an orderly shutdown, and if the folks there did know or care, they couldn't do much to warn you about a power failure, giving you time to use the Shut Down command.

You can keep your computers running long enough to complete an orderly shutdown of all your software and the operating system if you have an *uninterruptible power supply* (UPS). A UPS is a mega-battery that you plug into the wall, and you then use the UPS outlets to connect your computer and monitor. If your power fails, your computer draws power from the battery, giving you enough time to shut down everything.

UPS units come in a variety of power configurations (measured in watts). Some have line conditioning (see the next section "Understanding and fixing low-voltage problems") in addition to the battery feature. Some have software that performs the orderly shutdown for you. (The UPS unit connects to your computer through a serial port in order to communicate.) This is a nice feature if your power dies while you're away from the computer. The cost ranges from about $75 to several hundred dollars, depending on the wattage and the features you want. The best-known (and, in my opinion, most reliable) UPS units are made by APC. They're available anywhere computer peripherals are sold.

Understanding and fixing low-voltage problems

Sometimes, when everyone in town is using electrical gadgets at the same time, an area's all-around voltage drops. This is called a *brownout.* Computers — especially their hard drives and motherboards — are extremely sensitive to brownouts.

Well before you see the lights flicker, your hard drive can react to a brownout. Most of the time, that reaction destroys the part of the drive being accessed, and the result is that your drive develops bad spots — parts of the drive that can't be written to or read from. You can mark the bad spots to prevent the operating system from using those spots to hold data, but if the spots that go bad already have data on them, that data goes bad, too. (See Chapter 14 for a discussion of the Windows tools that can help you find and mark bad spots on your hard drive.)

You can prevent most of the problems associated with bad spots caused by brownouts, and you can overcome those problems that you can't prevent by purchasing a *voltage regulator.* This clever device constantly measures the voltage coming out of the wall and brings it up to an acceptable minimum and sells for about $50 to $100 (depending on how many devices you want to plug into it). Several companies make voltage regulators (try TrippLite, www. triplite.com), and some UPS units have voltage regulation built in.

If you purchase a voltage regulator in addition to a UPS unit, plug the voltage regulator into the wall. If you're also using a surge protector, the surge protector is always plugged into the wall, with any other devices plugged into the surge protector.

Here are some of the causes of low voltage, along with possible fixes:

✔ **Too many appliances are plugged into the same circuit as your computer.** This is something you can fix. Move stuff around, buy some very long heavy-duty extension cords to get to an outlet on another circuit, or call an electrician and get more outlets connected to empty breakers.

✔ **An appliance that's a voltage pig (central air conditioning, electric heating systems) kicks on, disrupting voltage throughout the house.** Plug your computer into a voltage regulator.

✔ **Your laser printer (or powerful inkjet color printer) is plugged into the same circuit as your computer.** See the section "Protecting Printers," later in this chapter. You shouldn't plug these printers into the same circuit as your computer. If you have no choice, plug the computer into a voltage regulator. Do not plug the printer into the voltage regulator.

✔ **The electric company is sending low voltage into your home.** Sometimes, the electric company just can't keep up with demand, and it delivers lower-than-normal voltage to your home. When the voltage really drops, the electric company calls it a brownout. This frequently occurs during very hot weather, when air conditioners in your area are running constantly and working hard.

The solution? Plug your computer into a voltage regulator.

Preventing static electricity damage

Static electricity is responsible for more damaged computers than most people realize. One day, when some hardware component mysteriously dies, you may not realize that you zapped it yourself.

Static electricity charges that zap your computer come from you. You pick up static electricity, carry it with you, and pass it along when you touch any part of the computer. Usually, the keyboard receives your first touch, and even though it's connected to your computer, it doesn't always pass the electricity along to the computer.

However, if you touch the monitor or the computer box, you can pass a serious or fatal amount of electricity to the motherboard (fatal to the computer, not to you) or to any component in your computer (including chips).

You must discharge the electricity from your body before you touch the computer. Touch anything metal (except an electric appliance such as a computer or a lamp). A filing cabinet is good if one is handy. If nothing metal is within reach, attach a metal bar to the desk or table that your computer sits on.

Computers and carpeting create the ideal atmosphere for zapping. New carpeting is really dangerous, followed by carpeting with a thick pile. If you can't pull the carpeting up, go to an office supply store and buy one of those big plastic mats that goes under the desk and your chair. If you don't, each time you move your feet, you'll collect static electricity and eventually pass it to the computer.

Caring for Network Hardware

If you receive an error message while trying to move files between computers or when you open the Network Neighborhood window, it's time to check your network hardware.

The network hardware, connectors, cable, and NICs may require some maintenance. In the following sections, I list the hardware components in the order in which they usually cause problems. Connector problems are the most common, then cable problems, and finally bad NICs.

Checking connectors

Cable connectors are the weakest link in the network hardware chain. Because of this, you should check the connectors first when your computers can't communicate.

If you wired your network with 10Base-T (twisted-pair) cable, you should check the following:

- ✔ See if the connectors are properly inserted in the NICs.
- ✔ Make sure that the connectors are properly inserted in the concentrator.
- ✔ Be sure that the concentrator is plugged in. (A concentrator usually doesn't have an on/off switch — if it's plugged in, it should be working.)

Here's what to check if you're using your household telephone line for your network:

✔ Make sure that the connectors are firmly seated in both the NICs and the wall jack.

✔ If you're using a splitter (also called a *modular duplex jack*) to plug in both a telephone and the network cable, make sure that the splitter is firmly positioned in the jack.

Splitters weigh more than the fraction of an ounce that the connector on the end of a phone cord weighs, and sometimes this extra weight pulls the splitter out of the jack just a bit. Frequently, you don't notice this problem when you look at the connection, but if you push on the connector, you do notice that it isn't all the way in the phone jack. Here are reasons why the splitter may have come out of the jack:

- The cable between the splitter and whatever the other end of the cable plugs into (either the telephone jack or the NIC) is taut.

- The telephone is moved, because either it's placed somewhere else or a person using the telephone walks around while chatting.

Checking cables

Make sure that the cables aren't pinched or bent to the point that they can't handle data. Have you ever sharply bent a water hose? The water stops flowing. The same thing can happen to cable.

If you have excess cable, don't twist it into a knot to avoid having it spill on the floor. Gently roll the cable into a circle and use a twist tie to keep it together. (Don't tie it tightly.)

I pounded thin nails into the backs of the tables that hold my computers, and I hang coils of excess cable on those nails to keep the cable off the floor.

Checking NICs

It's unusual for a NIC to give up, roll over, and die (unless you had a power surge or did something dumb like stick a bobby pin in the connector).

However, sometimes NICs — like all hardware — just stop working. If your NIC has a light on the back panel near the connector, it should glow green. If no light is glowing and you've checked the connectors and the cable, the only way to check the NIC is to replace it. If the new NIC works, the old NIC was bad. If the new NIC doesn't work, recheck your connectors and cable. Take the new NIC back to the store and get a credit.

If your NIC has two little light bulbs and the red one is glowing, your NIC is working but isn't receiving or sending data. You can be fairly sure that you have a connector or cable problem.

Monitoring Monitors

Monitors require some special attention, and too many people maul and mishandle them. By no coincidence at all, those are the same people who have to buy new monitors more frequently than should be necessary.

A monitor's screen attracts and collects dust — it actually sucks it out of the air. You can't avoid monitor dust, but you can remove it by wiping the screen with a soft, dry cloth. It's best to turn off the monitor before cleaning it. (Static electricity, which is responsible for attracting the dust, can build up to explosive levels when you rub the screen.)

If you're a person who points to the screen when you show somebody a beautiful sentence you just composed or a mind-blowing graphic you just created, you probably have fingerprints on your monitor. Fingerprints are oily and don't always disappear with a dry cloth. Office supply stores sell pre-moistened towelettes for cleaning monitors. You just pull one out and wipe the screen. (Remember to close the container's lid to keep the remaining towelettes moist. They're like the towelettes you use on infants when you change diapers, although I assume that the moistening agent is different and isn't so gentle on a baby's bottom.)

If you want to use the bottle of window cleaner that you keep around the house, spray it on a cloth, not on the monitor; the monitor isn't sealed properly to avoid leaks. Then wipe the moistened cloth across the screen.

You can also use a cloth moistened with window cleaner on the keyboard and mouse (the other collection points for fingerprints and dust).

Protecting Printers

You should perform a few maintenance chores regularly to make sure that your printed documents look terrific and your printers perform without errors:

- Don't overfill paper trays — doing so results in printer jams.
- If you have to clean up a printer jam, unplug the printer. Never yank on the jammed paper. Pull it steadily and gently.
- Always clean a laser printer when you change toner cartridges, following the directions that come with the cartridge.
- Dust is the printer's biggest enemy. Keep printers covered when they aren't in use.
- Don't put label sheets back into the printer for a second pass. If you only used a couple of labels on the sheet, throw away the sheet. The chemicals on the sheet can damage the internal mechanisms of the printer.

✔ Use paper that's compatible with your printer. (Check the documentation that came with your printer.)

✔ When you use heavy paper stock, labels, transparencies, or envelopes in a laser printer, open the back door to let the paper go through the printer in a straight path. That way, the stock doesn't have to bend around the rollers.

✔ Use the features in the software that came with your color inkjet printer to check the alignment of the color cartridge. (No alignment maintenance is required for monochrome cartridges — you simply replace the cartridges when they run out of ink or dry up.)

Besides protecting your printer, you also need to protect your computer from your printer, especially if you use a laser printer or a powerful color inkjet printer. These printers use a lot of power, and if they're on the same circuit as your computer, you're probably causing minor brownouts for the computer, which can harm your hard drive and your data.

Establishing a Plan for Backing Up Data

If you take the time to establish a plan of attack, you can fight back when disaster strikes. For computers, the best plan of attack is a well-designed plan for backing up your data. Your plan must provide protection for important files and must be so easy to implement that you won't be tempted to skip doing it.

Learning to love canned air

Office supply stores sell cans of air. It's not just air; it's air that comes out of the can with enough pressure to push dust out of places it shouldn't be in. The cans come with little straw-like tubes that you can attach to the sprayer so that you can get inside your removable drives, between the keys of your keyboard, and in the paper pathway in your printer.

Spray every opening, pore, and vent in your computer frequently. Built-up dust can interfere with the operation of your computer. CD-ROM drives and floppy drives that stop reading files usually have nothing wrong with them except dust. (Don't tilt the can when you're spraying air — if the can isn't upright, you won't get the power blast you need.)

I use canned air everywhere. It's the handiest cleaning tool I have in my house. I spray all the openings on my CD player, television set, radio, and cable box. It works great on the ridges that hold my storm windows and screens, too.

You should back up files on all the hard drives in your home network every day. But you won't. Nobody does, until they have a disaster and they realize how long it's been since they did a backup. That's an awful situation, and it provides the impetus for backing up religiously (at least for a while, until the memory fades).

Back up often

Computers die. Sometimes only one part of a computer dies, but it's usually one of the important parts, like the hard drive. You have to approach the use of computers with the attitude that one of the machines on your network could go to la-la land, or a hard drive could go to hard-drive heaven, tomorrow.

If you don't plan for a sudden demise of your equipment, the computer fairies figure it out — they notice that you're complacent (they call it smug), and they break something. Computer fairies must be the culprits — nothing else explains the fact that most computers bite the dust the day after the user has finished writing the greatest novel in the history of literature or an important report for the boss that's sure to mean a promotion, and no backup files exist.

Making a backup doesn't prevent the death of a computer. And there's no proof that skipping a backup invites a serious problem — it just seems to happen that way. But just in case, backing up important files every single day is imperative.

You need to back up your data files religiously. If you have a tape backup system or a large removable disk, such as a Jaz drive, you can back up everything on each computer in the network, but it's really only important to back up essential data.

Configure computers for easy backups

If something bad happens to one of your network computers and you haven't backed up, you can reinstall the operating system and all your software, but you can kiss that letter to grandma and that promotion-earning PowerPoint presentation goodbye. Say "so long" to that fat inheritance check and that office with a view.

The easier it is to back up data files, the more likely it is that you'll actually perform the task every day. Think about it: If you keep the vacuum cleaner in the hall closet, your house will stay cleaner than it would if you kept the vacuum cleaner in the attic. Convenience is an invaluable assistant.

Store all data files in the My Documents folder, and make sure that all the people who use the network do the same. If you like to organize files by type, either by software application or by some other scheme (perhaps separating letters from other documents), create subfolders for each type of file. When you copy the My Documents folder, you copy all of its subfolders.

Some software applications (for example, Quicken) have a backup routine built into the software. If the software backs up your data files to a floppy disk, that's best. If, however, the software backs up your data files to a separate backup directory on your hard drive, redirect that backup to a subfolder under your My Documents folder. Otherwise, you have to take the time to back up that separate folder in addition to your My Documents folder.

Safeguard software CDs and disks

If a hard drive on the network dies, you have to install Windows on the replacement drive. Then, if you have a total backup of your entire drive, including the Registry, you can restore that backup and put everything back the way it was before the demise of your equipment. You usually have to do a bit of tweaking, but essentially, the move to the new drive goes pretty smoothly.

If you don't have a total backup of your drive, all isn't lost. As long as you backed up the data files, you can reinstall the operating system, reinstall your software, and then restore the data files that you backed up.

This plan works only if your original software CD or disks are available. Storing the original disks for Windows and the software that you purchased in a safe place is important. I recommend that you use one of those fireproof boxes that you can buy in office supply stores.

If you have software that you downloaded from the Internet, copy it to a folder under the My Documents folder so it's backed up. If you have a large removable disk drive on your system, dedicate one cartridge to downloaded software programs (most downloaded programs won't fit on a floppy disk).

Safeguard backup media

Whatever backup media you choose — whether it be floppy disks, Zip or Jaz cartridges, or backup tapes — make sure that you have more than one disk, cartridge, or tape on hand. Don't back up on the same disk, cartridge, or tape that holds your last backup — if something goes wrong during the backup, not only do you not get a good backup this time, but you also destroy your previous backup.

The ideal situation is to have a disk, cartridge, or tape for each day of the week. If that seems too difficult or too expensive (in the case of cartridges and tapes), create one set of disks, cartridges, or tapes marked Odd (for odd days) and another set marked Even (for even days).

If a fire, flood, or any other catastrophe strikes, then after you clean up the mess you can replace the computers. You can replace and reinstall software, but you have no way to restore all those important documents, accounting information, and other data that you created on your computer unless you have a backup stored out of harm's way.

That's why, once a week, you should take your backup media out of the house and leave it with a neighbor, at work, or at your vacation home. Don't forget to bring the backups back the following week so that you can put a current backup on the media and take it away again. You'll probably be able to find a neighbor with a computer and backup media who wants to do the same thing, so the two of you can trade disks or tapes.

Using Microsoft Backup

Microsoft provides backup software with Windows, and because I operate on the theory "if it's free and it works, why not use it?" I find Microsoft Backup to be an excellent choice for safeguarding my files. In this section, I walk you through using Microsoft Backup to ensure a safe computing environment.

Installing Microsoft Backup

Microsoft Backup is not installed during a typical installation of Windows (except for Windows 2000 Professional). Unless you performed a customized installation of the operating system and installed the backup software at that time, Backup won't be available. Windows 98 and Windows Me have different methods for installing the backup software.

Installing Windows 98 backup software

Here's how to install Microsoft Backup in Windows 98:

1. **With your Windows CD in the CD-ROM drive, choose Start⇨Settings⇨ Control Panel.**

   The Control Panel window opens.

2. **Double-click the Add/Remove Programs icon.**

   The Add/Remove Programs Properties dialog box appears.

3. **Click the Windows Setup tab.**

4. **Click the System Tools listing (not the check box) and then click the Details button.**

5. **Select Backup from the list of components and then click OK.**

   The necessary files are transferred to your hard drive. A message appears to tell you that you must restart your computer to finish the installation process.

6. **Click Yes to restart the computer and finish installation.**

After the restart, the backup tool is on your menu system. When you want to run the program, simply choose Start➪Programs➪Accessories➪System Tools➪ Backup.

Installing Windows Me backup software

If you upgraded to Windows Me from Windows 98 or Windows 95, and you had installed the backup program in that previous operating system, you don't have to install the Windows Me backup software (the programs are almost identical, and either Backup software works fine in Windows Me). Instead, use the backup software you installed while you were running Windows 98 or Windows 95. Here's how to activate that software:

1. **Choose Start➪Programs➪Accessories➪Windows Explorer.**

2. **Click the plus sign next to My Computer and then click the plus sign next to drive C.**

   The folders on drive C are displayed in the left pane.

3. **Click the plus sign next to Program Files to expand it.**

   The subfolders under the Program Files folder are displayed in the left pane.

4. **If you upgraded from Windows 98, click the plus sign next to Accessories to expand it and then select the Backup subfolder. If you upgraded from Windows 95, select the Accessories folder.**

   You can see the backup software file in the right pane: `msbackup.exe` (for Windows 98 upgraders) or `backup.exe` (for Windows 95 upgraders).

5. **Right-click on the file and choose Send To➪Desktop (Create Shortcut) from the menu that appears.**

   The shortcut to the backup software appears on the desktop.

For easier access to the program, drag the desktop shortcut to either or both of the following locations:

✔ **The Start button.** The program is added to the top of your Start menu.

✔ **The Quick Launch bar.** You have one-click access to the backup software.

If you didn't upgrade to Windows Me, or you upgraded but you'd never installed the backup software, follow these steps to install Microsoft Backup in Windows Me:

1. **With your Windows CD in the CD-ROM drive, double-click the My Computer icon on your desktop.**

2. **Right-click on the icon for your CD-ROM drive and choose Explore from the shortcut menu that appears.**

   An Explorer-like window opens to display the contents of the CD (see Figure 13-1).

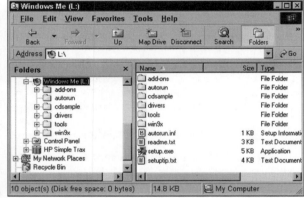

Figure 13-1: You must navigate through the contents of your Windows Me CD to find the backup software.

3. **Click the plus sign next to the Add-ons folder to expand it.**

   The subfolders appear in the left pane.

4. **Select the MSBackup subfolder.**

   The files in the subfolder are displayed in the right pane.

5. **Double-click** `msbexp.exe`.

   Installation of the backup program begins. The necessary files are transferred to your hard drive, and the system displays a message announcing that it's finished.

6. **Click OK.**

   A message appears to tell you that you must restart your computer to finish the installation process.

7. **Click Yes to restart the computer.**

After the restart, the backup tool is on your menu system. When you want to run the program, simply choose Start⇨Programs⇨Accessories⇨System Tools⇨Backup.

Configuring Microsoft Backup

Microsoft Backup for Windows 98 and Windows 95 uses floppy drives, network drives, removable drives, and tape drives as the target media when you make a backup. The *target media* is the drive onto which the backup is copied. When you use Microsoft Backup for the first time, you need to create a backup job (a set of instructions to tell Microsoft Backup which files to back up and when they should be backed up). You have three configuration options in a backup job:

- ✔ The folders and files that you want to back up
- ✔ Whether you want to back up all the files you've selected or only those that have changed since the last backup
- ✔ The target media

After you configure the backup options, you can give the backup job a name. For example, if you select a full backup, you might name it *full,* whereas you might name a backup of your My Documents folder *docs.* Thereafter, when you start the backup software, you can select an existing job or create another job with a different configuration.

Backups are not like copies. You can't retrieve the individual files from the target media, because the entire backup is one big file. The backup software makes a catalog that it displays if you need to restore any files. You must select the individual files from the catalog — you won't see the filenames on the media.

For full explanations of backing up and restoring your computer, read *Windows 98 For Dummies, Windows 2000 Professional For Dummies,* or *Microsoft Windows Me For Dummies,* all written by Andy Rathbone and published by IDG Books Worldwide, Inc.

Backing Up Data on Floppy Disks

You can back up your data files to floppy disks. You have a couple of methods to choose from for getting your files on the disks:

- ✔ **Using Microsoft Backup:** You can configure the backup software that's available with Windows 98 and Windows 95 to back up to floppy disks. Just select your floppy drive as the backup target when you're configuring your backup.

- ✔ **Using Send To:** You can copy files to a floppy disk to create a backup. Select all the files that you want to back up and right-click on any file. Choose Send To from the shortcut menu that appears and then choose the floppy drive.

When the disk is filled to capacity, an error message appears to tell you that the disk has no more room on it. Put another formatted, empty floppy disk in the drive, and then click Retry. Keep doing this until all your document files have been copied to floppy disks.

Send To doesn't really *send* the file; it copies it. The original file stays where it was.

Backing Up Data to Removable Drive Cartridges

Removable drives are terrific backup targets! You can use them with Microsoft Backup or with the Send To command (or by clicking your way through the files and folders in Windows Explorer if you like to do things the long way).

You can use a removable drive for backing up, and it doesn't have to be attached to your computer. Remote drives (drives attached to another computer on your network) work just fine.

Using Microsoft Backup with removable drives

Microsoft Backup works beautifully with removable cartridges. If you're using a Jaz drive or another large-capacity drive, you can probably back up everything on your computer. If you're using a Zip drive, you probably have to be more selective about the files you're backing up because you have less space. Make sure that you back up all your data files, and if any room is left after that, you can back up some of your software folders, which is especially useful for software you've configured, tweaked, and manipulated until it's just perfect.

You can do a full backup on a cartridge that's smaller than the amount of hard drive space you're using as long as you have extra cartridges. The backup software tells you when it's time to put another cartridge in the drive.

Using Send To with removable drives

You can use the Send To command that appears when you right-click on a folder or file to copy that folder or file to a removable drive. Oops, you just looked at the Send To choices, and you don't see a removable drive as one of the options? Okay, you're right, it's not on the Send To submenu. Wouldn't it be handy if it were? Well, go ahead and put it there! It's not hard to add a removable drive to the Send To submenu. Just follow these steps:

1. **If the removable drive is on your computer, double-click the My Computer icon. If the drive is on a remote computer, double-click the Network Neighborhood (or My Network Places) icon and then double-click the icon for the computer that holds the drive.**

   The icon for the removable drive appears.

2. **Right-drag the removable drive's icon to the desktop.**

   A menu appears when you release the right mouse button.

3. **Choose Create Shortcut(s) Here from the menu.**

   The shortcut appears on the desktop.

4. **Drag the shortcut to one side of the desktop.**

   This step is important because you need to see the shortcut after you open the SendTo folder window.

5. **Choose Start⇨Run and then type** sendto **in the Open text box.**

6. **Click OK.**

   The SendTo folder appears on your screen.

7. **Left-drag the shortcut from the desktop to the SendTo folder.**

   That's it! The removable drive is on your Send To command list. Cool!

The title under the icon in the SendTo folder is the command that appears on the Send To submenu. If you want to change the title (and therefore the command), click the icon and press F2. Then enter a new name. I like to change the name because I think it's tacky to see *shortcut to Kitchen Jaz* (if that's the name of the shared resource) and prefer to see something like *Remote Jaz Drive* on the menu.

Now you can select folders or groups of files and use the Send To command to copy them (back them up) to the removable drive.

One disk drive, so many users

If you're backing up to a removable drive, you're sharing the drive, not a disk that goes into the drive. You must have a separate disk for each user that backs up to the drive; otherwise, each user's backup process will overwrite the last user's backup.

Put a paper label on each disk to identify the user. You should also have at least two disks for each user. Label one *odd days* and label the other one *even days.* That way, if something goes wrong with the backup, you have the previous, good backup. The ideal is to have seven disks for each user, one for each day, but that's expensive.

Backing up data on tapes

Zip and Jaz drives may be all the rage right now, but the capacity of tapes is usually much larger than any removable drive cartridge. Tape systems vary widely in price, starting at several hundred dollars (up to thousands of dollars for business systems).

You can also use Microsoft Backup to back up to a tape drive if your tape drive is supported by Microsoft Backup. Check the documentation that came with your tape drive.

One disadvantage of using tapes is that they wear out. The edges fray, the tension disappears, and an assortment of other problems can show up. Tapes are not as durable as the cartridges for removable drives. So protect your tapes by keeping them in sealed boxes, away from moisture and direct sunlight.

If you purchase a backup tape system, software comes with it. Not all backup programs perform exactly the same way, so I can't tell you exactly how to configure and use your particular software. But here are some basic guidelines for getting the most out of your tape backup system:

- **Pay attention to the configuration options available in your backup software.** Remember that you're likely to need the tape to restore files if your hard drive dies. Therefore, if the software presents an option to put a copy of the catalog on the tape, select that option. (The *catalog* is the list of folders and files that you backed up.) The catalog on the hard drive dies with the drive. Although the software will recreate the catalog by reading the contents of the tape, the process takes a very long time, so a preloaded catalog on the tape saves time.

- **Always configure the backup software to include the Registry in your backup files**. That way, if you have to restore everything, you also restore the Registry. The *Registry* is a database that keeps track of the configuration options, software, hardware, and other important elements of your Windows system.

- **Verify the backup.** Select the option to verify the backup, which means that the software makes sure that the copy of the file on the tape matches the copy on your hard drive.

- **Clean out the catalogs.** Many backup software programs keep copies of every catalog. These copies take up a lot of hard-drive space, so do some hard-drive housekeeping and get rid of the catalogs that you no longer need. When you record over a previous catalog, you can get rid of the original one.

Backing Up to Remote Computers

One easy way to back up your data files is to use another computer on the network. If your network has two computers, each computer uses the other as the place to store backups. If your network has more than two computers, you can pick one of the other computers. In fact, you can back up your data to every remote computer in a frenzy of cautiousness.

This technique works if you operate on the theory that it is highly unlikely that all the computers on the network could die at the same time. The fact is that a fire, flood, or power surge from lightning could very well destroy every computer on your network. If you use remote computers for backing up, you should also back up on some sort of media, whether it be floppy disks, removable-drive cartridges, or tapes, on a weekly or monthly basis.

Start by creating a folder for yourself on the remote computer. Make it a shared resource and call it *Fred* (unless your name isn't Fred). To find out about creating shared resources, refer to Chapter 7.

After you create a backup folder, perform these steps every day to use Windows Explorer to back up data to a remote computer:

1. **Double-click the Windows Explorer icon on your own computer.**

2. **Right-click on your My Documents folder and choose Copy from the shortcut menu that appears.**

3. **Click the plus sign to expand the Network Neighborhood listing in Windows Explorer and also expand the computer that has your backup folder.**

4. **Right-click on your personal folder and choose Paste from the shortcut menu that appears.**

If you're making another backup on another remote computer for safety's sake (who, me, cautious?), repeat the preceding steps.

Chapter 14

Using Windows Maintenance Tools

● ●

In This Chapter

▶ Checking the condition of your hard drives

▶ Managing hardware

▶ Automating maintenance tasks

● ●

*W*indows has a virtual toolbox built into the operating system. This toolbox features a bunch of handy programs you can use to perform maintenance checkups and even repair some of the problems that may crop up with the computers in your network.

Checking Your Hard Drive for Damage with ScanDisk

ScanDisk is a program that checks the condition of your hard drive, looking for two specific problems:

✔ Damaged sections of the drive

✔ Pieces of files that don't seem to belong anywhere (or the operating system can't figure out where they belong)

If a damaged section is identified, ScanDisk takes files off the damaged section (if possible) and moves them to a good spot on the drive. Then the program marks the damaged section as bad so that the operating system won't use it to store files again.

If pieces of files are found and ScanDisk can't figure out where they belong, the software puts the pieces into files that you can look at to see whether you can identify them. However, usually you can't do anything with them except delete them. Those files are placed in the root folder (right on the hard drive, not in any folder) of your hard drive, and they're named `FILE0000.CHK`, `FILE0001.CHK`, and so on. You could try to read them, but even if they're readable (most of the time they're not text, so you can't decipher them), you can't do anything with them. Just delete them.

Why hard drives develop problems

I bet you're wondering how you get pieces of files floating on your drive. As I explain later in this chapter in the section on using Disk Defragmenter, Windows keeps track of the location of a file on the hard drive every time you save it. The information about file locations appears in the File Allocation Table (FAT).

However, if your computer unexpectedly shuts down while files are open, the operating system has no opportunity to tell the FAT where all the files or parts of files were placed on the hard drive. The data is on the drive, but the FAT doesn't contain any reference for them. This means you may lose parts of any open files, both data and software, because Windows doesn't know where they're located on your drive.

Unexpected shutdowns aren't limited to sudden power failures. If you shut off your computer without going through the Shut Down dialog box, that counts as an unexpected shutdown and can do just as much damage to your file system as a power failure. In fact, after an unexpected shutdown, ScanDisk runs automatically the next time you start your computer.

If you enabled power-management features for your monitor and your screen goes dark while ScanDisk is running, do not press the spacebar or the Enter key to bring the display back. Pressing either of those keys stops ScanDisk (in fact, the safe keys to press are Ctrl or Alt). If you want to watch the ScanDisk progress and your monitor goes dark after the specified amount of time of inactivity, use any key except the spacebar or Enter to bring the monitor back.

Running ScanDisk in Windows 98/Me

In Windows 98 and Windows Me, the ScanDisk tool is on the menu system. In Windows 2000 Professional, it's not (see the following section for details). Here's how to run ScanDisk in Windows 98 and Windows Me:

1. **Choose Start⇨Programs⇨Accessories⇨System Tools⇨ScanDisk.**

   The ScanDisk window opens, as shown in Figure 14-1.

2. **Select the drive you want to check.**

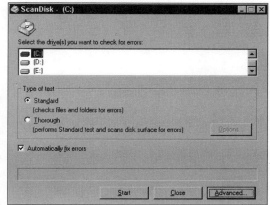

Figure 14-1:
Select the
drive you
want
to check
up on.

3. **Choose one of the following types of tests to run:**

   • **Standard.** This test checks the files and folders on your hard drive.

     Most of the time the Standard test is sufficient, because the files
     and folders are where most system errors are found.

   • **Thorough.** This test examines the surface of your drive, looking for
     physical errors (bad spots).

     This test takes much longer. It isn't necessary to select a Thorough
     test unless you've seen some peculiar behavior, such as messages
     that say there's an error trying to read or write from the drive.

4. **Select the Automatically Fix Errors check box.**

   After all, there's no point in running a test if you don't fix any problems
   that are found. If you don't select this check box, the errors are reported
   to you, and then you have to run ScanDisk again to fix them. Why do
   twice the work?

   If you want to, you can click the Advanced button to see the ScanDisk
   Advanced Options dialog box, shown in Figure 14-2, where you can
   specify the test procedures more precisely.

   There is a slight difference in the choices in this dialog box for Windows Me.
   The second-to-last choice in the right column is Prompt Before Fixing Errors
   on Improper Shutdown. Check Host Drive First is no longer an option.

5. **Click Start.**

   ScanDisk runs, and if your drive is large and has a lot of folders and files,
   ScanDisk may run for quite some time. When the program finishes, it
   issues a report of the results (see Figure 14-3).

6. **Click Close to close the report and then click Close again to close the
   ScanDisk window.**

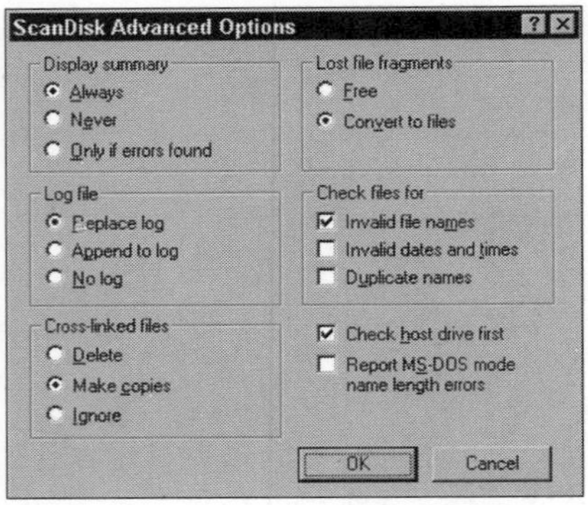

Figure 14-2:
You can
decide for
yourself
what you
want
ScanDisk to
check.

Figure 14-3:
ScanDisk
reports on
its findings.

Running ScanDisk in Windows 2000 Professional

Windows 2000 Professional is a more powerful and protective operating
system, and running ScanDisk isn't the one-two-three-done procedure it is in
Windows 98 and Windows Me. In order to fix file system errors, ScanDisk
locks the drive. But because the drive is in use, it can't be locked. Catch-22!

To get around the problem, if you want to fix errors, ScanDisk offers to run
the next time you start your computer. If you've been seeing errors when you
attempt to open or save files, you should run ScanDisk in its fix-stuff mode
the next time you reboot.

On the other hand, if you just want ScanDisk to check the disk, looking for
bad sectors (and marking them as bad so files aren't saved there), you can
perform that task without rebooting. You should be aware that this process is
much more thorough than it is in Windows 98 or Windows Me, and takes
quite a bit of time. You may want to start the process at the end of the day.
The report will be waiting for you when you go back to the computer.

To run ScanDisk in Windows 2000 Professional, follow these steps:

1. **Open My Computer.**

   The My Computer window opens, displaying the drives on your computer.

2. **Right-click on the icon for the drive you want to check and choose Properties from the shortcut menu that appears.**

3. **Click the Tools tab of the Properties dialog box.**

4. **Click the Check Now button in the Error-Checking section of the dialog box.**

   The Check Disk dialog box opens, displaying options for checking the drive.

5. **Select the Scan For and Attempt Recovery of Bad Sectors option, or the Automatically Fix File System Errors option, or both (depending on what you think is necessary).**

6. **Click Start.**

   If you selected only the option to check the bad sectors, ScanDisk begins checking the disk. Now would be a good time to have lunch, clean the bathroom, or take a nap. The process takes many minutes. The larger your drive, the longer it takes. On my system, a 2GB drive that's half filled took about 20 minutes.

   If you selected the option to fix file system errors, ScanDisk displays an error message telling you that it cannot fix errors because the drive is in use. The program then offers to run ScanDisk the next time the system boots. Click OK. If you want, you can shut down your computer immediately to get the task moving.

Defragging Your Hard Drive

Disk Defragmenter is a program that takes fragments of files and puts them together so that every file on your drive has its entire contents in the same place. This makes opening files a faster process.

Before I discuss the Disk Defragmenter tool, it's important to understand a piece of jargon. Nobody who is hip (well, as hip as a computer geek can be) uses the term *Disk Defragmenter*. In fact, nobody uses the terms *fragmented* or *defragmented*. Instead, when your disk is *fragged*, you "run the *defragger* to *defrag*" it. If you're not already a tech geek, at least now you can talk like one.

Files get fragmented (oops, I meant fragged) as a matter of course; the fragging (there — I've redeemed myself) isn't caused by anything you do or any problem with your computer. The more a drive fills up with files, the more likely it is to become fragged.

Dealing with physical hard-drive problems

If there's a physical problem with your hard drive, you'll probably see one of these messages (substitute the letter of your hard drive for X):

- Serious Disk Error Writing Drive X
- Data Error Reading Drive X
- Error Reading Drive X
- I/O Error
- Seek Error — Sector not found

If you get any of these error messages, your hard drive may have a serious health problem that could even be fatal.

Perform a backup immediately, as explained in Chapter 13 (although there may be some files that cannot be read from the drive and won't be backed up). If the backup doesn't work without producing error messages, manually back up as many important data files as you can.

Then take your computer to a computer store to see whether your hard drive can be fixed or you need to buy a new drive.

Why hard drives get fragged

After you've used your computer for a while, your hard drive starts to fill up. One day, you launch your word processor and open a document that's on your hard drive. That document is 50,000 bytes in size. You add more text to the document, and when you save the document, it's 75,000 bytes. The particular section of the drive where the file was originally stored has room for 50,000 bytes, so the operating system puts 50,000 bytes of your new version back where it was and finds another spot on the drive to lay down the remaining 25,000 bytes.

The sequence of events that takes place goes a little something like this:

1. Windows makes a note about that file, and the note says something like, "I stuck the first 50K here and put the next 25K there." The note isn't a note, though; it's an entry in a part of the operating system that's called the *File Allocation Table,* which acts like an index or a table of contents. It's from that component that we get the acronym FAT (which is not meant as an insult) for the file system used in Windows.

2. The operating system fetches all those fragments, in the right order, after checking the FAT to see where the pieces of the file are.

3. Because you're never satisfied, you feel compelled to add even more information to the file. When you're finally satisfied (at least for the moment), you resave the file.

4. The operating system puts the first two sections back where they were and then finds another spot for the additional bytes needed for your additions and changes.

5. The next time you open the file to add to it or make other changes, more sections of the disk are used to hold the pieces of the file (When will you ever be finished?), and the various file fragments must be fetched from more and more separate locations.

   This process continues for as long as you keep making changes. (Won't you just give it up, already?) In fact, this is the standard process that occurs with files you create and save in all your other software programs.

So, you're saying to yourself, "Big deal. As long as my computer knows where to get all these fragments so I can obsessively re-edit and add to my documents, what do I care how the process works?" Well, after a while, your system slows down as a result of all this searching and piecing file fragments together. You may notice that loading and saving documents takes a lot *longer*. That's because your operating system must do all this legwork to fetch and lay down the file parts.

Eventually, you need to tell the operating system to pick up all the parts and put them together, making all the parts of every file contiguous. This is what the Disk Defragmenter does. Read on to find out how to use this tool.

If you're using Windows 2000 Professional and chose to install the NTFS file system instead of the FAT file system, you don't have a FAT — you have a MFT (Master File Table). Also, your drive doesn't frag as quickly as it would with FAT, because NTFS is a much more efficient file system. However, you still need to run the defragger occasionally.

How to defrag your drive

The Disk Defragmenter juggles file parts, holding some in memory while it finds room for them and moving some stuff on the drive out of the way to make room for the stuff in memory. Although the process may seem tedious (how would you like to search out and find every piece of data that creates a whole document?), the process is pretty pain-free. Follow these steps to defrag your drive:

1. **Choose Start⇨Programs⇨Accessories⇨System Tools⇨Disk Defragmenter.**

   The Select Drive dialog box opens.

2. **Select the drive you want to defrag (usually C). Then click OK.**

   In Windows 98 and Windows Me, the program begins defragging the drive immediately. In Windows 95, the program checks the current state of the drive, and if the drive isn't badly fragmented, a message appears telling you that the drive doesn't really need defragging. You can opt to run the program anyway, if you want to. In Windows 2000 Professional, the program window offers a button named Analyze, which you can click to display a report on the level of fragmentation to help you decide whether to defrag the drive.

During the defragging process, the program displays a progress report so that you can see how much work remains to be done.

3. **Click the Show Details button to see a full-color representation of your hard drive and its fragmented files.**

You can watch the pieces of files being put together as the defragging proceeds.

Here are a few points about the defragging process:

- Technically, you can do work on your computer during the defragging operations, but things go very slowly (because the computer and the hard drive are very busy), and the defragmenter program itself is slowed by your actions. Go grab a bowl of cereal and watch a few commercials instead.

- If you absolutely must perform some task at the computer during this procedure, click the Pause button in the Disk Defragmenter dialog box. After you finish your work, click Resume. You can also click Stop to end the process.

- If you pause or stop the Disk Defragmenter, the response isn't immediate. The program finishes the file it's currently working on and updates the FAT information. Then it responds to your selection.

A message lets you know when the defragging is complete. After the defragging, you should notice a much peppier response when you load or save files. Of course, you're going to continue to open and save files, so the fragging starts all over again; eventually your system will slow down, and you'll have to defrag again.

Managing Devices with the Device Manager

The Windows Device Manager is a powerful tool. You can use it to view all sorts of information about the hardware in your computer. You can also use it to make changes to the way hardware is configured or the way it behaves.

To use the Device Manager in Windows 98 and Windows Me, right-click on the My Computer icon and choose Properties from the shortcut menu that appears. When the System Properties dialog box opens, click the Device Manager tab. All the hardware categories that exist in your computer are displayed, as shown in Figure 14-4.

Figure 14-4:
The list of devices for your computer may differ, depending on the hardware you have.

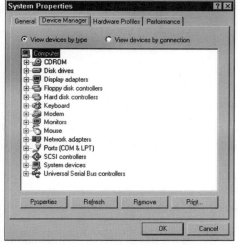

In Windows 2000 Professional, open the Device Manager by right-clicking on My Computer and choosing Properties. Move to the Hardware tab and click the Device Manager button. The Device Manager window is a Microsoft Management Console (MMC), but the device listings look very much like Figure 14-4.

The following few sections describe what you can do with the information in the device listings.

Viewing a specific device

The first list that appears when you open the Device Manger window is a list of hardware types, not the actual hardware that's installed in your computer. Click the plus sign to the left of a device type to see the actual hardware that's installed on your system. You usually see an exact description, sometimes including a brand name and model.

Select the specific device and click Properties to see information about the device and the way it's configured. The information in the Properties dialog box differs according to the type of device you're examining.

You can change the configuration for some devices right in the Properties dialog box. Just select the setting that needs to be changed and enter a new setting.

Managing device problems

If any device is experiencing a problem, the specific device listing appears when you first open the Device Manager window, because Windows expands the device type listing to show you the problematic device. An icon appears in the listing, indicating the type of problem. The icon may be a red *X,* which means Windows can't find or communicate with the device; or a yellow exclamation point, which means Windows has a problem with the settings for the device.

Select the device and choose Properties to see a message explaining the problem. Sometimes, the problem isn't so serious, and the device continues to operate. Other times, you may have to reinstall or reconfigure the device. The Properties dialog box usually provides enough information to guide you to a resolution.

Printing a report about devices

It's a good idea to have a list of all the devices in your system and the resources they use. I've found that such a list is handy in a couple of situations:

- ✔ If you have to reinstall everything when you replace a hard drive, all the configuration information for each device is available in your list.

- ✔ If you want to install additional devices, you know which resources on your computer are available by viewing your list.

To print a report on all the devices in your system, click the Print button in the Device Manager dialog box. Select the option to print a summary, unless you want to use up a whole ream of paper.

Determining Who's On Your Computer

Net Watcher is a handy tool that you can use to keep an eye on visitors — that is, those users working on other computers on the network who are accessing your computer. Net Watcher gives you all kinds of who, what, and where information.

To open Net Watcher, choose Start⇨Programs⇨Accessories⇨System Tools⇨Net Watcher. The window that opens displays a list of visitors, if any other users are accessing your computer (see Figure 14-5).

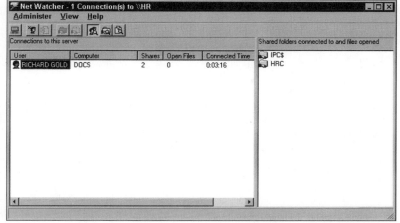

Figure 14-5:
Keep an eye
on users
who access
files on your
computer.

By default, the window displays a User view, which provides the following information about each visitor:

- ✔ The user name
- ✔ The name of the remote computer
- ✔ The number of shares in use
- ✔ The number of open files
- ✔ The length of time the visitor has been connected to your computer

You can select a specific user and see which shared folder that user is accessing (the information appears in the right pane of the Net Watcher window).

The Shared Folders view (choose View⇨Shared Folders) displays all the shared folders on your computer. You can double-click any folder to see the name of the user accessing the folder. This view is not named correctly because it not only displays shared folders, but it also lists all the shared resources on your computer (printers, removable drives, and so on).

The Show Files view (choose View⇨By Open Files) lists all the open files in use by visitors. Incidentally, only software program files are tracked, not data files. In addition to the name of each open file, the name of its shared folder is listed, as are the name of the remote user and the type of access (Read-only or Full).

In addition to viewing all this information, you can perform a number of tasks in the Net Watcher window, including the following:

- ✔ Close a file that somebody's using.
- ✔ Add a new shared folder to your computer.

✔ Stop sharing a folder that's currently shared.

✔ Change the properties of a shared folder (such as passwords and access options).

✔ Disconnect a user.

Some of these options sound like dirty tricks — I mean, after all, disconnecting a user? But if you think of Net Watcher as a security measure, you'll understand why this tool can be important. Suppose that your son and his friend are using a computer and decide to open the family budget or personal letters. If you use Net Watcher, and as a result, discover that remote users are accessing files and folders you'd prefer to keep private, you can adjust the way you configured your shared resources.

Cleaning Up Files with Disk Cleanup

Using the Disk Cleanup tool is like bringing in a housekeeper to clean up all that junk you never use — the stuff that's been lying around taking up space.

In your house, that stuff could be old magazines, newspapers, or clothing you haven't been able to fit into for years. On your computer, that stuff is files you don't use and probably don't even realize are stored on your drive. Those are the files that Disk Cleanup looks for and offers to sweep out.

Follow these steps to run the Disk Cleanup program:

1. **Choose Start➪Programs➪Accessories➪System Tools➪Disk Cleanup. Then choose the drive you want to clean.**

   Alternatively, you can double-click the My Computer icon and right-click on the drive you want to clean. Choose Properties from the shortcut menu that appears and click the Disk Cleanup button on the General tab of the Properties dialog box.

   The Disk Cleanup dialog box opens, as shown in Figure 14-6. File types that are candidates for safe removal are already selected.

2. **Scroll through the list of file types in the Files to Delete list box and select any additional file types you want to remove. (Click each file-type listing to see more information in the Description box.)**

   You should add the Old ScanDisk Files in the Root Folder file type to the list. These are the files I discuss in the section on ScanDisk, earlier in this chapter. These files contain lost data, but you can't do anything with them.

   The last item in the Files to Delete list box is Non Critical Files. If you select this file type, the cleanup is not automatic. Instead, the files are displayed so that you can decide which of them you want to delete.

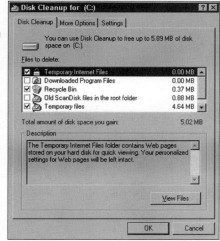

Figure 14-6:
Files that
seem
safe to
remove are
preselected,
and you can
select
additional
file types if
you want to
clean more
aggressively.

3. **When you're ready to clean out all this stuff, click OK.**

   Disk Cleanup asks if you're sure you want to delete these files.

4. **Click Yes to proceed, or click No if you suddenly panic.**

Working with System Information

The System Information tool (available only in Windows 98 and Windows Me) is misnamed, because it's not a tool — it's an entire toolbox. It starts off look- ing like a nifty, handy-dandy tool, but then you discover a menu item named Tools that leads you to more cool tools. In this section, I cover the System Information tool (*SI* for short) and then follow up with sections for some of the embedded tools in its toolbox.

The primary focus of SI is to gather information and diagnose problems. Just choose Start➪Programs➪Accessories➪System Tools➪System Information.

SI for Windows 98 is slightly different than SI for Windows Me. Figure 14-7 shows the SI window in Windows 98, and Figure 14-8 shows the SI window in Windows Me.

The differences between the two versions aren't terribly important in the ultimate scheme of things (a fancy way of saying that the job gets done in both versions). The Windows 98 version is missing the Applications category, which lists all the programs you've installed. The Windows Me version runs as part of the Help system. That means that after you select System Information from the menu, you have time to brew a pot of coffee, mow the lawn, or take a short nap. If they ever award a prize called "the most annoyingly slow to load component in the history of computers," the Windows Me Help system will win, hands down! All the fancy Web-like, graphical (and therefore, slow) components in the Help system are less important to me than getting information quickly, but on the other hand, whenever I need to open the Help files, I know I have time to leave the computer and take care of some household task.

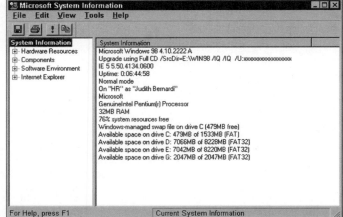

Figure 14-7:
Windows 98 system information.

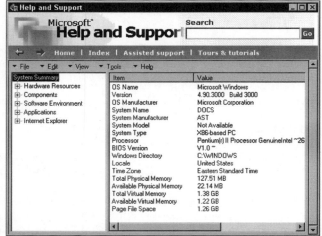

Figure 14-8:
Windows Me system information.

General System Information

Selecting the System Information category in the left pane displays general information about your computer in the right pane. You can't do anything with this information — it's purely informative.

Hardware Resources

Click the plus sign to the left of the Hardware Resources category and select a subcategory to view information in the right pane. Here are the subcategories for Hardware Resources:

- ✔ **Conflicts/Sharing.** This subcategory lists any resource conflicts. It also identifies resources that are being shared by Peripheral Component Interconnect (PCI) devices. This information can be helpful when you're trying to discover whether a hardware conflict is to blame for a device problem.

- ✔ **Forced Hardware.** Select this subcategory to see a list of devices that have user-specified resources instead of resources assigned by the system. Sometimes this information is helpful when you're having trouble installing a Plug and Play device that should have been easy to install.

- ✔ **I/O.** Selecting this subcategory produces a list of all the I/O addresses (parts of memory assigned to a device) currently in use. The devices that occupy each address range are also displayed. You can use this information to avoid the occupied addresses when you're configuring a new device.

- ✔ **IRQs.** Select this subcategory to see a display of the IRQs in use, along with the devices that are using each IRQ. (An IRQ is a channel of communication that a device occupies.) This subcategory also contains a list of unused IRQs, which is handy when you're configuring a new device.

- ✔ **Memory.** This subcategory displays a list of memory address ranges being used by devices. Most of the time this information is used when you're troubleshooting a device, especially if you call the manufacturer's customer support line. Support technicians often ask for this information.

Components

The Components category contains all sorts of information about your computer's configuration, including information about the status of device drivers as well as a history of all the drivers you've installed (it's not unusual to upgrade drivers when they become available from manufacturers or from Microsoft). Information about components in your system is available, including all sorts of highly technical data about memory addresses. Most of the time the data is incomprehensible, but if you're on the telephone with a support person, this technical mumbo-jumbo may be significant. This category also contains a summary of devices that the System Information tool suspects are not working properly.

Table 14-1 lists descriptions of the subcategories in the Components list.

You can change the view in the right pane in order to change the level of information. The choices are Basic Information, Advanced Information, or History (for device drivers).

Table 14-1	Components Category Descriptions
Subcategory	*Information Provided*
Multimedia	Lists installed sound cards and joysticks. Other subcategories provide specific information about audio, video, and CD-ROM configuration.
Display	Informs you about your video card and monitor.
Infrared	Provides information about infrared devices you've installed.
Input	Tells you about your keyboard and mouse.
Miscellaneous	Gives information about printers you've installed (both local and network), as well as about a potpourri of other devices.
Modems	Provides information about your modem.
Network	Offers information about network adapters and client services and protocols you've installed.
Ports	Gives you information about serial and parallel ports in your computer.
Storage	Tells you all about your hard drive(s), floppy drive(s), and removable media.
Printing	Tells you which printers and printer drivers (including drivers for printers on other computers) are installed on the computer.
Problem devices	Gives you the status of devices that have problems.
USB	Tells you about the Universal Serial Bus (also known as Plug and Play) controllers installed.
History	Gives you the history of all the drivers that have been installed on the computer, including updates and changes. Use this subcategory to see all the changes you've made to the system if something goes wrong.
System	Tells you all about the Basic Input/Output System (also called the BIOS), motherboard, and other key built-in devices.

Software Environment

The Software Environment category covers information about the software that's loaded in your computer's memory. Included are drivers, software programs, tasks that are currently running, and all sorts of technical data that's hard to understand. However, the information can be useful to support desk personnel if you're calling for help.

Internet Explorer

The Internet Explorer category displays information about the version, the temporary files, and security settings.

Saving system information to a file

You can save all the information that the SI tool provides in a file and then use that file as a reference when you configure new devices or call a support desk. To send the data to a file, choose File⇨Export from the System Information menu bar. A Save As dialog box opens so you can name the file and select the folder in which to save it. The file is a text file, so you can open it and print it in WordPad (it's usually too large to use Notepad).

Checking Windows 98 system files

Windows 98 provides a tool called the System File Checker that you can use to, well, check your system files. *System files* are the files that Windows 98 installs to make the operating system run. All the files for all the Windows components you install are transferred to your hard drive during the installation process. Most of the files end up in the Windows folder or one of the subfolders under the Windows folder.

Sometimes a system file gets corrupted or disappears. The System File Checker verifies the files on your hard drive, and if any of them are corrupt or missing, they're replaced from the original Windows 98 CD.

Incidentally, if a system file disappears, you can bet that it wasn't an accident, and somebody probably deleted it. It's very dangerous to open Windows Explorer and delete files from the Windows folder or one of the subfolders.

Windows Me does a better job of protecting system files, but if one of those files is corrupt or missing, the operating system has an automated process for fixing stuff.

Follow these steps to run the System File Checker from the SI window in Windows 98:

1. **Choose Tools⇨System File Checker from the SI menu bar.**

   When the System File Checker dialog box opens, the Scan for Altered Files option is already selected, as shown in Figure 14-9.

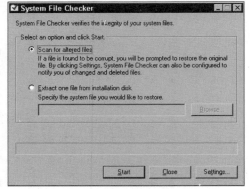

Figure 14-9:
The System File Checker determines whether any system files are having a problem.

2. **Click Start to have the System File Checker go through your hard drive(s) and check all the Windows system files.**

   The process takes a couple of minutes.

   If any files have been altered, you're prompted to restore the original file from the Windows CD (or the Windows 98 files folder if your computer came with the operating system preinstalled).

   If you're a control freak, you may want to click the Settings button so that you can configure the way the System File Checker works. The available options are self-explanatory, and if you're not sure about an option, you can right-click on it and get information from the What's This dialog box that opens.

If you're very comfortable with computers and operating systems, you can click the Tools menu item on the SI window in either Windows 98 or Windows Me, and run any of the tools listed on the drop-down menu. Some of these tools are complicated, dangerous, or both.

Automating Maintenance Tasks

Available only in Windows 98 and Windows Me, the Maintenance Wizard is a nifty way to make sure that important maintenance tasks are performed regularly and automatically. In addition, you can schedule these chores so they take place at times that won't interfere with your work.

To open the Maintenance Wizard, choose Start⇨Programs⇨Accessories⇨ System Tools⇨Maintenance Wizard. Each wizard window presents a question to answer or an option to select. Click Next to move through the wizard's windows.

If your computer isn't running the FAT32 file system, every time you open this program you're asked if you'd like to convert to FAT32. You probably should — it's a more efficient file system than FAT16. Basic operating system configuration is beyond the scope of this book, but you can find out more about file systems in *Windows 98 For Dummies* and *Microsoft Windows Me Millennium Edition For Dummies,* both written by Andy Rathbone and published by IDG Books Worldwide, Inc.

The opening window of the Maintenance Wizard offers these two configuration options:

- ✔ **Express,** which automatically configures the wizard for the most common maintenance settings
- ✔ **Custom,** which allows you to select your own settings

The common maintenance settings differ according to the software and Windows features you've installed in your system. However, the following programs usually run:

- ✔ ScanDisk
- ✔ Disk Cleanup
- ✔ Disk Defragmenter

The following sections explain the Express and Custom setup options in more detail.

Doing an Express setup

With the Express setup option, you schedule the three maintenance programs listed in the preceding list. You also choose the time at which the Maintenance Wizard performs its tasks. The Maintenance Wizard usually takes about three hours to complete its tasks, and the computer must be running. The schedule options are as follows:

- ✔ **Nights — Midnight to 3:00 AM,** which is convenient because it probably won't interfere with your work

✔ **Days — Noon to 3:00 PM,** which is handy for households with folks who work or go to school during the day

✔ **Evenings — 8:00 PM to 11:00 PM,** which may be convenient if the members of your household don't work at the computers after dinner.

Click Next to see a summary of the wizard's plans (see Figure 14-10). If you want, you can instruct the wizard to run all the tasks now and then follow your schedule in the future. (Only run the tasks now if you know you don't want to use the computer for a few hours, and nobody else on the network needs the computer.)

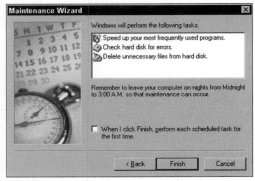

Figure 14-10:
The wizard
presents
the results
of your con-
figuration.

Doing a Custom setup

With the Custom option, you can specify a day and time for each individual task, rather than run all of them back-to-back.

After you select the Custom option in the first window of the Maintenance Wizard, follow these steps:

1. **In the Select a Maintenance Schedule Wizard window, select a schedule option and then click Next.**

   Select the Custom option if you're planning to create a schedule that differs from the available schedules.

   The wizard shows you a list of programs that runs every time you start Windows.

2. **Deselect any program that you want to remove from the startup list.**

   Removing a program makes booting your computer a faster process.

If you run Quicken, you'll probably see Billminder in this list. Quicken doesn't put Billminder in the Startup folder of the Programs menu, where you could easily remove it. Instead, the Quicken programmers use a hidden (okay, I call it *sneaky*) method to start Billminder every time you start your computer. Most Quicken users don't care if the Billminder feature isn't operating and wouldn't notice if it disappeared. The Billminder program takes up memory, and it does not have to be running all the time — Quicken does everything you need it to do without wasting precious memory and computer resources on this feature. Take this opportunity to kill it.

3. **In the following windows, the wizard presents each of the maintenance programs individually, so you can decide whether you want to run the program and when. In each window, do one of the following and then click Next:**

 • Click No if you don't want to run the program automatically (you can run all of these programs manually, as described earlier in this chapter).

 • Click Yes if you do want to run a program and then click the Reschedule button to create your own schedule for it.

 Figure 14-11 shows a custom schedule for ScanDisk.

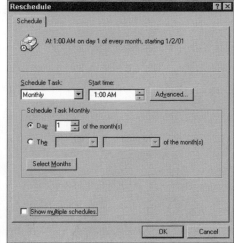

Figure 14-11:
You can schedule each maintenance program individually.

Each schedule interval (monthly, weekly, and so on) has its own options for fine-tuning the schedule.

You can also develop multiple schedules for any maintenance tool. For example, you may want to schedule a program to run monthly every three months at 3:00 a.m. and then also run it at 1:00 a.m. every week on a Friday. Actually, I've never found a good reason to develop multiple schedules for any of these utilities, but the option exists, so I'm mentioning it.

When you're finished scheduling tasks, a window appears, summarizing the tasks that you've scheduled.

4. Click Finish to complete the wizard.

The Maintenance Wizard is a good way to make sure that health checkups are performed regularly. Being able to run these programs in the middle of the night is a definite advantage. After all, even if you aren't planning to use your computer for a couple of hours in order to run maintenance programs, you're running a network — which means that other users on other computers may need to get into your computer.

Part V
The Part of Tens

The 5th Wave   By Rich Tennant

"Oddly enough, it came with a PCI bus slot."

In this part . . .

The Part of Tens is a tradition in the *For Dummies* series. In this book, it's also a breath of fresh air and a release from the other chapters, which put you through technical twists and turns, forcing you to concentrate on minutiae and geeky details. In this part, you discover ten fun things that you can do on your network, as well as find out ways to keep the Internet safe for children.

Chapter 15

Ten Fun Things to Do on Your Network

. . . .

In This Chapter

▶ Playing a game across the network

▶ Setting up message centers, bulletin boards, and other "communications-central" features

▶ Creating central locations for data that everyone uses

. . . .

*B*elieve it or not, a networked computer system isn't just about connections, cables, and user profiles. After all that setup stuff is finished, there are a zillion handy reasons for having a home network. Well, perhaps "zillion" is an exaggeration, but it isn't hard to think of ten things, and here they are.

Play Hearts

In my house, we play Hearts across the network for lots of really excellent reasons:

- ✔ We don't have to search the house for a deck of cards.
- ✔ We don't have to clean off the kitchen table to make room for playing cards.
- ✔ We don't argue about whose turn it is to keep score.
- ✔ We don't have to search for a pencil and paper to keep score.
- ✔ We don't argue about the score because computers don't make math errors.
- ✔ We don't have to argue about who should put the cards away.

People who stop by while we're playing get a kick of out us — you can hear the "gotcha" yells from different rooms in the house. This ritual seems strange to visitors, but we think of it as normal.

Hearts is built in to Windows 95, 98, and Me, and you can play it alone or with other players on the network. In fact, the game is built for network use. Its proper name is The Microsoft Hearts Network (check the title bar of the game's window). Up to four people can play Hearts across the network. If fewer than four human, breathing, players are available on the network, the computer provides the missing participants.

Even if you play the game alone (with the computer representing all the other players), the first time you open Hearts after a reboot, there's a delay before the game appears while the program searches the network to see if anyone else is currently playing the game.

Windows 2000 Professional doesn't come with Hearts (after all, it's built from the ground up for business users), and although you can install a copy on a Windows 2000 computer, it's a single-player game — it won't find the other players on a network. If you're running a Windows 2000 Professional computer on your network and you want to play Hearts by yourself, you need to copy two files from a computer that's running Windows 95, 98, or Me: Mshearts.exe and Cards.dll. Make sure that you put both files in the same folder.

You can open Hearts by choosing Start⇨Programs⇨Accessories⇨Games⇨ Hearts. But that's far too many steps for my taste, so I suggest creating a shortcut to it. To do so, position your mouse pointer on the Hearts listing and right-drag the listing to the desktop. Then choose Create Shortcut(s) Here from the menu that appears. For even quicker access, you can drag the shortcut to the Quick Launch bar rather than the desktop.

Follow these steps to play Hearts across the network:

1. **Open Hearts and select the I Want to Be Dealer option, as shown in Figure 15-1.**

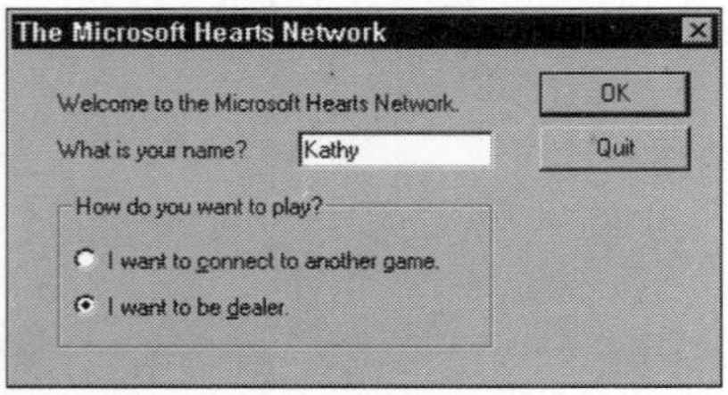

Figure 15-1:
First up?
You're the
dealer.

> **The Microsoft Hearts Network**
>
> Welcome to the Microsoft Hearts Network.
> What is your name? | Kathy
>
> OK
> Quit
>
> How do you want to play?
> ○ I want to connect to another game.
> ● I want to be dealer.

Windows automatically fills in the name that was entered when the operating system was first installed on the computer.

2. **Enter a different name, if you want. Then click OK.**

Along the bottom of the Hearts window, you can see a message that Hearts is waiting for others to join the game.

3. **If you're playing against the computer because nobody else is on the network, or nobody else on the network wants to play, press F2 to begin playing alone.**

4. **If someone else wants to play the game, have that person choose the I Want to Connect to Another Game option and click OK.**

5. **Enter the name of the computer that the dealer is using in the Locate Dealer dialog box. Then click OK.**

   The Hearts window opens, displaying a message at the bottom that everyone is waiting for the dealer to start the game — that's you!

If you don't like the names the computer chooses for the non-human players (or if a computer name duplicates a human player's name), you can change them. Choose Game➪Options and enter names you like better.

Set Up a Message Center

A computer-based household message center is a place to leave notes for other members of the family. This type of message center is much more efficient than the old system of hand-scrawled notes left on the blackboard in the kitchen, or the less-organized system of dashing off incomplete words and phone numbers on the back of an envelope with your youngest child's crayon. With a message center, you're less likely to run out of room when you take a message for your family members (especially from your teenage daughter's friend, Mindy, who just, like, got back from the mall and can't wait to talk about her, like, new shoes), and even more important, no one has to try to decipher your chicken-scratch handwriting.

Creating a shared folder for the message center

Choose one computer to serve as the message center, and then follow these steps to set up a shared folder on it:

1. **In Windows 95 or 98, choose Start➪Programs➪Windows Explorer; in Windows Me and Windows 2000 Professional, choose Start➪Programs➪Accessories➪Windows Explorer.**

   Windows Explorer opens. In Windows 98, drive C is expanded and selected. In Windows Me and Windows 2000 Professional, click the plus sign next to the My Computer listing and then select drive C.

2. **Choose File⇨New⇨Folder.**

   A new folder appears in the right pane. The name *New Folder* is high-lighted, which means the name is in edit mode. As soon as you press any key, the characters you type replace the name.

3. **Name the folder.**

   Naming the folder *Messages* seems like a good idea.

4. **Right-click on the new folder and choose Sharing from the shortcut menu that appears.**

   The Sharing tab of the Message Properties dialog box appears, as shown in Figure 15-2.

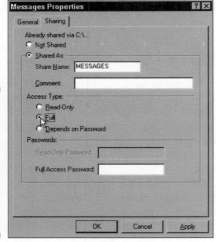

Figure 15-2: Windows automatically names the share *MESSAGES,* which seems appropriate.

5. **Select the Shared As option and configure the share for Full access.**

   Don't password-protect the share.

6. **Click OK.**

   Now the share is visible when network users open Network Neighborhood (or My Network Places) and double-click the computer you used to create the message center (see Figure 15-3).

Creating individual message boards

After you create the Messages folder, you're ready to create the individual message board files for every member of your family. The best way to create a message center file is to take advantage of a nifty feature that's available in Notepad. Notepad can create a date and time stamp on every entry that's put into a file. Here's how to set up this electronic wizardry:

1. **On the message center computer, choose Start⇨Programs⇨Accessories⇨ Notepad.**

   The Notepad window opens.

2. **Type** .LOG **and press Enter.**

   Make sure that the period is the first character on the line and that you use capital letters for the word LOG. And no spaces please.

3. **Choose File⇨Save.**

   The Save As dialog box appears.

4. **Save the file in the Messages folder, using your name as the filename.**

   Use the arrow to the right of the Save In box (at the top of the dialog box) to navigate to the Messages folder. In the File Name box, enter your first name or nickname — Windows automatically adds the extension .txt to the filename. Then click Save.

   The title bar of the Notepad window shows the filename, which is Yourname.txt (of course, your *real* name is on the title bar, not *Yourname*).

5. **Choose File⇨Save As and then save the file under another user name.**

   You're creating the same file for another user in your household. Repeat this step for every household member.

6. **When you're finished creating files, exit Notepad.**

Figure 15-3: Shared folders automatically appear in Network Neighborhood and My Network Places.

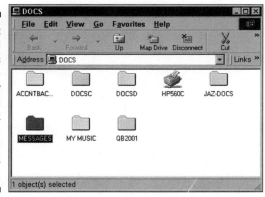

Now the message center (the Messages folder on the message center computer) contains an electronic message board for every user on your network. Everyone on the network can open other users' files in order to leave messages. And every time you open one of those messages, a time stamp appears.

Testing the message boards

The files you created in the preceding section are designed to work as message centers, noting the date and time of each entry. Make sure that the time-stamp feature is working by opening one of the files. Here's how:

1. **On the message center computer, open Windows Explorer and select the Messages folder in the left pane.**

2. **In the right pane, double-click a message board file.**

   The file opens in the Notepad window. The current date and time is preentered, and your cursor is waiting for input on the next line, as shown in Figure 15-4.

Figure 15-4:
Is this time-stamp feature cool, or what?

If you don't see a time stamp, you made an error when you entered the original text. Make sure that no characters, not even a space, appear in front of or after the text .LOG. Also make sure you entered a period, not a comma (a common error). Make corrections, save the file, and open it again to test it.

Tricks and tips for using the message center

After you have the message center in place, here are some tips for getting the most out of it:

✔ **Leave a blank line at the end of messages.** After you type a message in a user's file, be sure to press the Enter key to force a blank line to appear before the next automatic time stamp. The blank line makes it easier to separate the individual notes in the file.

✔ **If you don't want to save a message, close Notepad and click No when prompted.** If you open another user's file and change your mind about leaving a message (perhaps you opened the wrong file, or perhaps you just changed your mind), close Notepad and click No when Windows asks if you want to save the changes you made to the file. If you click Yes, the time stamp remains in the file with no message below it. This will drive the user nuts.

✔ **Use the file to write notes to yourself.** Most of the time, you'll open your message board file just to read the text, not to add text. You can, of course, use the file to write notes to yourself, perhaps entering reminders about tasks or appointments. However, don't enter any information you don't want others to see.

✔ **Clean out old messages to keep message files as small as possible.** You can delete each message as you read it, save some messages for future reference and delete others, or save all the messages forever. However, if the file grows too large for Notepad, when you double-click your file, Windows offers to open it in WordPad instead. WordPad doesn't support the time stamp feature. *Note:* The Windows 2000 Professional version of Notepad has no size limit.

✔ **Delete the time stamp that was automatically added when you opened the file.** Before you save and close your message file, after you've deleted the messages you don't need to keep, remember to delete the time stamp that was automatically inserted when you opened the file.

Keep a Family Shopping List

Many families keep a shopping list on a blackboard, usually in the kitchen, and everybody in the family adds items to the list. Personally, I don't see the point. Does the person who is heading for the store take the blackboard down and carry it to the store? If not, then the person who's heading for the store has to get a pen and paper and write down everything that's on the blackboard. Hello? Sorry, I'm too lazy for this scheme (and I'm usually the person heading for the store).

The next best plan is to keep a pad and pen (or pencil, if you have one — I haven't seen a pencil in my house since my kids got out of elementary school) in a central location, like the kitchen. Everybody can add items to the shopping list, and the person (Dad?) who next heads for the store just takes the list with him. Much better, wouldn't you say? Except, in my house, people "borrow" the pad, which always involves moving it to another room. Even more frequently, people take the pen. In fact, putting a cluster of pens next to the pad doesn't work; it's only a matter of a few days before those pens are all in pocketbooks, pockets, and other rooms.

The best place for a family shopping list is in a document on a computer. This list is easy to use and easy to print. Nobody can put the computer in his pocket (or in her pocketbook) and walk away with it, so the list is always available.

Creating the shopping list

In order to create a shopping list, follow these steps:

1. **Choose a computer to hold the shopping list.**

2. **Create a folder on that computer to hold the shopping list file and then share that folder.**

    Use the steps outlined in the "Creating a shared folder for the message center" section, earlier in this chapter, to create and share the folder.

    If you also set up a family message center, as described earlier in the chapter, you can use that same folder for your shopping list. (It's not necessary to create a time-stamp document for a shopping list.)

3. **Have all the users create shortcuts to the folder on their own desktops.**

    Refer to the "Creating a shared folder for the message center" section for information on how to create shortcuts.

4. **Use the computer that holds the shared folder to create the shopping list file: Open the software, enter the first item on the list, and save the file in the shared folder. You can name the file *Shopping List* or choose something more clever or creative.**

    You can create the file in any software that is available to everyone on the network. Notepad and WordPad come installed on every Windows computer, so either one of those programs will do. If everybody uses the same word processor, you can also use that software.

Using the shopping list

Any person in the household who wants to add an item to the shopping list can open the shortcut to the shared folder, double-click the file to open it, and add athlete's foot cream, zit zapper, prune juice, or another desperately needed item. Be sure that everyone knows to save the file. Easy, huh?

Hold all my calls! Gaining easy access to the message center

I'm sure everyone in your family gets a lot of phone calls, and I'm sure everyone agrees that the easiest way to do something is the best. That's why you should create a shortcut to the message center for each user on the network. That way, when the phone rings, you don't have to go through the whole folder hierarchy just to find the message center folder.

To create a shortcut, follow these steps:

1. **Locate the message center folder and right-click on it.**

2. **Choose Create Shortcut from the menu that appears.**

   Windows opens a message box that says you cannot create a shortcut here, and offers to create the shortcut on your desktop.

3. **Click Yes to create a shortcut on your desktop.**

For even quicker access to the message center (when you're working in software, you can't always see the desktop), drag the shortcut to the Quick Launch bar, or drag it to the Start button to put the shortcut at the top of your Start menu.

If multiple users share a computer, each user must log on to the computer and create the shortcut. Desktop shortcuts are linked to the profile of the user who created them. See Chapter 8 for information about user profiles.

Always press the Enter key before you add an item to the list so the item is on its own line. This extra space makes the list much easier to read when the designated shopper prints it out.

Managing the list's efficiency and workability is important, or else the concept dies. Then you may have to go back to copying lists from a blackboard. Yuck! When removing items, be sure to remove items from the list, *not* the file itself. You can either remove all the items on the list and "clean the slate," so to speak, or manually remove only the items you found at the store — and leave "12 pounds of caviar" on the list for next time. I'll leave that for you to decide. I find it's easy to just tell my family that there'll be no caviar this week; if they need that much caviar that badly, they'll find a way to get it on their own.

Here's some other organizational advice regarding shopping lists:

✔ **You can create separate shopping lists for different types of stores.** Your shopping list probably contains food items, paper goods, cleaning supplies, and other items available in your local supermarket. Create a file named *hardware* if you tend to purchase nails, tools, propane cylinders, and other hardware store items frequently. Do the same for other types of stores.

You could create a file for clothing, but the thought of a single household member shopping for clothing for teenagers makes me laugh. Come to think of it, the thought of sending another household member out with a list of clothing items for me makes me nervous.

✔ **You can create shopping lists for special items for each person in the household.** Be careful about naming the files if you're using message files — don't overwrite the time stamp file for any user. Instead, choose a filename that indicates the contents are a shopping list, for example *Fred-Shopping* (a dash is an acceptable character in a filename).

Individual shopping list files for household members are also great wish lists. Consult another user's shopping file before his birthday.

Collaborate on Documents

If everybody on the network is using the same word processing software, two of you (or all of you) can collaborate on documents. Common collaborative documents include the annual holiday letter to friends and relatives, a note to a family member who's away at school, or a family wish list for vacations, household repairs, and so on. All modern word processors provide a mechanism for handling multiple-user input. In fact, you can collaborate on documents several ways, but I discuss only the easiest and most straightforward method here. I'm using Microsoft Word for this discussion, because it's the most popular word processor. If you use another product, you shouldn't have trouble figuring out which commands to use to accomplish these tasks — just consult the program's Help system.

Deletion tips for the designated shopper

Pass on these simple tips to the person who does the shopping for your family, and make sure that if Dad's doing the shopping, he also maintains the list:

✔ To remove everything in the file, press Ctrl+A (which selects all the text in the file), press the Delete key, and then save the now-empty file.

✔ To remove an individual item, place your pointer at the beginning of the item. Hold down the Ctrl and Shift keys, and press the ↓ key; this selects the entire paragraph. Then press the Delete key. Repeat for other individual items and save the file.

✔ For multiple items that are listed contiguously, follow the instructions in the preceding bullet, but continue to press the ↓ key to add those items to the selected text. Then press the Delete key and save the file.

If you're using Notepad for your shopping file, hold down the Shift key while you move the ↓ key, instead of holding down the Ctrl and Shift keys.

The trick to managing a document that has input from multiple users is to configure the document to show each person's input. In Microsoft Word, that feature is called Track Changes. Here's how to use it to track changes made to a document:

1. **Open the document that you want to edit.**

2. **Choose Tools⇨Track Changes⇨Highlight Changes.**

   The Highlight Changes dialog box appears, as shown in Figure 15-5.

Figure 15-5: Configure the document to show changes.

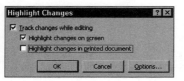

3. **Select the Track Changes While Editing and Highlight Changes On Screen check boxes.**

   These options enable you to see what changes you're making to the document:

   • All of your edits appear in a specific color. If more than one user edits the document, each user is assigned a different color automatically. Everything red came from one user, everything blue came from the second user, and so on.

   • Deleted text isn't really deleted; it has a line through it.

   • Additional text is underlined.

   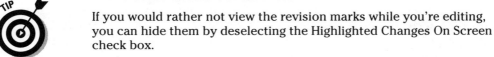

   If you would rather not view the revision marks while you're editing, you can hide them by deselecting the Highlighted Changes On Screen check box.

4. **Edit the document by adding and deleting text, as appropriate, and then save the document.**

   Make sure that you save the document with the same filename and in the same folder on the original computer.

5. **If additional people want to edit the document, have them repeat these steps.**

If more than one person has edited a document, you can see the name of the person who made a change by positioning your pointer over any changed text (see Figure 15-6). You can also find out what color is assigned to that user.

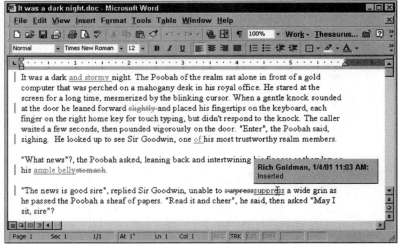

Figure 15-6:
You can't
see the
colors here,
but you can
see that the
document is
changed
and that
it's easy to
see the
changes.

You can accept some changes and reject others, or you can accept or reject all the changes at once. When you accept or reject a change, the text reverts back to regular formatting so it looks as if you wrote it. Check the Help files in your word processor to see how to perform these actions (in Word, choose Tools⇨Track Changes⇨Accept or Reject Changes, and use the dialog box that appears).

Set Up a Family Budget

Setting up a budget center on a home network is a clever idea, especially for finance-conscious families. A budget center not only gives you a way to see the latest and greatest version of the household budget, but can also help kids learn how to manage their own money.

Selecting a software program for your budget

You don't necessarily have to spend money on a bookkeeping program like Quicken. You can prepare your budget using several types of software. Most word processors have a Tables feature that you can use to create lists and columns of numbers, and the software adds up those numbers for you. Spreadsheet programs are designed for budget-type documents.

If you are using a bookkeeping program, you may not be able to separate the budget file from the other data files, but you can usually discover a way to export the budget to a format that you can use in a word processor or in spreadsheet software.

Setting up and using the budget center

After you select a software program, set up a shared folder on one computer so that everybody in the household can access the budget files (follow the instructions in the "Creating a shared folder for the message center" section, earlier in this chapter). Then save any budgets that you want to share in the budget center folder.

The real budget — the one that you use to run the household — must have a column in which you can enter the actual numbers. But you can also create other specialized budgets, such as a savings plan for a vacation, a new car, or college tuition. Budget regular contributions and then update the document each time you make a deposit.

If you want to play "what if" games with your budget, copy the budget and save it with a different filename. Then you can change figures in the budget to see how it affects the results. What if you put $100 a month into a mutual fund and reduce other budget categories to make up for that expenditure? You figure out quickly whether the tradeoff is worthwhile.

The budget center is also the place to track your investments. And, if you track investments online, you can save financial updates that you download from the Internet in your budget center folder.

You may want to have one budget center share for everyone in the household and then create a second share for the "real" budget. Password-protect the second share and give the password to your spouse if you don't want to share it with the kids.

Set Up a Family Document Library

Lots of documents that family members create are of interest to everyone in the family, so it makes sense to create a library where anyone can find these documents.

Follow the instructions in "Creating a shared folder for the message center," earlier in this chapter, to set up a shared folder on one computer so everybody in the household can access the documents. If you want to keep the documents you create on your own computer, you can just copy them to the share you're using as the document library. See Chapter 10 to find out how to move files around the network.

Set Up a Download Center

If family members download files from the Internet, it's a good idea to maintain a download center on the network. Here are a few reasons why:

- ✓ **You can run your antivirus software using the download folder as the target.** Running antivirus software on downloaded Internet files is important because many viruses enter computers this way. However, most people don't run virus scans on their computers as often as they should, because it takes so much time. Running anti-virus software on one particular folder is quick and easy.

- ✓ **A download center avoids duplicates that waste disk space.** If several members of the family want to download a game or a music file, checking the download center first avoids parallel downloading.

Choose the computer with the most disk space for this shared folder. And, clean the folder out frequently, to get rid of files that are no longer needed.

When you download a file, a Save dialog box opens because you're actually saving the file on your local drive. That dialog box usually has default selections for the folder that accepts the downloaded file, as well as the filename. Use the tools in the Save dialog box to change the destination folder to the network download center. (Don't change the filename.)

Have a Family Meeting

Windows comes with a nifty program called NetMeeting. This software lets you run a meeting across the network — it's sort of like bringing everybody into a chat room. Here's how to open the software:

- ✓ In Windows 98, choose Start➪Programs➪Accessories➪Internet Tools➪ NetMeeting.

- ✓ In Windows Me and Windows 2000 Professional, choose Start➪ Programs➪Accessories➪Communications➪NetMeeting.

The first time you open NetMeeting, a wizard walks you through the setup. Answer the questions and supply information as prompted (remember, you're configuring NetMeeting for a LAN (local area connection) instead of for over the Internet.

It's beyond the scope of this book to go over the instructions for using NetMeeting, but the Help files should get you rolling quickly.

While you're all together in the meeting, you can share documents, open a Whiteboard (a blank graphic screen in which every participant can enter comments, text, or whatever), or participate in a chat with all or selected participants (see Figure 15-7).

Figure 15-7:
A private
chat on the
side.

Send WinPopup Messages

Windows 98, Windows 95, and Windows Me have a cool message program — called WinPopup — that you can use to send a message to another user on the network (or to all the users).

Here's some information about how WinPopup works:

- If you want to receive a pop-up message, WinPopup must be running. However, Windows won't open WinPopup for you when a message comes in. This means you must open WinPopup every time you start your computer. It also means you don't close WinPopup after you've opened it; you minimize it instead.

- If the recipient is logged on to the network, WinPopup considers the message delivery successful. It doesn't check to see if WinPopup is running on the target computer(s). So even if you receive a success message, you can't be certain that the recipient received it.

- If the recipient opens WinPopup two hours after you send a message, the message won't appear on-screen. Because WinPopup's messages aren't files in the strict definition of the word *file,* they don't really exist, can't be tracked and saved, and can't be loaded into a WinPopup window later.

- If you send a message and enter a user or computer name incorrectly, or the user or computer name you specified is not currently logged on to the network, WinPopup displays an error message telling you the user couldn't be found on the network.

Sending messages in Windows 2000 Professional

Windows 2000 doesn't have WinPopup; instead it has a command-line utility called net send. To use this utility, open a command window and enter **net send <computer name> "message"**. Substitute the name of a computer for <computer name> and put quotation marks around the message. A window pops up on the other machine with your message, along with an indication of the name of the computer that sent it.

Windows 98, Windows 95, and Windows Me can't receive messages from the net send utility, and Windows 2000 computers can't receive messages from WinPopup. Therefore, if you're running a mixed network, the only way to send a quick message to a user on an incompatible machine is to yell.

Finding WinPopup

WinPopup is usually installed during the installation of the operating system, but it never appears on the menu system. This makes it a bit difficult to open the program. Here's how to make WinPopup available:

1. **Open My Computer.**

2. **Double-click the icon for drive C.**

3. **Press F3 to search drive C.**

   The Find dialog box (Windows 98 and Windows 95) or the Search dialog box (Windows Me) opens.

4. **Enter** winpopup **as the file to find and click Find Now or Search Now (depending on your version of Windows).**

   Windows searches the drive and should find `WinPopup.exe` in the Windows folder. Other files named WinPopup are also located, but it's the file with the extension `.exe` that you need.

5. **In the list of found files, right-click on** `winpopup.exe` **and choose Create Shortcut from the shortcut menu that appears.**

   A message appears to tell you that Windows can't create a shortcut here but that it can create a desktop shortcut.

6. **Click Yes and then close the Find/Search dialog box.**

   A shortcut to WinPopup now appears on your desktop.

If the operating system can't find `Winpop.exe`, you have to install WinPopup. To do so, open the Control Panel and double-click the Add/Remove Programs icon. In the Windows Setup tab of the Add/Remove Programs dialog box, WinPopup is listed under the category System Tools. Put the Windows CD in the CD-ROM drive, select WinPopup, and then click OK twice.

To avoid having to open WinPopup every time you start your computer, copy the desktop shortcut to the Startup folder of your Programs menu. Windows will then launch WinPopup every time you start your computer. To accomplish this, read the section on moving shortcuts to user profiles in Chapter 8. WinPopup will start every time your computer starts. After it opens, minimize the window (don't close the software).

Using WinPopup

Double-click the WinPopup shortcut (see the preceding section if you haven't yet created a shortcut) to open the WinPopup window. The first thing to do is to choose Messages⟹Options and select the Pop Up Dialog on Message Receipt option. This option means WinPopup automatically opens when you get a message (this should be the default setting).

To send a message to a user or computer, follow these steps:

1. **Click the Send icon on the toolbar (or choose Messages⟹Send from the menu bar).**

   The Send Message dialog box appears, as shown in Figure 15-8.

Figure 15-8:
Send a pop-up message instead of bellowing through the house.

2. **Select the User or Computer option and enter either a user name or a computer name.**

   Most of the time, it's easier to use the computer name, because you can check the computer names in Network Neighborhood or My Network Places. The user name you enter isn't the user's real name — it's the user's logon name. Most of us don't know (or care about) the logon names selected by other members of the household.

If you want to send a message to everybody on the network, select the Workgroup option and enter the name of your network workgroup. Enter the message text and click OK. After a few seconds, WinPopup displays a dialog box saying that the message was successfully sent. Don't believe it; it ain't necessarily so (hey, wouldn't that make a good song title?).

If WinPopup is running on the recipient's computer, the user sees the message in the WinPopup window (see Figure 15-9).

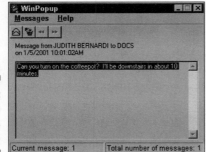

Figure 15-9:
Message
received,
10-4, Roger.

Meet George Jetson: Automate Everything That Isn't Stapled Down

Is anyone besides me old enough to remember that show about space-age families? Well, today that cartoon is a reality, and you can automate almost anything in your home from your computer.

Here's what you can do:

- ✔ Control the on/off state of any electric appliance.

- ✔ Operate your front door lock — let people in from your computer instead of walking to the front door.

- ✔ Operate a camera security system (useful before you perform the tasks in the preceding item).

- ✔ Pre-program lights, stereo systems, and so on to go on and off at specific times.

- ✔ Lots more.

Here's how you do it:

✔ You install remote-control software in every computer on the network.

✔ You buy special plugs for the electrical outlets into which you plug the electric appliances you want to control.

✔ Your computer software sends signals to the special plugs.

For example, you can plug an electric plug dohickey into the outlet that controls one of the lights in your living room. Then you can sit at one of the computers on your network (perhaps the one in the den) and turn the light off and on. Or you can move the dohickey into the kitchen and turn the coffeepot on from the computer in the bedroom, which could be a real time-saver in the morning.

I'm calling it a "dohickey" because different companies call the device by different names. The thing to look for if you're interested in automating your home from your computers is X10 technology (X10 seems to be the technology that will become the standard).

You can find out about available software at www.x10.com. You can look at all sorts of nifty remote control devices at www.smarthome.com.

Chapter 16

(Almost) Ten Ways to Make the Internet Safe for Children

In This Chapter

▶ Helping children understand what's dangerous about the Internet

▶ Using filters to prevent children from visiting undesirable Internet sites

▶ Setting guidelines for games and violence-oriented Web sites

*P*arents worry about the kind of stuff kids can run into on the Internet, and they're not being paranoid — Internet safety is a real issue. Fortunately, you can do some things to help make the Internet safer for your children, which is good, because you probably can't keep them away from it.

Kids love the Internet. In fact, in most households, the kids can find an Internet site faster than the parents. While parents wade through vague searches, due to vague search criteria, kids seem to guess right instinctively. They're at the site they need, reading or downloading, while their parents are still trying to figure out which site holds the stuff they're looking for.

Because you're sharing the Internet across your network, if you're working at a computer while your kids are on other computers, you can't see what your kids are doing. In this chapter, I discuss some software solutions for controlling Internet access. They work to some extent, and reviewers have offered mixed opinions. In the end, however, there is no substitute for vigilant parents.

Talk to Your Children About the Internet

Like any other danger, the Internet is less threatening if you have an open and frank discussion with your children about the perils they can encounter online. Approach this subject head on; you can't pussyfoot around it. You didn't mince words when you warned your kids not to get into a stranger's car — use the same approach to warn your kids about the Internet.

Be aware that just because you have a definition in your own mind about terms like pornography, hate crimes, child molesters, bomb-making, violent games, and so on (sorry, but those are some of the dangers on the Internet), your kids may not have a clearly defined notion of their meanings. Depending on the kids' ages, you'll have to decide on what explanations are appropriate for them. But the bottom line is, discuss these issues.

Place Your Computers in the Right Locations

The best way to keep your kids away from the Web sites you don't want them to visit is to provide a deterrent. The best deterrent is sort of a psychological deterrent — one that implies they could get caught if they don't follow the rules.

My best advice is don't put a computer in a child's room. It's actually a bad idea on several levels, according to many educators and child psychologists who point out that part of a healthy childhood is interaction with other children. Kids who have computers in their rooms tend to spend much more time alone, using the computer (mostly on the Internet), than kids who use computers that are in less private locations.

Put computers in rooms where it's normal and natural for other household members (especially parents) to walk through those rooms.

Use Internet Rating Services

A number of services rate sites for a variety of standards, including a "kid-safe" standard. When you use a rating service, your Web browser accommodates its recommendations.

To use a rating service in Internet Explorer, follow these steps while you're connected to the Internet:

1. **Choose Tools⇨Internet Options.**

   The Internet Options dialog box appears.

2. **Click the Content tab, and in the Content Advisor section, click Enable.**

3. **Enter a password and then enter it again to confirm it. When you're finished, click OK.**

   The Content Advisor dialog box opens.

   In some versions of Internet Explorer, the request for a password may appear after you click OK to close the dialog box.

4. **Click the General tab and click the Find Rating Systems button.**

   Internet Explorer takes you to Microsoft's rating system Web page. On this page, you can get information on rating systems and add the system you prefer to your browser. Each rating system provides instructions for adding its services to Internet Explorer.

5. **When you're finished, click OK to close the dialog box.**

After a rating service is enabled, any site that is not approved by the rating service is blocked (unless the user knows the password you entered in Step 3). This feature is known as *filtering*.

To use rating services in Netscape Navigator, use the Netwatch function (consult the Help files for instructions for your version of Netscape).

Create a List of Sites to Filter

In Internet Explorer, you can create your own filters, which are useful in the following circumstances:

- ✔ You don't want to use a rating service.
- ✔ The rating service you use permits access to a site you don't like.
- ✔ The rating service you use blocks access to a site you feel is appropriate for your children.

Use these steps to create a list of sites that you want to filter for:

1. **Choose Tools⇨Internet Options.**

   The Internet Options dialog box appears.

2. **Click the Content tab, and in the Content Advisor section, click the Settings button.**

   If you haven't previously used this feature, the Settings button is grayed out. If this is the case, click the Enable button to open the Content Advisor dialog box and then skip ahead to Step 4.

3. **Enter your password.**

   The Content Advisor dialog box opens.

4. **Click the Approved Sites tab (shown in Figure 16-1).**

5. **Enter the URL for a Web site you want to filter for and then click the Always or Never button. Repeat this step as many times as you want.**

   If you click the Always button after entering a URL, that site is always accessible, even if you're using a rating service that disallows it. Furthermore, sites designated as *Always* never require your password. Sites designated as Never require a password.

6. **When you're finished, click the OK button to close the dialog box and save your changes.**

   If this is your first time using this feature, you're prompted to create a password.

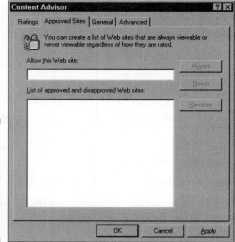

Figure 16-1:
You can create your own list of allowed or forbidden sites.

Use Software to Filter Sites

A number of software programs are available that control and/or monitor Internet activities. Following is a list of several programs that have received reasonably good reviews, along with their URLs:

✔ Net Nanny at www.netnanny.com

✔ KidDesk at www.edmark.com

> ✔ Cyber Patrol at `www.cyberpatrol.com`
> ✔ Cyber Sentinel at `www.securitysoft.com`

These programs work similarly to the rating services: They filter access to Web sites. The advantage you gain by using software is the ability to config- ure the software to create the filters. Your children's ages, interests, and your own general attitude about censorship can be reflected in your configuration choices.

For a comprehensive list of filter software, go to `www.worldvillage.com/wv/ school/html/control.htm`.

Use AOL Restrictions

If you use AOL, filtering doesn't take place via the AOL browser; filtering is built in to the user's screen name. When you create a user name for your child, you can designate an age group. Your choices are Kids Only, Young Teen, Mature Teen, and Unrestricted Access (intended for the parents). These different categories determine to what extent AOL filters content. Unlike Internet Explorer, AOL does not allow you to set any additional filter- ing options in the software; you and your children live with the judgments and value systems of the AOL programmers.

You can also use the Parental Controls feature to restrict e-mail so that kids can only send or receive e-mail from a selected group.

Be Wary of Chat Rooms

Kids love chat rooms. They make virtual friends. They get a chance to create a persona and become the person they'd like to be. Reality and truthfulness are in short supply in chat rooms.

Chat rooms abound on the Internet, although many parents aren't aware that they exist outside of AOL. Many chat rooms are dedicated to special interests and topics, but most kids hang out in generic chat rooms, some of which are organized by age group.

One concern for parents is that the language used in chat rooms can be offen- sive, violent, and (to many parents) disgusting. But the inherent problem with chat rooms is that you don't really know who you're chatting with. Neither you nor your children have any way of verifying that that person is indeed who he says he is. Your son may think he's chatting with a 12-year-old boy when in fact he's chatting with an adult who's posing as a young boy. Predatory adults — mostly child molesters — often hang out in chat rooms and try to befriend young children. The organizations devoted to finding missing children point out that some missing children were lured from their homes to meet chat room friends.

Make sure that your children follow these safety tips:

- ✔ Use a generic, asexual screen name that doesn't indicate your age or location. Often, online handles reflect some physical or other characteristic, but for children that's a no-no. If you're an esoteric parent, you can have a lot of fun picking strange names. (How about *Orange, Wallpaper,* or *Lantern* for screen names?)

- ✔ Never reveal your real name, address, or telephone number to any chat room acquaintance. Don't even reveal the region you're from, the name of your school, or the name of your little league team. With enough personal information, nefarious types can piece together more than you realize.

- ✔ Never, ever accept an invitation to meet a chat room acquaintance.

Find Acceptable Sites for Your Children

One way to control what sites your children visit is to steer them toward sites that you've picked out and approved. The Internet contains tons of great sites geared for kids — not just homework helpers (oh, Mom, borrrring), but games, puzzles, book sites (Judy Blume has a site at `www.judyblume.com`), and others. For parents who are overwhelmed at the thought of trying to ferret out new sites for their kids, here are a few places to look for ideas:

- ✔ **Family PC Magazine** (`familypc.zdnet.com`): This computer-related site is a great source for links to other computer-related sites.

- ✔ **ABC's of Parenting** (`www.abcparenting.com`): This site offers a wide range of topics such as recommendations for Web sites for kids, and also has chat rooms for parents who want to discuss parenting issues.

- ✔ **Parent News** (`www.parent.net`): This site covers lots of topics of interest to parents, including Web safety, good Web sites, and parenting hints unrelated to computers.

- ✔ **FamiliesConnect** (`www.ala.org/ICONN/familiesconnect.html`): This site provides great info for parents about Internet issues.

Set Guidelines for the Level of Violence in Computer Games

Almost every time the headlines announce a tragic shooting by a teenager, usually at a school, the background information on the accused includes the fact that the child was devoted to violent computer games — some of which are available for children to play interactively on the Internet.

No research exists that shows that a perfectly normal kid can be turned into a mass murderer as a result of a violent game. But the experts are polarized and locked into extreme positions, and parents have a hard time knowing whom to believe. Violent games are fascinating and popular, especially among boys (according to research), so knowing where you stand as a parent is essential. Here's what you need to do:

✔ Talk to your children about violence in *all* media, such as movies, music, television, and computer games. Make sure the boundaries you set are clear to your children, and listen to their opinions.

✔ If you decide to let your kids play video games, develop guidelines for your children. These guidelines should explain your own value systems; your own definitions of, and reaction to, violence. For example, some parents object to anything that's connected to guns, whereas other parents explain that hurting another person isn't amusing. By setting guidelines, you can send your kids off to game land with some moral and emotional equipment, which will help them put their activities into perspective — this is a game, not life.

✔ If you decide that some of the games are indeed extremely violent, you have every right as a parent to forbid your kids to buy or play them. Get familiar with all the games popular with kids so you're credible in the eyes of your kids.

One of the best ways to stay on top of computer games is to search the Internet for reviews of games. For reviews, try these sites:

✔ Microsoft Computing Central (computingcentral.msn.com/games)

✔ ZDNet GameSpot (www.zdnet.com/gamespot)

✔ CNET Gamecenter.com (www.gamecenter.com)

✔ GamePower (www.gamepower.com)

✔ Learning Network (learningnetwork.com)

Many of these sites offer links to additional sites as well as offer newsletters you can subscribe to in order to keep up with the latest games.

Geeky Programming Tips to Automate Your Backups

• •

*Y*ou can create a high-tech geeky method for backing up your data files to another computer. This means you don't have to sit in front of Windows Explorer and click folders, and then copy and paste them. And, as an added benefit, you get to be a quasi-programmer.

The secret to this automation is a *batch file*. A batch file is a program, but you don't have to be a programmer to write it. All you have to do is create a plain text file in Notepad. The trick to turning a text file into a program is to enter a valid command on each line of the text file. The trick to that trick is knowing what constitutes a valid command. I cover all of these topics in this appendix.

Here's what you have to do in order to write your own backup program:

✔ Create a folder on a remote computer to hold your backed-up data. Share the folder and make sure that the Access Type is Full; however, do not password-protect it. (See Chapter 7 to find out how to share a folder.) Alternatively, you can back up to a Zip or Jaz drive on another computer, by sharing the drive.

✔ Do some homework so that the information you enter in your batch file is correct (see the next section for details).

✔ Write your batch file (see the section "Writing the programming code," later in this appendix).

Gathering the Information You Need

The purpose of your batch file is to move all the data files in your My Documents folder (and its subfolders) to your backup folder on the remote computer. The My Documents folder is called the *source folder,* and your backup folder is called the *target folder.* What your backup program does is copy the contents (your data files) from their *source folders* to their *target folders*.

Before writing a batch file, you need to gather information about the source folder and the target folder.

Getting the information about the source folder

For the batch file, you need to know the real name of your My Documents folder. The real name includes the system path (which is the drive the folder sits on) and the name of its parent folder (if a parent folder exists).

When users log on to computers by entering a user name and an optional password in a Logon dialog box, Windows creates folders that are dedicated to that user name. Everything that belongs to a user is contained in those folders. These belongings include the listings that appear on the user's Start menu, the desktop shortcuts, and the My Documents folder for that user. (See Chapter 8 for more details.)

The My Documents icon on your desktop is probably a subfolder under your user folder, which is in turn under a parent folder. The path statement for Windows 98 or Windows Me is `C:\Windows\YourLogonName\My Documents`. For Windows 2000 Professional, the path statement is `C:\Documents and Settings\YourLogonName\My Documents`.

Don't worry; you can reveal the path to your My Documents folder very easily. Right-click on the My Documents folder on your desktop and choose Properties from the shortcut menu that appears. The dialog box that opens displays the path to your own My Documents folder (see Figure A-1).

Figure A-1:
The complete path to your My Documents folder is displayed in the folder's Properties dialog box.

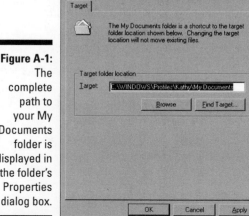

Write down the path because you'll need it when you type the command that identifies the source folder. If you cannot see the entire path statement in the Target text box (sometimes the path is quite long), use the arrow keys to expose the unseen characters.

Don't press any key except an arrow key, because the text is highlighted, which means it's in edit mode. Any character you type replaces the path. If you accidentally type a key, immediately press the Cancel button in the Properties dialog box and start this procedure again.

Getting the information about the target folder

Make sure that you know what to call the *target* (the folder that you created on another computer to hold your backup files). That folder also has a path, but it has a different format than the path for a folder on your own computer. The path statement for a folder on a remote computer is called a universal naming convention (UNC). It appears in this form: \\ComputerName\ShareName. For example, if you created a folder named KathyBackup and gave it a share name of Kathy (the share name you assign to a folder doesn't have to be the same as the folder's name) on a computer named Kitchen, the UNC for the folder is \\Kitchen\Kathy.

You can find out the UNC for the target by following these steps:

1. **Double-click the Network Neighborhood icon on the desktop (My Network Neighborhood in Windows Me and Windows 2000 Professional).**

   The Network Neighborhood window opens, displaying an icon for each computer in the network. In Windows Me and Windows 2000 Professional, you must double-click the Entire Network icon and then double-click the Microsoft Windows Network icon.

2. **Double-click the icon for the computer that holds the folder you created for your backup.**

   All the shared folders (shares) on that computer appear in the window.

3. **Right-click on the target folder that you created and shared for your backups. Then choose Properties from the menu that appears.**

   The computer name and the share name both appear in the Properties dialog box (see Figure A-2).

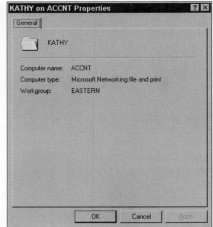

Figure A-2:
The share
name
appears at
the top of
the dialog
box, next to
the folder.
The
computer
name is
shown
below the
share name.

For the target folder shown in Figure A-2, the UNC is \\accnt\kathy
(the case doesn't matter).

4. **Write down the UNC or type it in your Notepad document (don't forget
   to save the document again).**

Creating the Batch File

After you gather the necessary information about the target and source folders, you're ready to write the programming code that copies your data from
its source folder to its target folder.

Writing the programming code

In general terms, here's what your code must do:

1. **Assign a drive letter to the target folder.**

   This is called *mapping* a drive, which is covered in detail in Chapter 10.

2. **Copy the folders from the source folder to the target folder.**

   You also provide special commands that specify some technical details
   about the copying process.

3. **Remove the mapping.**

   Removing the mapping releases the drive letter so that the next time you run your batch file, the first step (mapping a drive) doesn't produce an error message that says you already did that, yesterday.

In order to accomplish the tasks in the preceding steps, type the following commands in Notepad (choose Start➪Programs➪Accessories➪Notepad). Each line is a valid command (take my word for it). For this batch file, I use the folder names shown in Figures A-1 (my source folder) and A-2 (my target folder). For your batch file, you must substitute the names of your own source folder and target folder.

```
net use p: \\accnt\kathy
xcopy c:\windows\profiles\kathy\"my documents"\*.* p: /s/h/i/r/c
net use p: /delete
exit
```

You must pay attention to certain details when you're entering the text for your batch file, as described in the next three sections.

Spaces count

Spaces are important, because they tell your computer when commands end and when qualifiers for the commands begin. (A *qualifier* is the name of the object that the command acts on. For example, the command `xcopy` acts on the folders referenced in the rest of the typed line.) Note the following spaces:

- ✔ On the first line, between `net` and `use`, and between the colon (:) and the double backslash
- ✔ On the second line, after `xcopy`, after `*.*`, and before `/s`
- ✔ On the third line, between `net` and `use`, and before `/delete`

Folder names with spaces get special treatment

The folder name `"my documents"` is enclosed in quotation marks. Quotation marks are necessary whenever you type a folder or filename that contains a space. Otherwise, the system interprets the space between `my` and `documents` as the end of a command and the beginning of a qualifier. There is no valid command named `my`, so that won't work.

Miscellaneous details you should be aware of

A couple of details about the text you enter are noteworthy:

- ✔ The * . * in the second line tells the xcopy command to copy every file in the folder. Technically, the first asterisk means every filename and the second asterisk means every file extension.

- ✔ I chose the mapped drive letter p arbitrarily — you can use any letter that isn't already in use. I use p because it's far enough along in the alphabet to avoid any potential conflict with a drive letter than may be already in use.

- ✔ If you're curious about the meaning of all those forward slashes followed by letters, see the sidebar "Understanding command parameters." If you're not curious, just enter the parameters as I indicated and trust me that they'll work the way they're supposed to.

Understanding command parameters

A *parameter* is an option that controls the behavior of a command. A parameter is also called a *switch*. The xcopy command has lots of nifty parameters you can use to tell the command how to perform its work efficiently. For your batch file, you use the following parameters:

- ✔ /s tells xcopy to copy all the subdirectories of the source folder (in this case, My Documents).

- ✔ /h tells xcopy to copy any hidden and system files in the source folder. By default, xcopy ignores hidden files, but if you've hidden any document files, this ensures they are backed up.

- ✔ /i tells xcopy how to handle subfolders. In essence, it means that xcopy won't copy all your files into one folder on the remote computer; instead, it maintains the subfolder structure you created in your My Documents folder. Therefore, you don't have to create the My Documents folder on your target folder, and you don't have to create any subfolders in advance.

- ✔ /r tells xcopy to overwrite read-only files. By default, a file that is read-only can't be

changed (which means you can't copy the same file over it). This parameter enables xcopy to copy the current version of any read-only files.

- ✔ /c tells xcopy to continue copying even if a minor error occurs. For example, if you inadvertently leave a file open in a software window when you run your batch file, xcopy cannot copy it (files in use can't be copied). If you don't tell xcopy to move along, the command stops dead in its tracks waiting for you to tell it whether it's okay to skip this file. Because want to automate your backup, you probably won't be there to give xcopy the OK. This parameter makes sure that the command keeps moving on and that the remaining files are copied.

The /c parameter for xcopy applies only to minor errors, such as the failure to be able to copy a file. Major errors, such as not finding the target (in case the computer you're copying to isn't turned on) or finding something wrong with your network connections, stops the copying process.

Saving the file as a program

After you finish typing the commands in the Notepad window, you must save your file. Follow these steps to save the file as a program instead of a text file:

1. **Choose File⇨Save.**

   The Save As dialog box appears, as shown in Figure A-3.

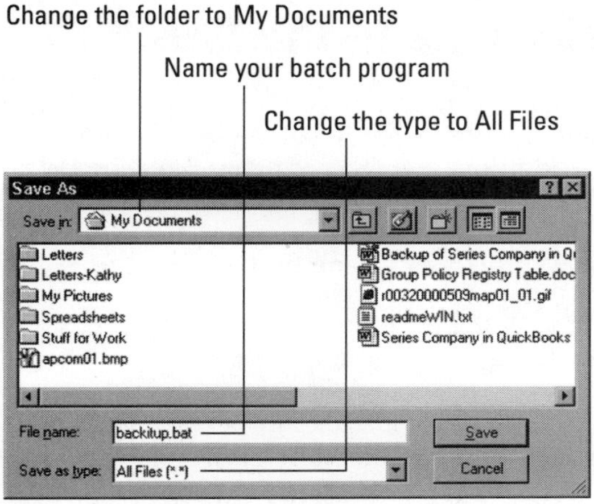

Change the folder to My Documents

Name your batch program

Change the type to All Files

Figure A-3:
The settings
you use for
saving the
text file are
important.

Save As	? X
Save in: My Documents	

Letters
Letters-Kathy
My Pictures
Spreadsheets
Stuff for Work
apcom01.bmp

Backup of Series Company in Q
Group Policy Registry Table.doc
r00320000509map01_01.gif
readmeWIN.txt
Series Company in QuickBooks

File name: backitup.bat — Save

Save as type: All Files (*.*) — Cancel

2. **In the Save In text box, select the My Documents folder.**

   This means your batch file is backed up along with all your other data files.

3. **Click the arrow to the right of the Save As Type text box and select All Files (*.*) as the file type.**

   Notepad uses the file extension .txt if you save the file as a text file. Changing the file type lets you use your own extension (in this case, .bat, which tells your computer that this is a batch file, and therefore a program instead of a data file).

4. **In the File Name text box, enter a name for this program and use the file extension .bat.**

   You can use any filename, but backitup.bat or kathybackup (substitute your own name for kathy) is a good reminder of this file's use.

If you think you may want to configure your backup batch file to run automatically (see the section "Scheduling Automatic Backups," later in this appendix), don't use `backup.bat` as the filename. Windows uses the name *backup* in the automated scheduler to schedule the backup software program that comes with your computer (discussed in Chapter 13).

5. **Click Save.**

6. **Close Notepad.**

Creating a shortcut to the batch file

It's a good idea to create a shortcut to the batch file. Otherwise, every time you use the batch file (every day, right?), you have to open Windows Explorer and find it. In addition, you can configure the shortcut to close the command window. Here's how to create the shortcut:

1. **Double-click the My Documents icon on the desktop.**

   The My Documents window opens.

2. **Right-click on the listing for your batch file.**

   The shortcut menu appears.

3. **Choose Send To⇨Desktop (Create Shortcut).**

   The Shortcut message appears to tell you that the new shortcut will be placed on the desktop. Click OK.

4. **Close the My Documents window.**

You can drag this shortcut to the Quick Launch toolbar for one-click access, or drag it to the Start button to place it at the top of your Start menu.

When you run the batch file, Windows opens a command window (because batch file programs are a series of commands that require the command prompt in order to run). After the batch file finishes its tasks, the command window remains open. You can close it by clicking the X in the upper-right corner, or you can tell your computer to close the window when the program finishes running with these steps:

1. **Right-click on the shortcut you created and choose Properties from the menu that appears.**

   The shortcut Properties dialog box opens.

2. **Click the Program tab (see Figure A-4).**

Figure A-4:
Tell
Windows to
close the
program
window
when the
program
ends.

3. **Select the Close on Exit check box.**

4. **Click OK to close the Properties dialog box.**

Now the command window closes automatically when your batch file ends, just like your software windows close when you exit the program. Slick!

Editing the batch file

If you want to view or change the contents of your batch file, don't double-click the shortcut (or the file itself). Double-clicking a program doesn't open the text file; it causes the program to run. Because your file has the file extension .bat, it's a program.

To open the batch file as a text file so you can view or change it, open the My Documents icon on the desktop and right-click on the listing for your batch file. Then choose Edit. Notepad opens with your batch file in the window.

If you want to add more source folders to copy to your target folder on the other computer, use the same format you use to copy My Documents. That means you enter the xcopy command, followed by the source (the folder you want to copy) and the target (the shared folder on the other computer that holds your backed-up data).

For example, if you use Quicken, you can back up your entire Quicken program and data by entering the following command on the line below the command that copies your My Documents folder:

```
xcopy c:\quickenw\*.* p:\quickenw /s/e/h/i/r/c/v
```

This command assumes that your Quicken software is installed in a folder named quickenw on drive C. If you installed Quicken in another folder, enter the path to that folder. For example, if you installed Quicken under the Program Files folder, you would use this command:

```
xcopy c:\"program files"\quickenw\*.* p:\quickenw /s/e/h/i/r/c/v
```

(**Note:** You use quotation marks around program files because the folder name has a space in it.)

Now your batch file looks like this:

```
net use p: \\accnt\kathy
xcopy c:\windows\profiles\kathy\"my documents"\*.* p: /s/h/i/r/c
xcopy c:\quickenw\*.* i:\quickenw /s/e/h/i/r/c
net use p: /delete
exit
```

Scheduling Automatic Backups

Because I'm a control freak and a total pessimist about computer crashes, I manually run my backup batch file at the end of every day. I never forget to back up. However, if you think you may forget to click that shortcut, you can tell your computer to run your backup batch file automatically.

To schedule automatic backups in Windows, you use the Task Scheduler, which is a cool program that's built into Windows. Here's how to create a scheduled task for backing up:

1. **Choose Start⇨Programs⇨Accessories⇨System Tools⇨ Scheduled Tasks.**

   The Scheduled Tasks window opens (see Figure A-5).

2. **Double-click the Add Scheduled Task icon.**

   The Scheduled Task Wizard opens.

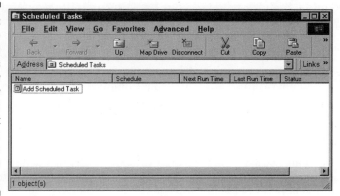

3. **Click Next to begin.**

4. **In the next window, click the Browse button to open the Select Program to Schedule dialog box.**

   Your batch file isn't in the list that the wizard displays, so you must click the Browse button and locate your program manually.

5. **In the Select Program to Schedule dialog box, change the folder location to My Documents, and select your batch file. Then click Open.**

6. **Enter a name for the task and select the schedule you want (see Figure A-6). Then click Next.**

   Select daily backups — it's the only way to go!

7. **Schedule a time for running your backup batch file program and then click Next.**

   Choose a time when you probably won't be using the computer (any files you are working on are considered open files and won't be backed up). I run my backups manually when I leave the computer to begin preparing dinner, so I'd schedule an automated backup for dinnertime.

   Both the computers must be up and running at the time the backup runs.

8. **Click Finish.**

   You can select the option to display advanced settings when you click Finish, but there's no need to. The advanced options don't usually apply to simple daily tasks like this one.

If you're using Windows 2000 Professional, the wizard asks for a user name and password for the user that will run this file. The password is a security measure of the Windows 2000 operating system, which has a high degree of security built into it.

Cleaning Up the Backup Folder

The problem with batch files that copy files to a backup location is that the target folder can get extremely crowded. Files that you delete from your My Documents folder aren't deleted in the backup folder on the other computer.

Eventually, every file you ever saved, including all the files you've deleted from My Documents, is contained in your backup folder. All these files take up a whole lot of disk space unnecessarily.

Every once in a while, perhaps once a month, delete the contents of the backup folder immediately before you run your backup batch file. Don't do it earlier in the day, just in case something happens to your computer before you can back up your data files.

Only delete the contents of the folder, not the shared folder itself. Here's how:

1. **Open Network Neighborhood or My Network Places.**

2. **Double-click the computer that has your backup share.**

   All the shared folders on the computer are displayed.

3. **Double-click the share that holds your backup.**

   All the subfolders and files in your backup share appear in the window.

4. **Press Ctrl+A.**

   All the subfolders and files are selected.

5. **Press the Delete key.**

   Windows asks if you're sure you want to delete these items?

6. **Click Yes.**

   Remember, you're working on a remote drive so the files aren't sent to a Recycle Bin — they're gone for good.

7. **Run your backup batch file.**

All the folders are re-created as the files are copied, because of the parameters you placed in your batch file.

Appendix B

Glossary

• •

10Base-2 cable: More commonly known as *coaxial cable* or *thinnet cable.* This network cable looks like a thin version of the cable that your cable television company uses. Today, many companies are abandoning their 10Base-2 systems in favor of 10Base-T cable. See also *10Base-T cable.*

10Base-T cable: Also called *twisted-pair cable,* 10Base-T is the current standard in network cable. 10Base-T looks like telephone cable, but the main difference is that it's designed to transmit data rather than voice. Two types of 10Base-T are available: unshielded twisted pair (UTP) and shielded twisted pair (STP). In STP, metal encases the cable wires, lessening the possibility of interference from other electrical devices, radar, radio waves, and so on. Using 10Base-T requires the purchase of a concentrator. Each network computer's NIC is connected to a length of 10Base-T, which is then connected to a concentrator. The concentrator disseminates data to the computers' NICs. See also *concentrator, NIC, star topology.*

AC adapter: A device that transforms alternating current (AC) electricity into a form that devices like laptops and notebooks can use.

active application: The software application you currently have open with the application's window appearing in the foreground of your screen. Other applications that may be open are in the background of your screen and are called inactive applications.

ADSL (Asymmetric Digital Subscriber Line) modem: This technology uses standard telephone lines to produce incredibly fast connections to the Internet. You need a special ADSL modem, telephone lines that support the technology (coming soon to most cities), and an Internet host server that supports ADSL technology.

arrow keys: Sometimes called direction or cursor keys. These keyboard keys have arrows pointing up, down, right, and left and are used to navigate around the screen.

ASCII (American Standard Code for Information Interchange): This standard assigns a number to each key on your keyboard. Internally, your computer uses the numbers to read and write keyboard characters.

ASCII text file: A file that contains untranslated ASCII characters without special formatting.

AutoPlay: A feature in Windows that automatically searches for and launches a CD's AutoRun file when you insert a disc into a CD-ROM drive.

backup: A copy of the files on your computer that you can use to restore data in the event of a computer crash.

banner: Also called a *separator page*. A form that accompanies each print job. The form displays the name of the user and prints ahead of the first page of each document so that multiple users of a printer can easily identify their documents. To print a banner, you must configure the printer for this feature.

barrel connector: A tube-shaped device that enables you to join two lengths of 10Base-2 cable in a network. See also *10Base-2 cable*.

baud rate: Also referred to as *bits per second* (bps). The speed at which information is transferred.

beta: A designation given to software that has not yet been released for distribution because it is still being tested. The beta version of software is usually in its second testing cycle (*alpha* versions are earlier releases) and is usually only available to particular users (called *beta testers*).

BIOS (Basic Input-Output System): Part of a PC that controls and manages the hardware in the computer.

bit: The smallest unit of digital information. A bit is either *on* or *off* (to the computer, on is 1 and off is 0).

bitmap: A graphic image stored as a pattern of dots (called *pixels*).

bits per second (bps): The speed at which data is transferred.

BNC connector: A round device shaped like a fat ring that locks male and female connectors together. A BNC connector looks like a smaller version of the connector at each end of your cable television cable. Installed at each end of a length of coaxial cable (also called 10Base-2 or thinnet), the BNC features a center pin (connected to the center conductor inside the cable) and a metal tube (connected to the outer cable shielding). The rotating ring on the metal tube turns to lock the male connector to the female connector. See also *10Base-2 cable*.

boot: The process of starting the computer and loading the operating system. Some people think the term originates from the adage "pulling oneself up by one's bootstraps."

brownout: A drop in electrical voltage that can destroy a variety of computer components (hard drive, chips, and so on). You can prevent brownout damage by purchasing a voltage regulator. See also *voltage regulator.*

bus: A slot on your computer's motherboard into which you insert cards, such as network interface cards. (Technically, the name of the slot is *expansion slot* — the bus is merely the data path along which information flows to the card. Nowadays, the common computer jargon is bus.) See also *NIC.*

byte: The amount of memory needed to specify a single ASCII character (which is 8 bits). Kilobytes and megabytes are usually used to describe the amount of memory a computer uses. See also *kilobyte, megabyte.*

cable modem: A modem that connects to your cable television company's cable lines (but doesn't interfere with TV transmissions). Cable modems are significantly faster than standard modems but aren't yet widely available. Cable modem speeds are measured in millions of bytes per second rather than in the thousands of bytes per second common in standard modems. See also *standard modem.*

cache: Random access memory (RAM) that is set aside and used as a buffer between the CPU and either a hard disk or slower RAM. The items stored in a cache can be accessed quickly, speeding up the flow of data.

cascade: An arrangement of open program windows on the desktop so that they overlap each other, with the title bar of each window visible.

cascading menu: Also called a hierarchical menu or submenu. A menu that is opened from another menu item. In Windows, a menu item has an arrow that points to the right if the item opens a cascading menu.

CD-ROM (Compact Disc-Read Only Memory): Discs that contain programs or data. CD-ROMs can hold over 600 MB of data. You can only read data on a CD-ROM; you cannot write (save) data.

CD-RW (Compact Disc-Recordable/Rewritable): Discs that will accept data, enabling you to copy files to the disc.

centronics interface: The connector on a printer cable (called a *parallel cable*) that attaches to the printer.

check box: A small square box in a dialog box that can be selected or cleared to turn an option on or off. When the check box is selected, an *X* or a check mark appears in the box.

client: A computer that uses hardware and services on another computer (called the *host* or *server*). Also called a *workstation.* See also *client/server network, host.*

client/server network: A network scheme in which a main computer (called the host or server) supplies files and peripherals shared by all the other computers (called clients or workstations). Each user who works at a client computer can use the files and peripherals that are on his individual computer (called the local computer) or on the server. See also *client, host, local computer.*

Clipboard: An area of memory devoted to holding data you cut or copy, usually used to transfer data between applications or between parts of a data file. Typically, you transfer data to the Clipboard by using an application's Copy or Cut command, and you insert data from the Clipboard by using the application's Paste command.

cluster: A unit of data storage for hard or floppy disks.

coaxial cable: See *10Base-2 cable.*

COM port: Also called a serial port. A connector into which you can plug a serial device cable, usually a modem. Most PCs have two COM ports: COM1 and COM2.

computer name: A unique name assigned to a computer on a network to differentiate that computer from other computers on the network.

concentrator: Also called a *hub.* The home base of a 10Base-T network to which all lengths of cable from the network computers are attached. (One end of each cable length attaches to the concentrator; the other end of each length attaches to a computer's network interface card.) See also *10Base-T cable, NIC, star topology.*

CPU (central processing unit): The chip that runs the computer.

default button: In some dialog boxes, a command button that is selected automatically if you press Enter. In most dialog boxes, the default button has a bold border to make it discernable.

defragment (or defrag): To take fragments of files and put them together so that every file on a hard drive has all of its contents in one place. Defragging makes opening files a much faster process because the operating system doesn't have to look all over your hard drive for all the pieces of a file that you want to open.

device driver: Software that allows your operating system to communicate with hardware (such as network interface cards) or peripherals (such as printers). For example, a printer driver translates information from the computer into information the printer can understand and manage. (Also called *drivers.*)

Dial-Up Networking: A feature in Windows that enables your modem to dial out and connect to a server, either on the Internet through an Internet service provider, or to a server in a company network.

directory: Part of the structure for organizing your files on a disk. A directory can contain files and other directories (called subdirectories). In Windows, directories are usually called *folders*.

document: A data file that you create in a software program.

document window: A window within a software program that contains an open document. Most software written for Windows can have more than one document window open at a time.

embedded network card: A network card built into a computer's motherboard.

Ethernet: The most widely used of the several technologies available for cabling local area networks. See also *LAN*.

evaluation software: A specially programmed version of commercial software. The software may stop working after a certain amount of time has elapsed or may be missing some features of the commercial version. See also *freeware, shareware*.

expansion slot: A slot on your computer's motherboard into which you insert cards, such as network interface cards. See also *bus*.

extension: The period (.) and characters at the end of a filename. An extension usually identifies the kind of information a file contains. For example, text files usually have the extension .txt, and Microsoft Word files usually have the extension .doc.

FAT (File Allocation Table): An entry in the operating system that acts like an index or a table of contents. The FAT keeps track of where all the fragments of a file are stored on a drive.

file sharing: The ability to allow more than one user to access the same file. Usually refers to software programs that are stored on a network fileserver.

firewall: Software that protects a computer on the Internet from unauthorized, outside intrusion. Companies that have one or more servers exposed to the Internet use firewalls to allow only authorized employees access to the servers.

fish: A tool designed for fishing cable. It's made out of flexible, thin, steel tape that has a hook at the end. The tape rolls out of a container (like a measuring tape). A fish is used by electricians and is sold in hardware stores, but you can fashion a homemade version by untwisting a coat hanger and using the hook at the end of the hanger to grab the cable as you run it through your house.

freeware: Software that's free — use it as much as you like without paying anyone a dime. See also *evaluation software, shareware.*

gigabyte (GB): 1,000 megabytes.

GPF (General Protection Fault): Also known as a *crash.* In Windows, this means the memory protection feature has detected an illegal instruction from a program, causing the program to crash, or stop functioning.

GUI (Graphical User Interface): Pronounced "goo-ey." A way of interacting with a computer using graphics instead of text. GUIs use icons, pictures, and menus to display information and accept input through a mouse and a keyboard. For example, software windows that have icons, and dialog boxes that have selection boxes, are GUI interfaces.

Home Phoneline Networking Alliance: An association working to ensure adoption of a single, unified home telephone line networking standard and to bring home telephone line networking technology to the market.

host: The main computer on a client/server network that supplies the files and peripherals shared by all the other computers. Also called a *server.* See also *client/server network.*

HTML (HyperText Markup Language): The language used to create Web pages, it defines the location and characteristics of each element on the Web page.

HTTP (HyperText Transfer Protocol): The protocol used for transferring files to and from World Wide Web (WWW) sites.

hub: See *concentrator.*

IDE (Integrated Drive Electronics): A type of hard drive.

install: Not only to physically set up a device but also to set up the files (called drivers) that Windows needs to communicate with the device. See also *device driver.*

interrupt: A signal that a device sends to the computer when the device is ready to accept or send information. See also *IRQ.*

I/O (Input/Output): The process of transferring data to or from a computer. Some I/O devices only handle input (keyboards and mice), some handle only output (printers), and some handle both (disks).

IP (Internet Protocol): The method by which data is sent from one computer to another computer on the Internet or on a network using the TCP/IP protocol.

IP address: A number that identifies a computer's location on the Internet or on a network using the TCP/IP protocol.

IRQ (Interrupt Request): An assigned location in memory used by a computer device to send information about its operation. Because the location is unique, the computer knows which device is interrupting the ongoing process to send a message.

ISA (Industry Standard Architecture) bus: A standard bus that has been used for a number of years. It's a 16-bit slot, which means that it sends 16 bits of data at a time between the motherboard and the card (and any device attached to the card). See also *bus, motherboard, PCI bus.*

ISDN (Integrated Services Digital Network) modem: A modem that offers faster transmission speeds than a standard modem. The drawback is that an ISDN modem is generally more expensive than a standard modem and requires a special ISDN phone line (which is more expensive than a standard phone line).

ISP (Internet service provider): A company that provides Internet access to individuals and businesses.

Java: A programming language produced by Sun Microsystems. Java is used to provide services over the Web. A Web site can provide a Java application (called an *applet*), which you download and run on your own computer.

JPEG: A format for graphic image files. JPEG images are usually smaller, due to compression features. However, the compression features are rather bad, so it may be difficult to reproduce the image properly.

jumper: A small piece of plastic in a network interface card that "jumps" across pins. Whether or not pins are "jumpered" determines IRQ and I/O settings for the NIC. See also *I/O, IRQ, NIC.*

keyboard buffer: An area in memory that keeps track of the keys you typed, even if the computer did not immediately respond when you typed them. If you hear a beep when you press a key, you've exceeded the size of the buffer.

kilobyte (K): 1,024 bytes. Used to describe the size of memory and hard drive storage.

LAN (local area network): Two or more computers connected to one another so that they can share information and peripherals. Your home network is a LAN.

laser printer: A printer that uses a laser beam to produce fast, high-quality output.

LCD (liquid crystal display): Technology used for laptop computer displays, as well as many other electronic devices.

local computer: The computer you sit in front of when you access a remote computer. See also *remote computer*.

local printer: A printer attached to the computer you're using.

LPT1: The name used to refer to the first parallel port on a computer. The second parallel port, if one exists, is called LPT2.

map: To assign a drive letter to a shared resource on another computer to more easily access that shared resource. You can map another computer's drive, folder, or subfolder. The drive letter that you use becomes part of the local computer's set of drive letters. The drives you create are called *network drives*. See also *local computer, network drive*.

megabyte (MB): 1,024 kilobytes (approximately 1 million bytes). Usually abbreviated MB.

megahertz (MHz): The speed at which a computer runs (set by the processor).

MIDI (Musical Instrument Digital Interface): The protocol for communication between electronic musical instruments and computers.

MIME (Multipurpose Internet Mail Extension): The standard for transferring binary information (files other than plain text files) via e-mail.

modem: A communications device that enables a computer to transmit information over a telephone line.

modular duplex jack: A device that plugs into a telephone wall jack to convert that single telephone jack into two jacks so that you can plug in two phones, a phone and a modem, or — in the case of a telephone line network — a telephone and a telephone line network cable. Also called a *splitter*.

monochrome printer: A printer that prints in black and shades of gray (rather than a color printer, which prints in, well, colors). Some people call this a black-and-white printer, despite the fact that no white ink is involved.

motherboard: For a PC, a plane surface that holds all the basic circuitry and the CPU.

multimedia PC: A PC that contains a CD-ROM drive, sound card, and speakers.

multiprocessor: A computer system that uses more than one CPU running simultaneously for faster performance.

NetBIOS (Network Basic Input/Output System): A software program that permits applications to communicate with other computers that are on the same cabled network.

network: Two or more computers connected to one another using network interface cards, cable, and networking software to communicate and exchange data. See also *client/server network, LAN, NIC, peer-to-peer network.*

network administrator: This is probably you if you're the one setting up a home PC network.

network drive: A drive that is located somewhere other than your local computer. See also *local computer.*

network printer: A printer attached to a remote computer on the network. (A printer attached to a local computer on the network is called a *local printer.*) See also *local printer.*

network resource: A device located in a computer other than the local computer. See also *local computer.*

network-ready computers: A new breed of computers that have telephone wiring adapters built into their motherboards for telephone line networking, eliminating the need to install telephone line networking NICs. See also *motherboard, NIC.*

NIC (network interface card): The primary hardware device for a network, a NIC attaches a computer to the network cable.

node: A connection point for distributing computer transmissions. Usually applied to computers that accept data from one computer and forward it to another computer.

OLE (Object Linking and Embedding): A software system that allows programs to transfer and share information. When a change is made to a shared object in the first program, any document in any program that contains that object is automatically updated.

packet: A chunk of information, or *data,* sent over a network.

parallel port: A connection on a PC, usually named LPT1 or LPT2, where you plug in a cable for a parallel device (usually a printer).

parent-child relationship: A hierarchy of shared resources with the following rules: If a hard drive is shared, all the folders on that drive are also shared. Folders are children of parent drives, and subfolders are children of parent folders. The most important thing to remember about this parent-child scheme is that when you configure folders as shares, you also configure the files contained in those folders as shares, and all files are children (the folders that contain them are their parents). You can interrupt this inheritance factor by changing the configuration of a child to be either more restrictive or less restrictive than its parent.

pathname: In DOS, a statement that indicates a filename on a local computer. When you use a pathname, you tell your computer that the target folder is on the local computer. Anyone working at another computer on the network must use a UNC statement to access that folder. See also *local computer, UNC.*

PCI (Peripheral Component Interconnect) bus: The PCI bus is built for speed and is found in most new computers. It comes in two configurations: 32-bit and 64-bit (32-bit means that the bus sends 32 bits of data at a time between the motherboard and the card; 64-bit means that the bus sends 64 bits of data at a time). Its technology is far more advanced — and complicated — than that of the ISA bus. See also *bus, ISA bus.*

PCMCIA (Personal Computer Memory Card Interface Adapter): A device for a laptop computer, such as a NIC or a modem, that works like an expansion slot (bus) in a desktop computer. A PCMCIA card is about the size of a credit card.

peer-to-peer network: A network in which all the computers communicate with each other — communication isn't limited to a client and a server. See also *client, client/server network, host, network.*

peripheral: Any device connected to a computer: monitor, keyboard, removable drive, CD-ROM drive, scanner, speakers, and so on.

permission level: A setting that controls users' access to shared resources on a network. The person who creates a shared resource decides which type of permission level to grant, such as Read-Only, Full, or Depends on Password.

persistent connections: Mapped drives linked to a user (a logon name) rather than a computer. If multiple users share a computer, the mapped drives that appear are those created by the user who is currently logged on. See also *map*.

Plug and Play: A software feature that reviews all the hardware in your computer during startup. When a new Plug and Play hardware component is detected, the software installation procedure begins automatically.

POP (Post Office Protocol): A protocol that permits a user to download e-mail from an e-mail server.

port: A connector located on the back of your computer into which you can plug a peripheral, such as a keyboard, mouse, printer, and so on.

POST (Power-On Self-Test): The test of internal circuitry, memory, and installed hardware that a computer performs on itself when you turn it on.

print queue: The lineup of documents waiting to be printed.

print server: On a network, a computer to which a printer is attached.

print spooler: The place on your hard drive where printer jobs are lined up, waiting to be sent to the printer. See also *print queue*.

protocol: Standardized rules for transmitting information among computers.

proxy server: A server that acts in place of a client computer. For example, a proxy server performs all the functions of a Web browser for all the individual computers accessing the Internet. See also *client*.

queue: The lineup of documents waiting to be processed — for example, the print queue is the lineup of documents waiting to go to the printer.

RAM (random access memory): The memory used by the operating system and software to perform tasks. The phrase *random access* refers to the ability of the processor to access any part of the memory.

Registry: A database that keeps track of the configuration options for software, hardware, and other important elements of your Windows operating system.

remote computer: On a network, a computer other than the one you're working on.

remote user: A user who's accessing one computer but sitting in front of another computer.

resolution: The number of dots (pixels) that make up an image on a screen or printed document. The higher the resolution, the finer and smoother the images appear.

RG-58 cable: The specific type of coaxial (10Base-2) cable used in networks. See also *10Base-2 cable*.

RJ-11 connector: The connector at each end of a length of telephone cable for telephones and telephone line networking schemes.

RJ-45 connector: The connector at the end of 10Base-T cable that looks like (but isn't) the connector at the end of a telephone cable. See also *10Base-T cable, RJ-11 connector*.

root directory: A section of a hard drive that is not part of a directory (folder). The root directory holds files needed for booting.

screen saver: A moving picture or pattern that appears on your screen when you haven't used the mouse or keyboard for a specified period of time.

scroll: To move through data on the screen (up, down, left, or right) to see parts of the data that cannot fit on the screen. You can use a variety of scrolling tools to move through the screen, such as the scroll arrow, scroll bar, and scroll box.

separator page: See *banner*.

server: See *host*.

shared resources: Drives, files, folders, printers, and other peripherals attached to one computer on a network that have been configured for access by remote users on other computers on the network. See also *remote user*.

shareware: Software that you use under an honor system — if you try it and like it, you should pay for it. See also *evaluation software, freeware*.

shielded twisted-pair cable: A type of 10Base-T cable. Metal encases the cable's wires, lessening the possibility of interference from other electrical devices, radar, radio waves, and so on. See also *10Base-T cable*.

slot: See *expansion slot*.

SMTP (Simple Mail Transfer Protocol): The protocol used to transfer e-mail between computers on the Internet. It is a server-to-server protocol, so other protocols (like POP) are needed to transfer e-mail to a user's computer.

sneakernet: The inconvenience you have when you don't bother setting up a network. With a sneakernet, information is exchanged between computers by copying files to a disk from one computer, walking to another computer (not necessarily wearing sneakers — you can wear your fuzzy pink bunny slippers and accomplish the task just as well), and then loading the files from the disk to the second computer.

splitter: See *modular duplex jack.*

standard modem: A modem whose speed is measured in thousands of bytes per second (Kbps), which is also referred to as the *baud rate* — 33.6 and 56 Kbps are common. See also *ADSL modem, cable modem, ISDN modem.*

star topology: A 10Base-T network with multiple runs from the concentrator to each computer on the network, forming an arrangement that can resemble a star when several computers are used.

surge: A sudden spate of very high voltage that travels from the electrical lines to your house and ultimately to your computer. A surge protector can help protect your computer equipment. See also *surge protector.*

surge protector: Also called a *surge suppressor.* A device that protects computers and other devices by absorbing the electricity of power surges.

system files: The files that Windows installs to make the operating system run.

T-connector: A T-shaped connector used to connect 10Base-2 to a NIC on a network without interrupting the cable run. See also *10Base-2 cable, NIC.*

TCP/IP (Transmission Control Protocol/Internet Protocol): A set of standardized rules for transmitting information. TCP/IP enables Macintosh, IBM-compatible, UNIX, and other dissimilar computers to jump on the Internet and communicate with one another, as long as each computer uses TCP/IP.

terminator: A device with BNC connectors that lets you "cap off" the empty crossbars of T-connectors at the beginning and end of a 10Base-2 cable run. See also *10Base-2 cable, BNC connector, T-connector.*

thinnet: See *10Base-2 cable.*

topology: The way a network is laid out. See also *star topology.*

twisted-pair cable: See *10Base-T cable.*

UNC (Universal Naming Convention): A formatted style used to identify a particular shared resource on a particular remote computer. The format is \\computername\resourcename. See also *pathname.*

unshielded twisted-pair cable: See *10Base-T cable*.

UPS (uninterruptible power supply): A mega-battery that plugs into the wall outlet. You plug your computer and monitor into the UPS outlets. If power fails, your computer draws power from the battery to give you enough time to properly shut down your computer.

URL (Uniform Resource Locator): An address system used on the World Wide Web (WWW) to identify the location of a resource on the Internet. For example, www.hungryminds.com.

user profile: The computer environment that belongs to a particular user. A profile lets you personalize your Windows desktop without risking ruin of your decorative efforts when the next person logs on to the computer.

virtual drive: A drive that doesn't really exist — you add a new drive letter, but you don't add any new physical drives to a computer. See also *map*.

voltage regulator: A device that constantly measures the voltage coming out of the wall and brings it to an acceptable minimum to protect against brownouts. See also *brownout*.

Web interface: In Windows 98, Windows Me, Windows 2000, or Windows 95 with Internet Explorer 4.0 installed, a graphical appearance that resembles the look of pages on the World Wide Web.

wizard: An interactive program that walks you through a software installation process.

workgroup: The group to which the computers on a network belong.

workstation: See *client*.

WYSIWYG (What You See Is What You Get): The ability to display on your monitor the same image that will appear on printed output. Pronounced "wizzywig."

Y-connector: An adapter shaped like the letter *Y* that connects two devices to one input device. For example, you can use a Y-connector to connect both a modem and a telephone line NIC to a length of cable that's inserted in a wall jack for a telephone line network. The two ends at the top of the Y connect to the back of the computer (one end connects to the modem; the other connects to the NIC). The single end at the bottom of the Y connects the cable between the computer and the wall jack. See also *NIC*.

Index

• Y •

• Z •

YOUR
ONLINE
RESOURCE

WWW.DUMMIES.COM

Discover Dummies Online!

The Dummies Web Site is your fun and friendly online resource for the latest information about *For Dummies* books and your favorite topics. The Web site is the place to communicate with us, exchange ideas with other *For Dummies* readers, chat with authors, and have fun!

Ten Fun and Useful Things You Can Do at www.dummies.com

1. Win free *For Dummies* books and more!
2. Register your book and be entered in a prize drawing.
3. Meet your favorite authors through the Hungry Minds Author Chat Series.
4. Exchange helpful information with other *For Dummies* readers.
5. Discover other great *For Dummies* books you must have!
6. Purchase Dummieswear exclusively from our Web site.
7. Buy *For Dummies* books online.
8. Talk to us. Make comments, ask questions, get answers!
9. Download free software.
10. Find additional useful resources from authors.

Link directly to these ten fun and useful things at
www.dummies.com/10useful

SURF THE NET

WWW.DUMMIES.COM

For other titles from Hungry Minds,
go to **www.hungryminds.com**

Not on the Web yet? It's easy to get started with *Dummies 101: The Internet For Windows 98* or *The Internet For Dummies* at local retailers everywhere.

Hungry Minds™

Find other *For Dummies* books on these topics:
Business • Career • Databases • Food & Beverage • Games • Gardening
Graphics • Hardware • Health & Fitness • Internet and the World Wide Web
Networking • Office Suites • Operating Systems • Personal Finance • Pets
Programming • Recreation • Sports • Spreadsheets • Teacher Resources
Test Prep • Word Processing

FOR DUMMIES
BOOK REGISTRATION

Register This Book and Win!

We want to hear from you!

Visit **dummies.com** to register this book and tell us how you liked it!

- ✔ Get entered in our monthly prize giveaway.

- ✔ Give us feedback about this book — tell us what you like best, what you like least, or maybe what you'd like to ask the author and us to change!

- ✔ Let us know any other *For Dummies* topics that interest you.

Your feedback helps us determine what books to publish, tells us what coverage to add as we revise our books, and lets us know whether we're meeting your needs as a *For Dummies* reader. You're our most valuable resource, and what you have to say is important to us!

Not on the Web yet? It's easy to get started with *Dummies 101: The Internet For Windows 98* or *The Internet For Dummies* at local retailers everywhere.

Or let us know what you think by sending us a letter at the following address:

For Dummies Book Registration
Dummies Press
10475 Crosspoint Blvd.
Indianapolis, IN 46256

FOR DUMMIES™

BESTSELLING
BOOK SERIES